Dear Ted,

What a wonderful surprise to hear from a "Nurdberger" — thanks to the good Lord that you come thru your cancer ordeal. Ted, I may be trite to say it — but you made my day. Your kind words were much appreciated by my wife and yours truly. I was impressed by the medallion and the fact that you designed it and specially by your service to our country. God bless you, our mayors are with you for your good fight victory over & against cancer. Stay well.

Sincerely yours,
Ed Mirasian
May 11, 2007

MUSA DAGH

A chronicle of the Armenian Genocide factor in the subsequent
suppression, by the intervention of the United States government,
of the movie based on Franz Werfel's *The Forty Days of Musa Dagh*

EDWARD MINASIAN

I agree — Brussels
was a great way to close
of our Nurnberg experience.
Cheers,

Cold Tree Press
Nashville, Tennessee

2-2-14

The colors used on the cover of the book represent the three horizontal bars of the Armenian flag. The red stands for the blood shed by Armenian soldiers from all wars, the blue stands for the sky of Armenia, hope and the unchanging character of the land, and the orange represents the courage of the people and the fertile lands of Armenia and the workers who work on them.

The author would like to convey a special thank you to Edward Toros Minasian. Without his support this book would not have been possible.

Library of Congress Control Number: 2007926420

Published by Cold Tree Press
Nashville, Tennessee
www.coldtreepress.com

In conjunction with

minas mulberry

Printed in the United States of America
ISBN 978-1-58385-159-3

In memory of the martyrs and the survivors of the Armenian Genocide, to Franz Werfel for "snatching from the Hades of all that was, this incomprehensible destiny of the Armenian nation,"[1] and to those who championed the film production of Werfel's The Forty Days of Musa Dagh.

---

1. Franz Werfel, *The Forty Days of Musa Dagh*, Viking Press, New York, 1934, Note.

BLACK SEA

CONSTANTINOPLE

TURKEY

SMYRNA

Brusa

Adapazar

Kutahya

ANGORA

Afion-Karahisar

Konia

T

Caesarea

TALAS

Yozgat

Marsovan

Amasia

Tokat

Samsoun

Ordou

TREBIZOND

Chebin-Karahisar

ERZERUM

BATUM

TIFLIS

RUSSIA

MEDITERRANEAN SEA

CYPRUS

NICOSIA

Port Said

CAIRO

EGYPT

JERUSALEM

BEIRUT

Saida

DAMASCUS

Alexandretta

Musa Dagh

ANTIOCH

ALEPPO

AINTAB

MARASH

Zeitoun

Hadjin

Adana

Tarsus

Mersina

SEBASTIA

SIVAS

Egin

Gurun

Malatia

MAMURET

UL-AZIZ

KHARPERT

DIYARBEKIR

ERZINGAN

BITLIS

Mouch

AGHABEKIR

ERZERUM

KARS

ANI

Gumri

Kirovagan

Lake Sevan

Echmiadzin

YEREVAN

Lake Van

Mt. Ararat

VAN

TABRIZ

Lake Urmia

SYRIA

Der-El-Zor

Euphrates

Tigris River

BAGHDAD

To Yezd

PERSIA

CASPIAN SEA

It was an event planned in conjunction with the commemoration of the sixty-seventh anniversary of the Armenian Genocide. Searchlights beamed into an evening sky accenting an auspicious event, patrons were dressed befitting an "opening night," an aura of electricity and intense nervous anticipation charged the Academy of Motion Picture Arts and Sciences Theater in Beverly Hills on the evening of April 30, 1982. The "first nighters" were looking forward to the motion picture world premiere of Franz Werfel's *The Forty Days of Musa Dagh*.

For the most part, the capacity audience was uninformed as to the actual events during the siege and deliverance at Musa Dagh in 1915 as well as Werfel's inspiration to capture the episode in a stunning novel, and, most particularly, of the controversy the film project had generated for almost fifty years.

Table of Contents

BOOK III

BABYLON-ON-THE-PACIFIC-AND-ON-THE-POTOMAC

BOOK IV

THE QUEST FOR SANCTUARY

BOOK V

BABYLON REDUX

BOOK VI

THE SEDUCTION OF THE SILVER SCREEN

TABLE OF CONTENTS

Acknowledgements

Investigating Hollywood's involvement in Franz Werfel's *The Forty Days of Musa Dagh*, a subject on which published information is sparse, was a rewarding challenge. The mission was primarily accomplished thanks to Samuel Marx, the story editor in 1981 at Metro-Goldwyn-Mayer (MGM) and during Hollywood's Golden Age of the 1930s. He interceded on my behalf to Herbert Nusbaum, Esq., of the studio's legal department. I shall be forever grateful to them for their support in making available the invaluable resource material in the *Musa Dagh File* in the MGM Archives at the studio in Culver City.

I wish to express my gratitude to the Armenian General Benevolent Union (AGBU) Alex Manoogian Cultural Fund and its chairman, Edmond Azadian, and to Joseph Matossian and the Tekeyan Cultural Association for grants to retire some of the expenses incurred in my research. John and Mary Kurkjian were most gracious in allowing me to tape a series of interviews in their home before and after their film production of *The Forty Days of Musa Dagh*. My thanks to Sarky Mouradian and Ed Vasgersian for relating their experiences in the Kurkjian production. I am also obliged to Hank Moonjean for recalling his involvement in Pandro Berman's *The Forty Days of Musa Dagh* film project and critiquing the film aspects of my manuscript. I am appreciative of manuscripts librarian Genie Guerard, UCLA Special Collections Library, who arranged clearance of the Franz Werfel Papers, as did Nicole Verity of the Barbara Hogenson Agency and the Wilder family for an excerpt in Thornton Wilder's *The Bridge of San Luis Rey*, and Barbara Perlmutter, the New York representative of S. Fischer Verlag, Frankfurt am Main, Germany, who secured permissions for *The Forty Days of Musa Dagh* and *And the Bridge is Love*.

I am indebted to *The Hairenk Weekly* and especially John Kefeyan for securing the relevant Musa Dagh data in the archives of the newspaper. Many thanks to Dr. Dennis Papazian (former director of the Armenian Center, University of Michigan, Dearborn), Marjorie Housepian Dobkin, Virginia Madajian, Jan Wall, Evelyn Garabedian, Arpena Mesrobian, and Mark Arax for their comments of the first draft. Thanks to Stan Minasian's prodigious efforts the publication of this book was made possible. My gratitude to a number of friends: Michelle Ekizian, Gladys Peters, Lala Hazarabedian, Richard Demirjian, Gilles Faget, Richard Kharibian, Jim Van Heuit, and Jack Bousian for their support.

A very special note of appreciation to Brooke Bryant of the *Contra Costa Times* for her "Monday Profile" personal interview that piqued the interest of CEO Peter Honsberger of Cold Tree Press to publish *Musa Dagh*. His staunch commitment to the book will always be remembered. Vahram Shemmassian's doctoral dissertation, "The Armenian Villagers of Musa Dagh: A Historical-Ethnographic Study, 1840-1915," UCLA, 1996, was indispensable in providing me with a better understanding of Musa Dagh and the Armenians who lived there. I appreciate the steadfast support of Dr. Shemmassian who was also instrumental in making available several of the Musa Dagh photographs, as was the Mousa Ler Association of California and Armine Antreassian for the photograph of her father, the Reverend Dikran Antreassian. At the

University of California, Los Angeles, Professor Richard Hovanissian and Gia Aivazian expedited access to the *Franz Werfel Papers* in the Special Collections Library. In Washington, D.C., on Casey Kazanjian's initiative, Raffi Manoukian and Mihran Toumajan obtained pictures from the National Archives and Records Administration for which I am grateful. Marc Wanamaker of Bison Productions was very helpful in offering the "Hollywood" photographs. Charles Kezerian provided yeoman service that was essential in the preparation of the manuscript's illustrations and the dust jacket photograph. His time and patience on the project will not be forgotten. My respects and appreciation to The Reverend Gregory Haroutunian and Vahack Haroutunian for the most recent pictures of the Musa Dagh region and of Anjar, Lebanon. I especially thank Dr. Vazken K. Der Kaloustian and the Red Mountain Committee (Armenian Revolutionary Federation) for the photographs in the book about his father, *Movses Der Kaloustian*.

I revere Franz Werfel for reawakening in me the determination to understand and appreciate my ancestral heritage. His heroic novel recounting the indomitable spirit and resilience of the strong and self-reliant Armenian people restored my ethnic soul.

And most especially, I would not have realized my mission without the encouragement, vital assistance, and unlimited patience of my wife Goldie and son Edward Toros. I shall always be sustained by my good fortune in their being part of my life.

Fridtjof Nansen. *The passport in his name as High Commissioner of the League of Nations made possible the emigration of many Armenians to Europe and the United States.*

2

A Personal Preface

In 1933, almost twenty years after the Armenian Genocide[1] of World War I, the German-language publication of Franz Werfel's novel *The Forty Days of Musa Dagh* injected renewed hope in the Armenian Diaspora. Werfel was inspired by an event during the Great War about a group of Armenian villagers who defended themselves atop Musa Dagh rather than submit to the Ottoman Turkish government's directives "to relocate." The eminent English historian Arnold Toynbee referred to that episode as "the single happy incident in the national tragedy of the Armenians in the Ottoman Empire."[2] Armenians were elated when Metro-Goldwyn-Mayer (MGM), the most powerful motion picture studio in Hollywood, announced in May 1934 the purchase of the rights to film Werfel's epic novel. A generation had passed since the tragic events of 1915 to 1923. The world had become indifferent to the Armenian Genocide. But then, for a brief moment, Armenians took heart. Someone big was going to reveal the twentieth century's first genocide through the epic story of Musa Dagh. At last, the Armenians were to have their "day in court" through the medium of film. December 1934 to November 1935 became a year of hopeful anticipation for Armenians, especially when MGM entrusted Irving Thalberg, Hollywood's wunderkind, to produce *The Forty Days of Musa Dagh* as a major motion picture.

The passion that drove me to research and write *Musa Dagh* stems from many sources. My ethnicity is a primary factor. My father, Toros Minasian of Chimishgadzek (Kharpert province), had immigrated to the United States in 1912. He had planned to send for his (first) wife and children but when war broke out in 1914, his hopes were dashed, especially with the Ottoman Turkish government's April 24, 1915, decree banishing the Armenians from their ancestral lands. His daughter Peprone was the only survivor of a family of five on the death march to the Syrian Desert. One of the most traumatic moments in my life occurred in 1976 when I first met my seventy-two year old half-sister Peprone. I learned for the first time of Haig, my father's three- year-old son, who had died of typhus on the death march to Der el-Zor. My father had never told me of Haig. Perhaps he was so traumatized by his inability to rescue his family that he blocked out this negative aspect of his life. In 1915, my nineteen-year-old mother, Haiganoush Naldjian Tabakyan, witnessed the rounding up of the able-bodied Armenian men of her native town of Amasia, including her twenty-three year old (first) husband. They were marched away carrying shovels, never to be seen again. Surviving six years of high anxiety, she and her eight-year-old daughter, Nevart (Rose), eventually found refuge in the United States in 1921, thanks in part to a Nansen Passport.[3] My parents began a new life in the United States when they married in 1924.

In December 1934, Nevart learned of a recent publication that had become the topic of conversation in the Armenian community. She soon owned a Viking Press first edition of Franz Werfel's *The Forty Days of Musa Dagh*. I was ten years old at the time and recall her enthusiastic interest in the book that is now part of my library, along with other editions of the novel.

The meeting with Peprone and her story about Haig, my frustration with my father's "secret," and unbridled anger compounded by the history of my parents' odyssey to America inspired me to channel my energy in a more constructive direction. And so my Musa Dagh mission was launched.

During my formative years in the Great Depression, I often found escape and solace at the movies. We lived in a third-floor tenement over my father's tailor shop in the Italian neighborhood in Lawrence, Massachusetts. From our window I could see "two houses of worship," the Grace Episcopal Church and the Capitol theater. Quite often, when I could scrape up ten cents, I chose the latter over the former on Sundays. I was often asked what I saw in that "dark place." That "dark place" was a refuge in the thirties, a safety valve and a classroom that aroused my curiosity and broadened my education. It was also the best entertainment value of the time for a budding movie fan. Before I read my first history textbook, the movies introduced me to history, literature, and music. They motivated me to separate fact from fiction as a regular patron of the public library. Over the years I became a movie buff, collecting movie memorabilia and stocking an extensive film book library. I am still a regular patron of the cinema.

I first read *The Forty Days of Musa Dagh* during World War II while serving in the U.S. Army Air Corps. Werfel's novel confirmed in my nineteenth year the stories I had heard from my elders about the Armenian Genocide. In time, Werfel's masterpiece became my second Bible. I have read *The Forty Days of Musa Dagh* more often than any other book. Each time I read it, I sense a rush of adrenaline. As a history teacher and longtime movie buff, I became concerned about Werfel's Armenian treasure in Hollywood.

While a G.I. Bill undergraduate and graduate student at the University of California in Berkeley following World War II, I researched my ancestral heritage. The result was a master's thesis, "They Came From Ararat: The Exodus of the Armenian People to the United States."[4] The challenge was to juxtapose Ottoman and Kemalist Turkish-Armenian policies with United States Armenian immigration statistics from 1890 to 1932. The study points out a definite correlation between the Armenian population in the United States then and the genocidal actions taken by the Turkish government. As late as 1960, the Armenian presence in the United States was overwhelmingly composed of the survivors of the Armenian Genocide and their first-and second-generation Armenian American (the author insists that he is not a hyphenated American) descendants. My research into non-Armenian primary sources (German, French, English, and American) also confirmed the extent to which the anti-Armenian policies of the Ottoman Turkish government were designed to eliminate the indigenous Armenians from their homeland. In the course of my investigation, I was reminded of the controversy surrounding Werfel's novel in Hollywood.

My interest in the book and film project led me to present a paper, "The Forty 'Years' of *Musa Dagh*," at Harvard University in May 1984. The co-sponsor of the event, the National Association of Armenian Studies and Research (NAASR), published the paper twice in its *Journal of Armenian Studies*.[5] Subsequently it was printed in The *Armenian Mirror-Spectator*, an English language weekly.[6] The response to the article gave me the incentive to expand my initial effort into a more definitive work tracing the *Musa Dagh* episode from its inception in 1915 to Werfel's inspiration for his novel and the controversy it has stirred as a proposed motion picture until today.

In the course of my research I uncovered the vital facts about *The Forty Days of Musa Dagh* film project in the MGM archives at Culver City, California. They proved to be a treasure trove of significant data. Through the Freedom of Information Act, I obtained the *Musa Dagh* documents from the State Department in Washington. Another important source was the *Franz Werfel Papers* at the University of California at

Los Angeles, Special Collections Library. The American Film Institute (AFI), Los Angeles, provided me with access to all the screenplays, adaptations, and other production related documents of *The Forty Days of Musa Dagh*. English-language Armenian newspapers provided the ethnic point of view in my research. The American news media also were a source of essential information during my inquiry. I then interviewed those available individuals who were significantly involved with the film project.

The objective of *Musa Dagh* is to focus primarily on the events and personalities involved in what the Hollywood trade paper *Variety* characterized as "possibly the most on again, off again major literary property in the history of American motion pictures."[7]

The result is a chronicle of an investigative report of the seventy-three-year ordeal endured by *The Forty Days of Musa Dagh* film project. It is a story that has never been completely told. *Musa Dagh* is one more chapter in the literature of memorials to the Armenian Genocide.

NOTES – A PERSONAL PREFACE

1. *The Armenian Genocide, History, Politics, Ethics,* Richard Hovannisian, ed., New York, St. Martin's Press, 1992, p. xv. Dr. Raphael Lemkin, a Polish Jew, who survived the Nazi invasion of Poland, created the term genocide. On January 12, 1951, the United Nations Convention on the Prevention and Punishment of the Crime of Genocide went into force. Article II declares genocide to mean the commitment of any of the following acts with intent to destroy, in whole or in part, a national, ethnical, racial, or religious group as such, including:

    a. Killing members of the group;

    b. Causing serious bodily or mental harm to members of the group;

    c. Deliberately inflicting on the group conditions of life calculated to bring about its physical destruction in whole or in part;

    d. Imposing measures intended to prevent births within the group;

e. Forcibly transferring children of the group to another group.

2.   Viscount James Bryce, *The Treatment of the Armenians in the Ottoman Empire,* 1915 -1916, Documents presented to Viscount Grey of Fallodon, Secretary of State for Foreign Affairs, Arnold Toynbee, ed., London: H.M.S.O., 1916, p. 511; also titled *The Blue Book,* Document 130, pp. 512-520.

3.   Fridtjof Nansen (1861-1930), famed explorer, headed the Norwegian delegation to the League of Nations in 1920. As high commissioner, he was responsible for the certificate that bears his name. The Nansen Passport made possible the emigration of many Armenians to the United States as well as other displaced nationals. Nansen also led the relief efforts to the famine-stricken Armenians. In 1922, he was awarded the Nobel Peace Prize for his humanitarianism. *Encyclopaedia Britannica,* Vol. 16, pp. 69-70, 1961.

4.   Edward Minasian, "They Came from Ararat: The Exodus of the Armenian People to the United States," master's thesis, University of California at Berkeley, 1961, 287 pages.

5.   Edward Minasian, "The Forty 'Years' of Musa Dagh," *Journal of Armenian Studies,* Vol. II, No. 2, Fall/Winter, 1985-1986, pp. 63-73; Vol. III, Nos. 1 and 2, 1986-1987, pp. 121-131, National Association for Armenian Studies and Research (NAASR), Cambridge, Mass.: Armenian Heritage Press.

6.   Edward Minasian, "The Forty 'Years' of Musa Dagh," *Armenian Mirror-Spectator,* Vol. LIV, No. 28, 1/24/87, pp. 8-10, Watertown, Mass.: Baikar Association.

7.   Variety, 4/16/69, p. 3.

Henry Morgenthau, *U.S. Ambassador to Turkey,*
1913–1916, was convinced that the Young Turk
Armenian policy was part of a premeditated plan
taken against the coming of a new generation
of Armenians.

3

Prologue

The Crucible of the Armenian Nation, 1915-1923

Except for a handful of scholars, most people are unaware of the fact that Armenians trace their history since the eighth century before Christ. Perhaps this can be attributed to the fact that since World War I, Armenia played no significant role in world affairs until 1946, when the Soviet Union launched a worldwide Armenian repatriation program and simultaneously pressed its unsuccessful demand for the annexation of the eastern Turkish (Armenian) provinces of Kars, Ardahan, and Erzerum to Soviet Armenia.

As the twentieth century was coming to a close, a series of events occured that kept Armenia and Armenians on the front pages. The episode that caught the world's attention was the devastating earthquake in Soviet Armenia on December 7, 1988, costing over 25,000 lives. Then with Mikhail Gorbachev's "glasnost" and "perestroika," the stage was set for the disintegration of the Soviet Union and Armenia's independence in September 1991. This was followed by the current Nagorno-Karabagh dispute with Azerbaijan and Turkey that led to the blockade of Armenia, adversely affecting the political climate in the Caucasus and the Middle East.

When Armenia became the first nation to adopt Christianity as its national religion in A.D. 301,[1] followed by the creation of a national alphabet a hundred years later, its national character and unique Christian identity were redefined. This combination of religion and a written language reinforced Armenia's racial solidarity and sustained the Armenian people as successive invaders tried to conquer them outright or force a foreign culture on them.

With the fall of Constantinople to the Ottoman Turks in 1453, the greater portion of the Armenian heartland in eastern Asia Minor (Anatolia) came under their rule. Under this new Muslim master, the Armenians were subjected to discriminatory and oppressive measures that have lasted into the twenty-first century.

The actions taken by the Ottoman Turkish government against its Armenian subjects in the nineteenth century eventually aroused the attention of Russia, Great Britain, and France. It offered them an excuse to intervene in the "Armenian Question" in order to protect their political and economic interests in the Dardanelles, the Caucasus, and the Middle East. The intent of the "Question" by the great powers was to promote reforms improving the welfare of the Armenians in the Ottoman Empire.

In July 1908 the Ittihad, a Turkish cabal called the Committee of Union and Progress, known more familiarly as the Young Turks, succeeded in taking over the Ottoman Turkish government and demoting Sultan Abdul Hamid to a figurehead monarch. The Ittihad leaders, a triumvirate composed of Minister of War Enver,[2] Minister of the Interior Talaat, and Minister of the Navy Djemal, were determined to resolve the "Armenian Question" once and for all.

When the Ittihad joined the war on the side of Germany and the Central Powers in 1914, the fate of more than 2,500,000 Armenians in the Ottoman Turkish Empire was sealed. By early spring of 1915, the Armenians recognized the real intent of the Young Turk oligarchs was to exterminate them.[3] The Young Turks saw the Armenian presence in Anatolia as an obstacle to their war efforts and an impediment to the realization of Turkish expansion. Their objective was to unite the lands from Constantinople to Central Asia by cleansing it of non-Muslims. The triumvirate was further encouraged when pro-Turkish Germans, proponents of Germany's expansion in the Near East (Drang nach Osten), did not protest the "relocation" of the Armenians.[4] Ottoman Turkey's final solution to the "Armenian Question" was initially implemented in a deliberate plan on April 24, 1915, when several thousand Armenian educators, writers, physicians, businessmen, attorneys, members of the Ottoman parliament, and community leaders were rounded up and executed on the orders of the triumvirate. By removing the Armenian leadership, the Ottoman Turkish government deprived the *Ermeni Millet* (the Turkish term for the Armenian people) of any possibility of united protest and resistance, thus paving the way for the slaughter of the innocents. What followed was one of the greatest systematized mass murders of the twentieth century. The thoroughness of the Turkish government's campaign to cleanse itself of its Armenian subjects by death and exile is borne out in a current statistic: Out of a population of over 2,500,000 Armenians in Ottoman Turkey in 1915 there are about 65,000 Armenians residing in Turkey today, the overwhelming majority of whom reside in Istanbul.[5]

While the immediate task of uprooting the Armenians was placed in the hands of the local authorities, the Turkish pattern of expulsion of the Armenian population was so similar everywhere that it underscores the existence of a calculated design from the center formulated by the triumvirate. Henry Morgenthau, the U.S. ambassador to Turkey from 1913 to 1916, was convinced that the Young Turk Armenian policy was part of a premeditated plan taken against the coming of a new generation of Armenians.[6] Concurrently, the Allies (Great Britain, France, and Russia) announced publicly that they would hold all members of the Turkish government and their agents personally responsible for their crimes against their Armenian subjects.[7] The admonition fell on deaf ears.

It was Count Paul von Wolff-Metternich, German ambassador to Turkey from 1915 to 1916, who singled out Minister of the Interior Mehmet Talaat as "the soul of the Armenian persecutions."[8] Talaat ordered the provincial governors and their underlings to exterminate every Armenian within the empire, regardless of age, gender, or physical or medical condition, and to do so without conscientious scruples.[9] The only way to escape death was to renounce one's Christian faith and convert to Islam.[10] To conceal their real intentions from foreign missionaries and the diplomatic corps, Enver and Talaat had personal cipher telegraph machines in their homes.[11] The "killing orders" were issued from there in tandem with commands requiring the destruction of all written orders so as to eliminate any incriminating evidence.[12] Due to the swift action taken by General Edmund Allenby's troops in Aleppo in 1918, numerous Turkish documents were seized. Among them were cipher telegrams relating to the Armenian Genocide exposing the culpability of the Ottoman government.[13]

At least one-third of the world's Armenian population, 1,500,000 people, perished between 1915 and 1923 due to the calculated genocidal policies initiated by the Ottoman Turkish government.[14] The decimation of the Armenian population was far greater than any other national ethnic group during World War I.

Justice was not meted out to all those responsible for perpetrating the Armenian Genocide. As time passed, it became the "forgotten Genocide."

Within a generation of the Great War, it gave license to the totalitarians to launch the Holocaust. The Armenian Genocide was a prelude to Auschwitz. Today, ninety years later, the tragic impact of the Armenian Genocide has not diminished. Independent and landlocked Armenia remains a Christian enclave surrounded by Muslim neighbors.

It is against this history of ethnic cleansing (1915-1923), that in a remote corner of the Ottoman Turkish Empire in 1915, a small colony of Armenians of the mountainous Musa Dagh region was forced to choose between submission to Ottoman directives that meant exile from their ancient homeland and almost certain death in the Syrian Desert, or active resistance. This was the incident that inspired Franz Werfel to pen his masterpiece, *The Forty Days of Musa Dagh* and created a tempest as a motion picture production in Hollywood.

NOTES - PROLOGUE

1. The Church of Armenia (the Church of the Armenian People) in the Armenian language, *Hayasdanyatz Yegheghetzi* is Apostolic, claiming the introduction of the nation to Christianity by the Apostles Bartholomew and Thaddeus in the first century A.D. Christianity functioned in Armenia underground until A.D. 301 when St. Gregory the Illuminator (Krikor Loosavoritch) enlightened the nation with the Gospel and converted King Drtad. As the first head of the Church of Armenia, Gregory established Etchmiadzin, "the place where the Only-Begotten (Jesus Christ) descended," as the Mother See of the Church. The term Loosavorchagan commonly refers to the Mother Church after its founder, St. Gregory, and to those Armenians who practice that faith.

2. *Contra Costa Times*, "Remains of Enver Pasha Given Military Honors in Istanbul Burial," 8/5/96, p. 43. Eighty years after the Armenian Genocide, the Turkish government led by President Suleyman Demirel accorded Enver a state funeral and burial on Memorial Hill in Istanbul. His tomb lies next to his co-conspirator

Talaat, "heroes" of the Young Turk revolution and motivators of the Armenian Genocide.

3. Henry Morgenthau, *Ambassador Morgenthau's Story*, an eyewitness account by the American Ambassador to Turkey, 1913-1916. Memorial edition honoring Henry Morgenthau and in commemoration of the 60th Anniversary of the Armenian Genocide, Plandome, N. Y.: New Age Publishers, p. 290, originally published in 1919 by Doubleday, Page & Co.

4. Vahakn N. Dadrian, *German Responsibility in the Armenian Genocide-A Review of the Historical Evidence of German Complicity*, Watertown, Mass.: Blue Crane Books, 1996, p. 114.

5. *Contra Costa Times*, 2/10/07, p. 47. Of Turkey's 70 million people, some 65,000 are Armenian Orthodox Christians, 20,000 are Roman Catholic and 3,500 are Protestant, mostly converts from Islam. Around 2,000 are Greek Orthodox and 23,000 are Jewish.

6. Morgenthau, *Ambassador*, p. 291.

7. *New York Times*, "Allies to Punish Turks Who Murder," 5/24/15, Section 1, p. 2.

8. Ulrich Trumpener, *Germany and the Ottoman Empire, 1914-1918*, Princeton, N.J.: Princeton University Press, 1968, p. 231, note 88. Cited by Kevork B. Bardakjian, *Hitler and the Armenian Genocide,* Zoryan Institute, Special Report 3, 1985, p. 35.

9. Arnold J. Toynbee, *Armenian Atrocities, The Murder of the Nation*, London: Hodder & Stoughton, 1915, pp. 12-13.

10. Ibid., p. 31. It raises the question: What would a DNA examination of the current Turkish population reveal?

11. Vahakn N. Dadrian, *The History of the Armenian Genocide: Ethnic Conflict from the Balkans to Antolia to the Caucasus*, Providence, R.I.: Berghahn Books, pp. 384-385.

12. Annette Höss, "The Trial of Perpetrators by the Turkish Military Tribunals: The Case of Yozgat," *The Armenian Genocide,* New York: St. Martin's Press, Hovannisian, ed., 1992, p. 219.

13. Marjorie Housepian, "The Unremembered Genocide," *Commentary*, Vol.

42, No.3, September 1966, New York: American Jewish Committee. The cipher telegrams were first published in the *London Daily Telegraph*, 5/29/22.

14. Maj. Gen. James G. Harbord, U.S. Army, "Report of the American Military Mission to Armenia," United States, 66th Congress, 2nd Session, *Senate Document 266*, 1920, pp. 6-8.

MUSA DAGH

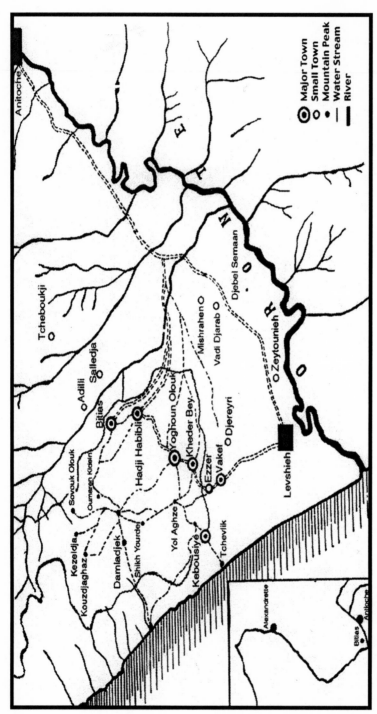

4 The Musa Dagh region in 1915.

BOOK I

Crucible:
The Sixty-Four Days
of Musa Dagh

... behold, I have set before thee an open door,
—The Revelation of St. John the Divine 3:8

Chapter 1

AN IDYLLIC COMMUNITY:
THE ARMENIANS OF MUSA DAGH

A self-contained community threatening no one

A Christian mountain, scarcely touched by the fall of man,
Under which, the rest of Asia Minor mourns.
It was as though, an archangel had been allowed
To linger in the lands around Musa Dagh,
Where experts in Biblical geography
Locate the Garden of Eden.
The villages round the mountain had shared
In this benediction.[1]

No matter the vantage point, Musa Dagh, the Mountain of Moses, looms like a stoic sentinel of the southernmost point of the Amanus mountain range. Overlooking the Mediterranean Sea to the west and the Antiochian plains of northwestern Syria to the east, the massif resembles a fortress. From time immemorial there has been an Armenian presence in the Musa Dagh region.[2]

Clustered on the eastern slopes of Musa Dagh in 1915 were six prominent Armenian villages: Bitias, Haji Habibli, YoghunOluk, Kheder Beg, Vakef, and Kabusiye and two neighboring hamlets, Upper and Lower Ezzeirs in the Sanjak (a large administrative district or state) of Alexandretta.

Muslims were interspersed throughout the region. The nearest city, Antioch, was eighteen miles east of Musa Dagh. Thirty-five miles north was Alexandretta[3] (Iskenderun) harbor. To the south was the rural town of Suedia and the Orontes River. The Armenian population of the Musa Dagh region at the time was 6311, comprising 1235 families[4], whose chief source of income was derived from sericulture (raising of silkworms).

The strong bond instilled in every member of the Armenian family was characterized by devotion to family, clan, church, and nation. It was this spirit inherent in the Armenian people that made for their presence on Earth despite catastrophic adversities throughout their history. And it still does.

Who were these Musa Daghians who dared to defy the Ottoman Empire as their fellow Armenians had resisted the Turkish armies at Van, Shabin-Karahissar, Urfa, and Zeitun?

Through hundreds of generations, the Armenians of Musa Dagh had come to master their skills and trades. The Armenian families of Bitias, the most northerly and scenic village, engaged in spinning, weaving, and marketing silk products. Haji Habibli, the largest Armenian settlement, was the center of the silk industry. Enjoying a central location in the area, the largest village, YoghunOluk, was the ideal gathering place and trade center. Many of the Armenians there were self-employed in bone and woodcarving (combs, pipes, cigarette holders, and the like), as well as the silk industry.

A fifteen-minute walk from YoghunOluk was Kheder Beg, whose many tributaries provided enough water to operate twenty mills and irrigate groves and fields there and south into the Suedia valley. Vakef and Kabusiye were nearest to the sea. Kheder Beg, Vakef, and Kabusiye had the advantage of rich black soil and an excellent water supply, which provided cereals, vegetables, and fruit for home consumption and export.

Intent on planting wheat, barley, and millet on every inch of arable land, residents created hundreds of small plots terracing Musa Dagh's eastern flanks to the very top of the mountain.

Collectively, the Musa Dagh villages were also noted for beekeeping, extracting licorice roots, and home manufacture of kitchen utensils, mesquite charcoal, linen goods, and clothing for sale in Cilicia, Syria, and Egypt. The Armenian villages had a few tailors, barbers, cobblers, tinkers, smiths (gold, iron, and gun) and stonecutters.[5]

Enhancing the beauty of the region's flora, rhodendrons and azaleas bordered homes, and the fields were lush with olive, apricot, peach, orange, apple, and pomegranate orchards, fig and mulberry groves, and vineyards. The area also provided sufficient grazing land for livestock. The Musa Daghians for the most part provided the basic necessities for their sustenance.

The prevailing Mediterranean climate and the bucolic setting of the region established Musa Dagh as a favorite summer retreat for foreigners and especially for Armenians in Syria. Visitors remarked that the locality reminded them of the villages near Naples, Italy.[6]

Under Ottoman rule, Turkish resentment, jealousy, and suspicion of the Armenians were primarily based on a combination of the Armenians' ethnicity, Christianity, cultural heritage, education, and business acumen. Ever threatening and without warning, the Turkish gendarmerie constantly searched for arms, illegal tobacco, and literature critical of the government or contrary to Ottoman history.[7] Taxes were particularly onerous, ranging from *ashar* (tithe) to *dish kirasi* ("tooth rent," the tax collector's personal share) that fell heavily on Christians.[8]

Like their compatriots to the north on the Anatolian plateau, the Musa Daghians revered the sacred Mt. Ararat (Massis) as the national symbol of Armenia's aspirations signifying the freedom that comes with independence. But they had another beloved mountain, the more familiar Musa Dagh (the Armenian term is Mousa Ler). The men and boys knew every crag and ravine of the steep and rugged mountain. It was the playground of their childhood. For those who could not afford the *bedel* (payment for military exemption) to avoid conscription or impressment, Musa Dagh was an excellent refuge for young men.[9]

On the eve of World War I, the Musa Daghians were a self-contained community who went about their daily business making a living and threatening no one. After April 24, 1915, the Turkish objective was to rid the area of its Armenian inhabitants.

Chapter 2

SIEGE AND RESISTANCE

A life and death struggle

On July 13, 1915, almost three months after the April 24 decree, the Antioch district lieutenant governor, Zeki Maaruf, issued an edict (Appendix I) notifying the Armenians of the Musa Dagh region that within eight days they would be relocated.[10] Posters were plastered on walls to alert the populace. The following day, in response to the edict, the leaders of the six villages gathered in Yoghon Oluk at the home of the village Armenian Apostolic priest, the Reverend Father Abraham Der Kaloustian.[11] The discussion ran the gamut from making a stand atop Musa Dagh by taking advantage of its commanding position as an excellent temporary sanctuary[12] to expressing concerns that disobeying the directive would certainly invite a harsh response. Others thought resistance would be impossible.[13] Hoping to find a way out, an official Musa Dagh delegation was sent to Antioch to beg or to bribe the Turkish authorities for an exemption from deportation. Their plea was rejected.[14]

The Reverend Harutiun Nokhudian, the twenty-five-year-old pastor of the Armenian Protestant community in Bitias, was among those who believed it was senseless to oppose the authorities. He thought it would be wiser for his congregation to await the Turkish gendarmerie because the Turks were known to be lenient to Protestants in fear of the American and German missionaries in Turkey. He was convinced that present supplies of food and ammunition would not suffice for the resistance. Furthermore, by provoking the authorities, Armenians would be endangered everywhere.[15]

Realizing the futility of defending themselves in the foothills, better than two-thirds of the Musa Daghians preferred to make a stand on Musa Dagh.[16] They reasoned that there would be no chance of survival in the wilderness against raids by lawless brigands and the Turkish "escort."[17] Besides, the news of the summons for the Armenians to evacuate the Musa Dagh region was already common knowledge, thus exacerbating anti-Armenian hatred among the Muslim populace.[18] YoghunOluk, Kheder Beg, Vakef, and Haji Habibli overwhelmingly opted for resistance. Bitias was divided. A few families of Kabusiye joined the fight. About two-thousand Musa Daghians eventually obeyed Maaruf's orders and prepared for exile.[19]

Working feverishly in the eight-day "grace" period, more than four-thousand Armenian men, women, and children prepared to climb Musa Dagh. Every able-bodied Musa Daghian had something to tote. Gathering as much food, clothing, and tools as they could carry, along with livestock and weaponry, they made their ascent. Climbing the mountain like ant columns, the entire contingent took three days to make it atop Musa Dagh.[20] Camps were set up in four different areas on the mountain with Damlayik as the encampment center. Meetings were held to establish a government that would supervise military and internal affairs.[21] Irrespective of their religious and political affiliations[22] and recognizing the odds against them, the Musa Daghians pulled together against the common foe.[23]

Once the Musa Daghians occupied the heights atop Musa Dagh, communications with the outside world were practically severed. They knew they could not rely on the American Protestant missionaries 120 miles to the north in Aintab or the Russian forces in eastern Asia Minor. But the knowledge that the Allied invasion in the Dardanelles might neutralize Turkey, along with the presence of an Allied naval force patrolling the eastern Mediterranean, gave them hope of rescue.[24]

By nightfall of the first day on Musa Dagh, the testing of the Armenian resolve began. As they were preparing camp and the evening meal, they were deluged by a cloudburst that continued for seven hours into the early morning.[25] Lacking tents, sufficient rain gear, and time to make shelter, everyone was drenched. To compound the misery, much of their bread was inedible. Only a few of those who possessed guns and powder were able to keep them dry. Reassessing their situation after the storm, they knew their first priority was to dig trenches at the most vulnerable points on the eastern approaches of Musa Dagh. Where earth was lacking, they rolled rocks together to make strong barricades. To brace their spirits, each of the village clergymen conducted daily services for their respective flocks.[26]

The evening following the rainstorm, a mass meeting was held to elect by secret ballot a Central Administrative Council responsible for law and order and the defense of Musa Dagh.[27] This executive body consisted of sixteen members representing the six villages.[28] The chairmanship of the council was entrusted to the twenty-seven-year-old Reverend Dikran Andreasian (Antreassian), one of the most educated men in Musa Dagh. Prepared by American Protestant Congregational missionaries for the ministry at Aintab and Marash, Andreasian displayed intelligence, governing skills, cool-headedness, and a knowledge of English, all of which proved invaluable. (By virtue of his administrative position, Andreasian's account of the events at Musa Dagh is the most definitive and authentic record published in English.)

The council had absolute authority over the six communities now joined together in a life-and-death struggle. Choosing from its ranks, the council appointed the Reverend Father Der Kaloustian's son, Movses (Moses), to be responsible for military operations. With more than half the men without arms, time was of the essence. The younger Der Kaloustian, with the assistance of two lieutenants,[29] promptly organized and trained the men capable of defending Musa Dagh into disciplined fighting units. To alert the fighters and the populace, armed sentinels were assigned to every pass on the mountain and every approach to the four encampments. The best marksmen and scouts were assigned specific duties. Forty-three squads comprised of ten men each with a corporal in charge, with a total of 120 modern rifles and shotguns and about 400 old flintlocks and horse pistols, had to defend more than 4000 Musa Daghians. Compensating somewhat for the shortage of weapons were the Musa Daghians' sharpshooting skills learned from long experience in hunting. In the absence of technical communications, "telephone boys" ranging from ten to twelve years old were positioned at ten-minute intervals as relay-team messengers. A "workers' brigade" composed of the older men and those without weapons provided shelters, prepared ramparts, dug trenches, cleared trees, and rolled boulders.[30] To keep the populace atop Musa Dagh informed and alert, town criers were appointed. Lacking a trained medical staff and supplies, first aid was a matter of applying warm water to injuries and wrapping and changing bandages. The women provided food and water to the fighters, and when the attacks came, many of them fought alongside the men. Gunsmiths proved resourceful in repairing guns, loading and reloading of empty shells, and distributing bullets, lead, and gunpowder.[31] The Musa Daghians, knowing the odds were overwhelmingly against them, were of one mind. It was better to fight than to submit.

Refusing to join the defenders on Musa Dagh, Pastor Nokhudian had convinced sixty families of his Bitias parish and about thirty families from the neighboring village of Haji Habibli to remain in their homes. Summoned by the Turkish military, Nokhudian was asked, "Why have these devils taken to the mountain?" The young minister shot back: "They choose to die fighting in their own faith rather than submit as lambs to the slaughter." The Turkish officer retorted: "I have been given orders to exterminate such rebels." The pastor was ordered to contact the defiant Armenians and demand their surrender. That evening, Nokhudian sent a message to the Reverend Andreasian apprising him of the situation. There was no response. Awaiting further Turkish instructions, Nokhudian and his flock witnessed the looting of the Armenian homes by their Muslim neighbors while Bitias was occupied by four hundred Turkish soldiers from Urfa, whom he described as the most wicked and unscrupulous in the Turkish army.[32]

On August 15, Nokhudian and his followers were informed that, because the Musa Dagh region was now a war zone, they would be escorted to Antioch. Forced to walk at a fast gait, within a day they joined another Armenian convoy and were redirected to Hama, a six-day southward trek. Guards were impatient with those who lagged behind. Cholera, typhus, and dysentery decimated the ranks of the exiles. As a result, many of the aged, infirm, and children were abandoned. In Hama they met hundreds of Armenian Protestants led by the Reverend Tigran Koundakjian, pastor of the Kessab Protestant community, who were en route to Der el-Zor in the Syrian Desert. Chairman Andreasian surmised that the Reverend Nokhudian and his congregation, having yielded to the Turkish authorities, were force-marched to the lower Euphrates, where they vanished. In reality Nokhudian survived the death march.[33]

In spite of the odds, the Musa Daghians were committed to defending themselves in the hope that, in time, the victorious Allies would deliver them from their enemies. Unfortunately, the Allied stalemate in the Dardanelles emboldened the Young Turk triumvirate to finalize their campaign against the Armenians.[34]

Before the outbreak of war in 1914, the triumvirate had sanctioned the creation of a German Military Mission in Turkey to reform and reorganize the Turkish army. After Ottoman Turkey joined the Central Powers on October 29, 1914, the Mission under Marshal Liman von Sanders grew to 800 German officers and 12,000 German troops. Every Turkish field commander of a unit was assigned a German officer as his chief of staff and advisor.[35] During the siege at Musa Dagh the Turkish forces in the region were under the command of General Fahri, chief of staff to the IVth Army commander, the triumvir Djemal. A German artillery officer, Count Eberhard Wolffskeel von Reichenberg, chief of staff of the VIIIth Army Corps, with the rank of major in the Ottoman army, was ordered by Fahri to serve at Musa Dagh. Wolffskeel considered the Armenians to be traitors who deserved deportation. As an observer during the siege at Musa Dagh, he was so unnerved by the Armenian resistance that in the ensuing attack on Urfa he led the bombardment that destroyed the Armenian quarter.[36]

On Wednesday, July 21, an advance force of 200 Turkish regulars launched the first attack. After almost five hours of combat, the Armenians repulsed the initial assault. The lack of Armenian casualties instilled great confidence in the defenders on Musa Dagh.[37] In the second strike, lasting from dawn to dusk, the Turks hurled 2000 troops at the defenders and brought up a field gun. Once gaining the range, the cannon threatened the major encampment at Damlayik. A volunteer Armenian sniper crept down through the shrubbery and rocks and, guided by the roar of the artillery piece, came within earshot of the cannoneers and dispatched them with five shots. The Turks bolted and pulled back the menacing field piece, giving the Musa Daghians a few days' respite.[38]

The experience learned from these attacks convinced commander Der Kaloustian to form a mobile force of three commando units under three chiefs.[39] Noted for their bravery and excellent marksmanship, the commandos were stationed at a central location, ready on a moment's notice to speed to the defense of endangered positions. These "minute men" were also charged to maintain discipline, police the fighters, and prevent desertions. Even though the commandos had the best rifles, their guns had a disadvantage—the cartridges were filled with ordinary gunpowder. Every time a gun was fired, the smoke betrayed its location. The Turks would then direct their fire toward the smoke. The Armenian fighters learned to continually change their positions.[40]

The Turkish commanders, having lost their first two encounters, in their frustration called for a jihad (holy war). When Governor Khalid Bey's demand for the Armenians to surrender was ignored, the Antioch arsenal provided rifles and ammunition to Muslim civilian volunteers for a third assault.[41] Together with 3000 gendarmes, the Turks laid siege to all the eastern approaches of Musa Dagh and eventually occupied the high ground overlooking the "town" enclosure on Damlayik. Since the seaward (western) side of the mountain sloped directly into the Mediterranean, it compounded the difficulty for a quick escape. The situation was ominous. Turkish rifles had a range superior to the firearms of the Musa Daghians. In the next attack, the Turks concentrated their forces on one particular mountain pass, killing several of the defenders. By sundown the enemy had three companies within four hundred yards of Damlayik.[42] Choosing comfort and security, the Turks miscalculated;

they bivouacked rather than attack at night. The defenders could not afford the luxury of a nocturnal respite. They boldly chose a dangerous initiative. Surreptitiously, they surrounded the foe in the darkness. On a given signal, the Armenians sprung the trap. Closing in, they suddenly set off a volley of withering shots and ended their sortie in hand-to-hand combat. Familiarity with the terrain made it possible for the Musa Daghians to do what the enemy could not. The lightning sally bewildered the Turks, who panicked. By morning the mountain was virtually clear of the enemy. It was a bitter humiliation for the Turks, further compounded by the fact that the rout had come at the hands of the "infidel" Armenians. As a boon to the defenders, many of the guns and ammunition abandoned by the retreating enemy were recovered.[43]

The upshot of these attacks reinforced the will of the Musa Daghians not to submit to the enemy. As never before, the defense of Musa Dagh had united the Armenians of the region in their common baptism of fire. The situation had become intolerable to the Turkish military. For the time being, rather than challenge the Musa Daghians again, the Turks decided to starve them out. During this phase of the siege, Pastor Andreasian became the proud father of a son, Movses (Moses), the first infant born during the resistance.[44]

The only food on the mountain were the supplies the 4000 villagers had brought with them. "Mujaddara" made of crushed whole wheat, cooked with lentils and oil was the typical noon and evening meal.[45] It was not long before they had consumed all their stores of bread, olives, and cheese. For weeks they had been spared from starvation by killing their livestock. Goat milk was reserved for the children and the sick. By the end of the sixth week of the siege, provisions were dangerously low. To compensate, men, women, and boys would steal into the villages at night foraging for food. During one of these episodes, some boys went into Bitias and captured an Arab who said the Turks had nine brigades ready to attack. The situation on Musa Dagh had now become so tenuous that the governing council discussed plans to accelerate their contact with friendly forces.[46]

One runner had already been sent to make the dangerous eighty-five mile journey through Turkish villages to Aleppo with an appeal for help to the American Consul, Jesse B. Jackson.[47] When the runner did not return, another volunteer crept through the Turkish lines hoping to sight an Allied ship in Alexandretta harbor thirty-five miles to the north, but he returned without success. Other appeals went to Boghos Nubar Pasha of the Armenian General Benevolent Union (AGBU) in Cairo and to the Armenian Prelacy in Aleppo.[48] In addition, three strong swimmers were always posted on the Mediterranean shore. Their mission was to brave the pounding surf and contact any passing ship to deliver an urgent message. The appeal was written in English by Andreasian and addressed to the Allies:

> To any English, American, French, Italian, or Russian Admiral, captain, or authority ... we appeal in the name of God and human brotherhood:
>
> We, the people of six Armenian villages, about 5000 souls in all, have withdrawn to that part of Mousa Dagh called Damlayik, ...
>
> The Government some forty days ago informed us that our six villages must go into exile.
>
> Rather than submit to this we withdrew to this mountain. We now have little food left, and the troops are besieging us. We have had five fierce battles ...
>
> Sir, we appeal to you in the name of Christ! Transport us, we pray you to Cyprus or any other free land ...

If this is too much to grant, transport at least our women, old people, and children, equip us with sufficient arms, ammunition, and food, and we will work with you with all our might against the Turkish forces. Please, sir, do not wait until it is too late!

Respectfully your servant, for all the Christians here.

September 2, Dikran Andreasian.[49] (Appendix III)

On Andreasian's recommendation, the women made two large white banners. On one, was printed in bold English letters CHRISTIANS IN DISTRESS. The second banner had a large red cross at the center. They were fastened to tall saplings atop the cliffs overlooking the Mediterranean. While a constant watch scanned the horizon, the intermittent rain, heavy mist, and fog contributed to the ever-increasing depression of the isolated enclave atop Musa Dagh.[50]

The Turks were well aware that the stranded enemy had been weakened by the dwindling supply of food. In the interim, they launched a psychological campaign by raising the decibel level at the base of the mountain with their threatening epithets. The obstinate Armenian foe was reminded that resistance was futile and that it would be useless to expect outside help. The Turkish commander demanded unconditional surrender. Realizing that their threats were futile and the siege was not working to their advantage, the Turks regrouped their forces for what proved to be their fiercest assault. Several thousand Turkish regulars, using a larger mob of armed Muslim residents as a shield, closed in on the defenders.[51] Making up for their lack of matching arms, the Armenians had prepared massive walls of logs and rocks. As the enemy approached the encampments atop Musa Dagh, the attack increased in severity. Then the wood and stone engines were let loose. The approaching

Turks met a devastating avalanche of logs, rocks, and boulders hurtling down the precipitous mountainside in addition to the Armenian firepower. It was another resounding victory that bolstered the spirits of the Musa Daghians and bought them precious time.[52]

Chapter 3

DELIVERANCE OF
THE UNVANQUISHED

A joint enterprise

And then, the miracle! On Sunday morning, September 5 (Andreasian says it was the fifty-third day on Musa Dagh), while Reverend Andreasian was preparing a sermon, a runner approached shouting:

> *Pastor! Pastor! A battleship is coming and has answered our waving. Praise God! Thank God! Our prayers are heard. When we waved the Red Cross flag, the battleship answers by waving signal flags. They see us and are coming in nearer shore!* [53]

Patrolling the Syrian coast, the *Guichen*, a French armored cruiser commanded by Captain Joseph Brisson, part of the 3rd Squadron of the French Mediterranean fleet based in Port Said, Egypt, had sighted the banners. A wireless message was immediately sent to the commander of the fleet, Vice-Admiral Dartige du Fournet, apprising him of the situation. [54] The Musa Daghians were frantic with joy. Captain Brisson sent a launch for a delegation [55] to come aboard and tell their story. Based on their information, he ordered the bombardment of the village and church at Kabusiye, which the Turks were using as a campground and arsenal. The shelling was also directed at the hills occupied by the

Turks. Shortly thereafter, the flagship, the armored cruiser *Jeanne d'Arc*, accompanied by the French warships *Desaix*, *D'Estrées*, and *Foudre* and a British warship joined the *Guichen*.[56]

The Musa Dagh representatives were aboard the *Jeanne d'Arc* within hours. They conferred with du Fournet, who assigned Captain Edouard Alphonse Vergos of the *Desaix* the task to evacuate the Musa Daghians. It was a fortunate happenstance that serving on the *Desaix* was a French Armenian officer, Lieutenant Charles Diran Tekeyan (nephew of the Armenian poet, Vahan Tekeyan), who acted as interpreter and intermediary. The Musa Daghians wanted their non-combatants removed from the war zone and the fighters to have enough guns and food to continue the fight. While sympathetic to the defenders' request, du Fournet ordered the evacuation of all the Musa Daghians. Once Tekeyan gave the evacuees their instructions and organized the refugees according to their villages, the embarkation got underway. As they moved down to the beach, the fighters remained behind to give cover. Descending the Mediterranean coast of Musa Dagh entailed a precipitous trek of about four hours through rugged terrain.[57] Haroutune Boyadjian in his *Musa Dagh and My Personal Memoirs* called the embarkation area "Salvation Valley."[58] In a few days, the Musa Daghians were evacuated from the mountain that had been their refuge for almost eight weeks. Despite the approaching enemy, high seas, and breakers, no one was lost thanks to the trained French naval personnel and the Musa Daghian fighters.[59]

According to Andreasian's statistics, about 180 Musa Daghians had died or escaped during the siege. Eighteen of them made the supreme sacrifice in combat; the youngest was seventeen and the oldest was sixty-one.[60] Their ashes are contained in separate urns at St. Paul Armenian Apostolic Church in Anjar, Lebanon.[61]

Among the possibilities discussed for resettlement were Algeria,

Tunisia, Morocco, Cyprus, Rhodes, Corsica, and the Caucasus.[62] After much diplomatic wrangling, the first contingent of Musa Daghians, after a two-day sail, arrived at the British refugee installation, Camp Lazaret (Lazarus) at Port Said, Egypt, on September 14. A tent city was set up and arranged the way the villages were located on the slopes of Musa Dagh.[63] Due to the tireless efforts and organizational skills of several British camp officials, the refugees were given excellent care. The Armenian Red Cross Society of Cairo, headed by the Armenian Apostolic Primate of Cairo, Bishop Torkom Gushagian, sent a staff of doctors and nurses.[64] Within a matter of days, all of the survivors were examined and inoculated. The Armenian General Benevolent Union of Cairo provided food and clothing at the camp. A school was soon set up for the children. Here at the Port Said encampment, Bishop Torkom, in the presence of several thousand Musa Dagh survivors of the siege, christened one of the new baby boys Movses Guichen.

Soon after their arrival at Camp Lazaret, Andreasian filed the following survivors report:

Babies and children under four years of age	*413*
Girls from four to fourteen	*505*
Boys from four to fourteen	*606*
Women above fourteen years of age	*1449*
Men above fourteen years of age	*1076*
Total number of souls rescued	*4049*[65]

According to Andreasian's calculations, the actual defense atop Musa Dagh lasted from July 15 to September 5, 1915, a total of fifty-three days. Using his "calendar," the Musa Daghians' ordeal equals sixty-four days from the date of receipt of the summons on July 13 to the arrival of the first contingent of survivors at Port Said on September

14, 1915. In his historic account of the siege and deliverance at Musa Dagh, Andreasian insisted that the stand taken at Musa Dagh was a joint enterprise of the entire Armenian population and that no single political party or religious group or individual could claim credit for the victory.[66]

Within a few weeks, about 600 Musa Daghians, including their military commander, Movses Der Kaloustian,[67] volunteered to fight in the French *Legion d'Orient*[68] led by Colonel Louis Romieu, under the command of General Edmund Allenby.[69]

The passion exhibited by the Armenians atop Musa Dagh reminds us that as long as there is an unvanquished human spirit and communal unity there is always the chance to triumph. The siege and deliverance of Musa Dagh has taken its rightful place in legend and in the annals of Armenian history.

Chapter 4

SUBSEQUENCE

The destruction of roads leading to Musa Dagh

Following the Allied defeat of the Central Powers in 1918, the Musa Dagh survivors gradually left the refugee camp at Port Said. Some of them settled in Cairo and Alexandria. As a result of the Allied prime ministers' agreement at San Remo, Italy, in 1920, the Sanjak of Alexandretta, was renamed Hatay and placed under a French-Syrian mandate guaranteed by France and Turkey in the Franklin-Bouillon Agreement of October 1921.[70] Under the impression that the Turkish presence in the Musa Dagh region had ended, the majority of Musa Dagh survivors returned to their native environs in the foothills of their beloved mountain fortress. Under French administration, they were able to reclaim their properties.

On Sunday, September 18, 1932, on the occasion of the seventeenth anniversary of the siege and deliverance at Musa Dagh, the survivors dedicated a memorial on Musa Dagh at Damlayik in remembrance of their martyrs and their victory. The monument resembled the prow and the funnels of a French warship centered by an Armenian Apostolic church altar. Inscribed on a marble plaque in Armenian and in French was the following text:

*For sixty days the Armenians of Musa Dagh resisted the
enemy heroically and were rescued from the danger of annihilation*

on September 14, 1915, with the help of the [French] marine
of the Syrian region, commanded by Dartige du Fournet.[71]

Participating in the ceremony was Musa Dagh's military commander Movses Der Kaloustian.

By 1936, the Armenians in Hatay numbered 24,911 (11.3 percent of the Hatay population). Ever since the occupation of the area, the French and Armenian presence there was a constant irritant to the Turkish government.[72] The Ataturk government exerted increasing pressure on France to cede the sanjak to Turkey. The overwhelming majority of the people living there, even some Turks, were vehemently against such action.[73] Ignoring their protests, France and Great Britain were more concerned about the ominous threats posed by Nazi Germany and Fascist Italy. The containment of Hitler and Mussolini and the security of the Dardanelles had priority. On the recommendation of the French military, France, wishing to retain favor with Turkey, made ready to return the contested area, contrary to the many treaties the Allies and Turkey had signed.[74] Protests from Armenians, particularly in Syria and Lebanon and the Armenian Catholicate in Antelias, Lebanon, were filed with the League of Nations, but to no avail.[75] The Turkish government urged the French to convince the Musa Dagh Armenians to remain. Ataturk, in a bold exaggeration, claimed that Armenians had descended from the Turkish race and should remain and labor with their Turkish kinsmen and yet he simultaneously ordered the destruction of all roads leading to Musa Dagh. The intent was to discourage French aid for the Armenians contemplating a second defense of Musa Dagh. The Musa Daghians, especially the survivors of the 1915 siege, had asked the French for support to defend themselves on the mountain, only to be rejected.[76]

With the Franco-Turco cession a fait accompli, from July 17 to 22,

1939, the Armenians evacuated Hatay, preferring Syria and Lebanon—particularly Beirut—rather than Turkish domination.[77] The Turkish response was to prohibit the exchange by the émigrés of 25 Syrian pounds or more and to admonish Turks from buying the properties of the evacuees. It legitimized the confiscation of 400 million French francs' worth of abandoned property and goods. In contrast, the Turkish government paid 35 million francs to France to compensate for the properties of French nationals.[78] A total population of over 219,000 in Hatay, including a majority of non-Armenians, was eventually reduced by emigration by over one-third by 1940. The Turks promptly reduced the Musa Dagh memorial to rubble.

Eventually, many of the Musa Dagh families founded a settlement in Anjar, Lebanon, near the Syrian border. In 1946, as a result of the Soviet Russian repatriation program, about half of the Musa Daghians in Anjar moved to Soviet Armenia.[79] As a consequence of the civil war in Lebanon, the Armenian population of 300,000 declined considerably after 1975. A great number of Lebanese Armenians established new homes in the United States, particularly in Los Angeles, Fresno, and San Francisco. Some of the Musa Dagh survivors and their descendants were among them. Their numbers have increased enough to sponsor Musa Dagh compatriotic organizations in those communities.

Every year in September, the victory at Musa Dagh is celebrated in the churches of the Diaspora Musa Dagh communities and in Armenia. A memorial service (hokeehunkist) remembering the event is highlighted in the ancient and traditional ceremony of the blessing of a "madagh" (sacrificial lamb).[80] "Hariseh," a porridge made of chicken or lamb and barley, is prepared.[81] Following the services, the symbolic meal is offered to the congregation to emphasize the unity of the community in the commemoration of the heroic epic of Musa Dagh.[82]

A sentimental journey to the Musa Dagh region by Armenian American tourists in September 1993 witnessed an area virtually void of Armenians. Bitias, now Teknepinar, is home to about 300 non-Armenians. What was once the Armenian Protestant church is now a mosque. In Vakef (Vakifli), the tourists were pleased to meet an Armenian family who still clung to such Armenian names as Ardemis, Viken, and Arshag.[83] Outside Vakef there was no evidence that Armenians had lived in the foothills of Musa Dagh before the time of Christ. Only Vakef retains its Armenian identity. For policing purposes, the Turkish government in 1939 had concentrated all the Armenians in the Musa Dagh region in Vakef. Today it is home to less than 40 Armenian families. It is the only village of its kind in all of Turkey completely populated by Armenians.

On August 9 and 10, 1997, the church in Vakef, having been rebuilt with the permission of the Turkish government, was reconsecrated as the Armenian Church of the Holy Mother of God (Soorp Maryam Asvadzazin/St. Mary) by the Armenian Patriarch of Constantinople (Istanbul), Archbishop Karekin Kazandjian. The title of "arch priest" was awarded to the ninety-three-year-old pastor of the village, the Reverend Serovpe Gulian. Following the Divine Liturgy, "hariseh" was served to hundreds of villagers and guests. On the same occasion, a bust of Kemal Ataturk was unveiled in the village square.[84]

Ninety years have passed since the onset of the Armenian Genocide of World War I. All that exists of the Armenian past in eastern Turkey (historic Armenia) are remnants discernible only to a knowledgeable eye. Any signs of Armenian monuments, culture, or glory are in a state of disrepair or in ruins. It is difficult to find restored, protected, and recognized Armenian historic sites in Turkey today. The ethnic cleansing of the Armenians of Turkish Asia Minor is a fait accompli. Turkey's solution is to remain in a state of denial that the Armenian Genocide ever happened.

Fifteen years after the siege and deliverance of Musa Dagh, it remained for an Austrian Jew, Franz Werfel, to remind the world of the first genocide of the twentieth century and to capture the soul and the fighting spirit of the Armenian people in *The Forty Days of Musa Dagh*.

NOTES - BOOK I
CRUCIBLE: THE SIXTY- FOUR DAYS OF MUSA DAGH

Chapter 1
AN IDYLLIC COMMUNITY: THE ARMENIANS OF MUSA DAGH

1. Franz Werfel, *The Forty Days of Musa Dagh*, Book One, Chapter 2, pp. 42-43.

2. The Armenians call the Mountain of Moses Mousa Ler. In Arabic it is called Jabel Musa. The Turkish name is Musa Dagh. Its elevation ranges from 410 to 4446 feet above sea level. At 902 feet above sea level, YoghunOluk and Kabusiye had the highest elevation of the six villages.

3. In 1915, Musa Dagh was located in the nahiye (sub-district) of Suedia in the kaza (district) of Antioch in the sanjak (a large administrative district or state) of Alexandretta. Werfel, in his novel, included the Ezzeirs as the seventh village.

4. Vahram L. Shemmassian, "The Armenian Villagers of Musa Dagh, A Historical-Ethnographic Study, 1840-1915," Ph.D. diss., University of California, Los Angeles, 1996, p. 26. These statistics are estimates of the Reverend Dikran Andreasian, chairman of the Central Administrative Council during the siege.

5. Ibid., pp. 9-21.

6. Dikran Andreasian, "A Red Cross Flag That Saved Four Thousand," *The Outlook*, 12/1/15, Vol. CXI, p. 799.

7. Haroutune P. Boyadjian, *Musa Dagh and My Personal Memoirs*, Fairlawn, N. J.: Rosekeer Press, 1981, p. 4.

8. Shemmassian, "Armenian Villagers," p. 58.

9. Interview of Joseph Matossian, President, Musa Dagh Compatriotic Union of San Francisco, by the author, Berkeley, Calif., 10/6/89.

Chapter 2
SIEGE AND RESISTANCE

10. Dates are based on the Western/Christian calendar and the Reverend Dikran Andreasian's records. Regarding the dates, there is a discrepancy between Andreasian's article, "A Red Cross Flag That Saved Four Thousand" in *The Outlook* and in the expanded account he wrote translated by Knarik O. Meneshian. To be consistent, the dates will be based on *The Outlook* article due to its proximity in time to the event.

11. In the text Armenian names are spelled to conform to the author's transliteration method based on Western Armenian pronunciation.

12. University of California, Los Angeles, Special Collections Library, *Werfel Papers*, Box 9; *New York Herald Tribune, Books*, "Werfel and *The Forty Days of Musa Dagh*, Comments by Survivors of the Tragedy on the Novel's Authenticity in Spirit and Fact," Interview of the Reverend Harutiun Nokhudian by Avedis Derounian, a reporter for *The Armenian Spectator*, 3/24/35, p. l0.

13. Andreasian, "Red Cross Flag," *The Outlook*, p. 800.

14. Shemmassian, "Armenian Villagers," p. 197.

15. Derounian/Nokhudian Interview, UCLA, *Werfel Papers*, Box 9; *New York Herald Tribune*, 3/24/35, *Books*, p. 10.

16. Shemmassian, "Armenian Villagers," p. 196.

17. *New York Times*, "Beat Off 4000 Turks," 3/12/16, p. 3.

18. Andreasian, "Red Cross Flag," *The Outlook*, p. 801.

19. Shemmassian, pp. 26,196.

20. Ibid., Andreasian says there were 4231 Armenians atop Musa Dagh during the siege while 2080 Musa Daghians followed Reverend Nokhudian into exile.

21. Knarik O. Meneshian, *Escape to Musa Dagh or the Banishment of Zeitoun and*

Suedia's Revolt. Translated from Dikran Andreasian's *Zeituni Antsnadviutuin yev Suedia Inknabashbanatuin (The Surrender of Zeitun and the Self-Defense of Suedia)*, Cairo, Egypt, 1915, Paramus, N.J.: Armenian Missionary Association of America, 1993, p. 37.

22. Shemmassian, p. 130. The active Armenian political parties were the Social Democratic Hnchakian, Armenian Revolutionary Federation (Dashnaktsutiun), and Reformed Hnchakian.

23. Ibid., pp. 98,104. The Musa Dagh Protestants numbered about six hundred. The Armenian Catholics were less than five hundred. The remainder of the Musa Dagh population was Armenian Apostolic (Loosavorchagan).

24. Andreasian, "Red Cross Flag," *The Outlook*, p. 801.

25. *Hairenik Weekly*, "80th Anniversary," 9/21/95, pp.10-11.

26. Boyadjian, *Memoirs*, p. 14.

27. Andreasian, "Red Cross Flag," *The Outlook*, p. 801.

28. Antreassian/Meneshian, *Escape to Musa Dagh*, p. 45. The members of the Central Administrative Council were: Chairman Dikran Andreasian (Antreassian), Secretary Mikael Gegejian, Hetoon Filian, Sahag Andekian, Hadjee Khatcher Mardirian, Hovnan Eskenderian, Eskender Kelemian, Jabra Kazanjian, Boghos Kabaian, Hovhannes Koboorian, Movses Der Kaloustian, Melkon Kouyoumjian, Krikor Tovmassian, Yesayee Ibrahimian, Simon Shemmassian, and Tovmas Aghayan.

29. Shemmassian, pp. 201-202. Serop Sherpetjian and Tigran Garajian were the lieutenants.

30. Antreassian/Meneshian, *Escape to Musa Dagh*, pp. 45-48.

31. Shemmassian, pp. 204-205. Three blacksmiths assisted master gunsmith Nerses Kazanjian.

32. Derounian/Nokhudian Interview, UCLA, *Werfel Papers*, Box 9, *New York Herald Tribune, Books*, Vol. VII, 3/24/35, p. 10.

33. Ibid.

34. The invasion, led by the ANZAC forces (Australian and New Zealand troops), at Gallipoli took place on April 25, 1915, the day after the Young Turks issued the directive that initiated the Armenian Genocide. When the Allied/ANZAC mission failed, the entire invasion force was eventually withdrawn by December 1915. The plan's architect was the First Lord of the Admiralty, Winston Churchill, who was dismissed from the Cabinet.

35. Vahakn N. Dadrian, *German Responsibility in the Armenian Genocide, A Review of the Historical Evidence of German Complicity*, Watertown, Mass.: Blue Crane Books, 1996, pp. 109-110.

36. Ibid., pp. 136-137.

37. Alexander A. Antrasian (brother of the Reverend Dikran Andreasian), "Memories," *Hairenik Weekly*, 9/27/35, p. 6.

38. Antreassian/Meneshian, *Escape to Musa Dagh*, p. 43. Bedros Kaloustian was the sniper.

39. Shemmassian, pp. 203-204. The chiefs were Esayi Yagupian, Petros Timlakian, and Petros Tutaglian.

40. Boyadjian, *Memoirs*, p. 17.

41. Ibid.

42. Andreasian, "Red Cross Flag," *The Outlook*, p. 802.

43. Boyadjian, *Memoirs*, pp. 17-20; Andreasian, "Red Cross Flag," *The Outlook*, p. 801; Antrasian, "Memories," *Hairenik Weekly*, 9/27/35, p. 6.

44. Andreasian, "Red Cross Flag," *The Outlook*, p. 802.

45. Boyadjian, *Memoirs*, p. 20.

46. Antreassian/Meneshian, *Escape to Musa Dagh*, pp. 48-55.

47. Shemmassian, pp. 209, 330 (note 118). Unknown to Andreasian, the Musa Dagh messenger delivered the pastor's letter to Jackson in August. In a statement issued three years later, Jackson, apprised of the situation at Musa Dagh through an Armenian emissary, believed he himself might have alerted the French fleet at Beyrouth. (U.S. National Archives, RG 59, File 867.4016/386, J.B. Jackson to Secretary of State, May 27, 1918.)

48. Antreassian/Meneshian, *Escape to Musa Dagh*, p. 62.

49. Andreasian, "Red Cross Flag," *The Outlook*, p. 802.

50. Ibid.

51. A. Antrasian, "Memories of a Survivor of Musa Dagh, the Rescue, the Sojourn, and the Return," *Hairenik Weekly*, 11/22/35, p. 4.

52. Andreasian, "Red Cross Flag," *The Outlook*, p. 803.

Chapter 3

DELIVERANCE OF THE UNVANQUISHED

53. Ibid.

54. Shemmassian, p. 211

55. Ibid., p. 221. Bedros Timlakian led the delegation.

56. Boyadjian, *Memoirs*, p. 25.

57. Shemmassian, pp. 213-218,332.

58. Boyadjian, *Memoirs*, p. 25.

59. Werfel's sources of the rescue came from documents furnished by the French War Ministry, which included Vice Admiral Dartige du Fournet's memoirs, *Souvenirs de Guerre d'un Amiral, 1914-1916*, Paris, 1920, and his official report of the events of September 1915 to the French Marine (Naval Command); *The Blue Book*, 1916, Document 131, "Report of Musa Dagh Rescue by Bishop Torkom of the Gregorian community in Egypt," pp. 521-529, which was most likely in the Mekhitarist Library in Vienna.

60. *75th Anniversary of the Heroes of Mousa Ler*, 1915-1990, Directory, translated from the Armenian, Mousa Lertzis, Bay Area and Fresno, Calif., 1990.

61. Shemmassian, pp. 263-264. In addition to Anjar, Lebanon, there are two other memorials dedicated to the heroes of Musa Dagh. In 1976, the Musa Dagh community in Soviet Armenia built an impressive monument and museum on a hilltop in the town of Musa Ler (midway between Yerevan and the Holy See of Etchmiadzin). At the entrance today is a large white bust of Franz Werfel. Since 1989, there has been an eagle-topped monument in Cambridge, Ontario, Canada.

62. Ibid., p. 222.

63. Boyadjian, *Memoirs*, p. 29.

64. Andreasian, "Red Cross Flag," *The Outlook*, p. 803. Arshak Fermanian of the Kodak Company and Professor Hovhannes T. Kayayan directed the relief efforts.

65. Ibid., See Appendix IV for Musa Dagh Chronology.

66. Antreassian/Meneshian, *Escape to Musa Dagh*, p. xiii.

67. Shemmassian, p. 203. After the victory at Musa Dagh, Movses Der Kaloustian served as an officer in the French *Legion d'Orient* in Palestine, Lebanon, Syria, and Cilicia. Following the war he was sub-district governor of Musa Dagh. Later he served as an Armenian deputy in the Syrian and Lebanese parliaments and as a member of the highest ruling body of the Armenian Revolutionary Federation. At the time of the siege he was in his early twenties.

68. Antrasian, "Memories," *Hairenik Weekly*, 11/22/35, p. 4.

69. Boyadjian, *Memoirs*, p. 36.

Chapter 4

SUBSEQUENCE

70. Avedis K. Sanjian, "Sanjak of Alexandretta (Hatay), A Study of Franco-Turco Relations," Ph.D. diss., University of Michigan, Ann Arbor, 1956, pp. 1-2, 15, 38.

71. Shemmassian, pp. 262-263.

72. Sanjian, p. 109.

73. Sanjian, pp. 109, 171.

74. Ibid.

75. *New York Times*, 6/16/38, 6/26/38.

76. Sanjian, *Alexandretta*, pp. 187b, 218a,b, 219a.

77. Kenneth Waring, "Armenians on March Again," *Christian Science Monitor*, 9/16/39, pp. 5, 15.

78. Sanjian, *Alexandretta*, pp. 219b,c.

79. Shemmassian, p. 263.

80. *The Armenian Observer*, "Fresno and San Francisco Musa Dagh Union," 8/20/86, p. 11.

81. Throughout biblical times and Armenian history it has been a custom to offer a "madagh" or sacrifice to give thanks to God for a success, triumph, or a return to health. When the Musa Daghians were saved from annihilation, they had offered a "madagh" (a lamb) to God for their salvation..

82. The author witnessed such celebrations at St. Gregory Armenian Apostolic Church, San Francisco, 9/17/89 and 9/17/95.

83. John Baronian and Richard Demirjian were interviewed by the author about their September 1993 visit to Musa Dagh in Moraga, California, 8/8/96.

84. *The Armenian Observer*, "Historic Pilgrimage to Moussa Dagh," 9/3/97, pp. 1, 13.

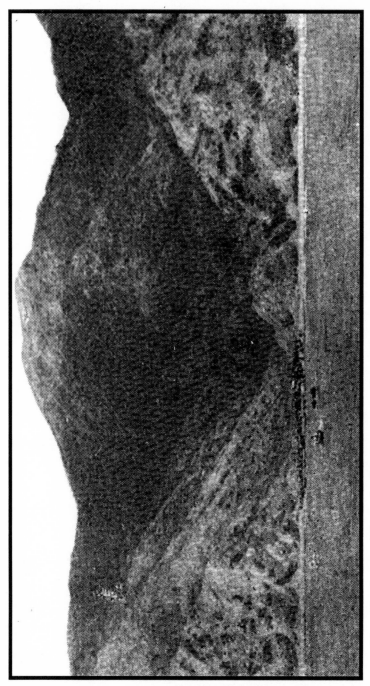

5   *Musa Dagh* viewed from the Mediterranean Sea. Armenians awaiting deliverance by the French Navy, September 1915.

6 *(Below)* Pastor Dikran Andreasian (Antreassian) Chairman, Central Administrative Council.

7 *(Above)* Movses Der Kaloustian, *Musa Dagh* military commander (1932 Photo).

8 *(Left)* Rev. Father Abraham Der Kaloustian of YogunOluk.

9 Damlayik (1999) Site of the main encampment on *Musa Dagh* in 1915.

10 View of the Mediterranean Sea from *Musa Dagh* (1999).

13 Serving aboard the *Desaix*, Lieut. Charles Tekeyan (11) acted as interpreter and intermediary. Vice Admiral Darrige du Fournet (12), Commander 3rd Squadron, French Mediterranean fleet, flagship *Jeanne d'Arc* (13), September 1915.

14 Rescue of the *Musa Dagh* Armenians by French naval personnel, September 1915.

15 The *Musa Dagh* Red Cross flag on display during religious services, Port Said, 1915.

16 Musa Dagh volunteers in training camp at Cyprus, 1915. Movses Der Kaloustian, middle row, sixth from left (wearing white kepi).

17 The *Musa Dagh* Memorial today, reduced to rubble by the Turkish Government in 1939.

(18, Left) The *Musa Dagh* Memorial dedicated in September 1932.

18

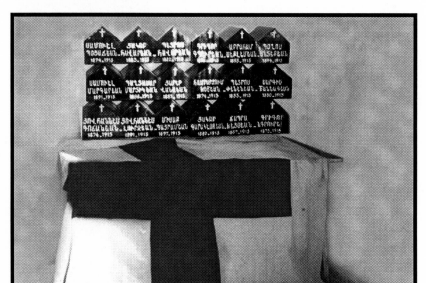

19 Red Cross flag sighted by the French armored cruiser, *Guichen*. Urns of martyred fighters, St. Paul Armenian Church, Anjar, Lebanon (1999).

20 Memorial honoring the French Navy, Anjar, Lebanon (1999).

21 The *Musa Dagh* monument, Musa Ler, Armenia.

BOOK II

The Catalyst
and
The Messenger

... a great voice, as of a trumpet.
—The Revelation of St. John the Divine 1:10

Chapter 5

THE PASSION OF FRANZ WERFEL

He had no peer

"I have not forgotten that I, too, am a victim of persecution," wrote Franz Werfel in his last work, *A Star of the Unborn*, a utopian narrative of an autobiography set a hundred thousand years in the future.[1] Werfel's victimization may have been a factor that compelled him to write an epic novel about another persecuted minority. Why would this Austrian Jew be so inspired to write a masterpiece that one day would be acclaimed by Armenians as their treasure?

Werfel was born September 10, 1890, in Prague, within the realm of the Hapsburg Austro-Hungarian empire. As the only son of a wealthy Jewish glove manufacturing family, he attended elementary and secondary schools in his native city, followed by a higher education at the universities of Prague and Leipzig. Much to his father's consternation, Werfel preferred to write rather than work in the family business. By his early twenties, he was a celebrated poet and a firm believer in the universality of man.[2]

With the outbreak of war in 1914, Werfel was conscripted into the Austrian army. While stationed on the Austrian-Italian front, he suffered a foot injury which plagued him the rest of his life.[3] Later, on the Galician-Russian front, Werfel unwittingly allowed enemy patrols to penetrate the Austrian lines while he wrote poetry. His literary pre-occupation resulted in a court-martial. Only the intervention of Max Reinhardt's secretary, Rudolf Kommer of the Austrian Secret Service, succeeded in commuting Werfel's death sentence.[4] Thanks to the intercession of Count Harry Kessler, a German aristocrat and patron of the arts and letters, Werfel was reassigned to the Army Press Division in Vienna and eventually discharged in 1917.[5] His military service convinced Werfel of the madness of war, instilling in him deep and abiding religious and pacifist convictions.

In October 1917, soon after making Vienna his home, Werfel met Alma Maria Schindler Mahler Gropius, a Roman Catholic and the belle of Vienna.[6] In her circle, Alma was recognized as "the wet nurse of geniuses."[7] She had been especially impressed by a particular passage in Werfel's poem *Man Aware*:

> *One thing I know:*
> *Nothing is mine to own;*
> *I possess alone*
> *This awareness ...*[8]

She was convinced that Franz Werfel's lifelong concern was exemplified by his driving credo: "How can I be happy while a single creature on earth suffers?"[9]

At the time of her encounter with Werfel, Alma was about eleven years his senior and was married to the eminent architect and founder of the Bauhaus, Walter Gropius. Ignoring convention, Werfel and Alma began an affair that eventually led to the permanent bonding of the two dynamic personalities. By January 1918, she was carrying their child.[10] Werfel considered the birth of their son, Martin Carl Johannes, to be "the most important moment in his life."[11] Within a few months they were traumatized by guilt feelings when the infant died.[12] They never had another child. Gropius proved to be most civil in recognizing the delicate situation that had engulfed the three of them; he divorced Alma in 1919.[13]

Werfel's prolific writings eventually earned him recognition as a literary genius and an extraordinary orator, lecturer, and storyteller on any subject. As a raconteur he had no peer.[14] By the early 1920s, Werfel was hailed as one of the most brilliant emerging young German language writers.[15] *Verdi: A Novel of the Opera* (1924) was so well received that it made Paul Zsolnay Verlag the most prominent publishing house in Austria.[16] It became Werfel's first American publication and was made into an Italian film. Between author and publisher, a personal relationship developed that paved the way for Alma's twice-divorced daughter, Anna Mahler, to marry Zsolnay.

Despite his marvelous attributes, Werfel also had debilitating habits that would plague him throughout his life. He was a coffee and tobacco addict. Ignoring doctors' advice, he chain-smoked cigars, cigarettes, and pipes.[17]

Werfel's flowering relationship with Alma and his war experience convinced many of their friends that he had become a secret convert to Christianity. He had told Gottfried Reinhardt[18] that the coming of Adolf Hitler and the charge of seeking favor prevented him from publicly converting to the Roman Catholic faith.[19] Reinhardt was convinced that Werfel had become a fervent Catholic in his heart and was "intellectually more Christian than Jew."[20] It was Werfel's piety, in part, that would set him on a journey that would have a profound impact on his literary career.

Chapter 6

APPOINTMENT IN DAMASCUS

El Greco faces

Intrigued by the wonders of the Middle East since their first trip there in 1925, Werfel and Alma made a second pilgrimage to the Holy Land in March 1929.[21] At his insistence, Alma consented to visit Damascus. It proved to be the propitious event that inspired Franz Werfel to write his crowning work. Despite warnings of danger, they set off from their base in Jerusalem, crossing the Syrian Desert in a car accompanied by a detective serving as both a bodyguard and guide. On the road to Damascus, armed mounted Arab Bedouins constantly harassed them. It was a harrowing ride, mitigated only by the presence of the armed escort.[22]

The unnerving trip was put behind them once they reached that most ancient of cities — Damascus. After refreshing themselves in their hotel they were eager to see the sights. Werfel was not one who thought that a traveler merely registered in hotel guest books and pasted exotic labels on luggage. He was the epitome of the peripatetic explorer whose insatiable curiosity compelled him to investigate the sights and sounds of every new environment.

To Alma, the Syrian capital was a typical Near Eastern sprawl of decaying buildings. After exploring some impressive mosques and lavish bazaars, they visited the largest carpet-weaving plant in the city to get a feel for what the Western world accepted as the typical industry of the Middle East. Georg Messon, the owner, graciously conducted them on a personal tour of his factory.[23] Passing along the rows of looms, the two tourists were shaken to see:

> *Emaciated children with El Greco faces and enormous eyes scurrying around the floor, picking up spools and threads, and wielding a broom now and then. Werfel inquired of the proprietor, "What strange children are these?" He replied, "Those poor creatures? I pick them up in the street and give them ten piasters a day, so they won't starve. They're the children of the Armenians killed off by the Turks. If I don't take them in, they starve and nobody cares. They can't really work; they're too feeble."* [24]

The sight of the haggard Armenian children brought home to Werfel the reality of the Armenian massacres.[25]

They left the factory stunned, traumatized by the encounter. They sought to regain their composure by relaxing at a nearby coffeehouse, but to no avail. Werfel had been so shaken by his contact with the scrawny Armenian children that his mind was seared by their wretchedness. One of the most enduring experiences in his life, it was the catalyst that inspired Werfel to set forth on a path that led to his magnum opus. This brief side trip to a Syrian carpet factory, probably lasting about an hour, shocked Werfel into an obsession. Like an earlier traveler on that fabled Damascus road, he went through a metamorphosis:

> *The miserable sight of some maimed and famished-looking refugee children, working in a carpet factory, gave me the final impulse to snatch from the Hades of all that was, this incomprehensible destiny of the Armenian nation.* [26]

The Damascus experience reinvigorated Werfel. Within a day he began to gather notes on the Armenian massacres until his hotel bed was covered with them.[27] Werfel's heart and mind were now consumed by the encounter with the Armenian children in Damascus and the story of the Armenian holocaust.[28]

Chapter 7

THE FORTY DAYS OF MUSA DAGH, THE NOVEL

He had a premonition

Upon his return to Vienna, Werfel arranged through his friend, French Ambassador Count Bertrand Clauzel, to obtain the file on the Armenian massacres from the French Ministry of War in Paris. Recognizing Werfel's literary credentials, the French granted permission to study the mass of records and documents indefinitely. Werfel was shocked at the enormity of the horrors of the Armenian tragedy.[29]

Under the heading "Scenarios and Plans, June 1930," Werfel began to compile his thoughts and ideas. By a stroke of luck, another of Werfel's most important resources was also in Vienna, the monastery and library of the Armenian Mekhitarists (an Armenian Roman Catholic monastic order). He credits his knowledge of the Armenian people to the revered Mekhitarist priests of Vienna, particularly Abbot Mesrob Habozian and Father Aginian. Respecting Werfel's desire to know as much as he could about the Armenians, the Mekhitarists granted him interviews and complete access to their library. For two years he immersed himself in the history, culture, and religion of the Armenian people. Determined to know as much about the Church of the Armenian People, Werfel used a German translation of the Armenian Apostolic Mass (Badarak) and other Armenian Church rites. Werfel was troubled to find that, despite the fifteen years that had elapsed since the onset of the Armenian disaster of 1915, the Mekhitarist fathers were still fearful of Turkish retaliation against Armenians. They asked him to omit their names and that of the monastery in his acknowledgments.[30]

In the process of his research, Werfel learned of the Armenian stands taken against Turkish "relocation" orders during the Great War at Van, Shabin-Karahissar, Zeitun, Urfa, and Musa Dagh. In June 1930, he decided to focus on the siege and deliverance at Musa Dagh because "it had so fascinated him that he wished to help the Armenian people by writing about it."[31]

Werfel never visited Musa Dagh and the surrounding environs. His knowledge of the area and the incident rests on diligent investigation and exacting scholarship, which won him the ultimate compliment of a Musa Dagh survivor:

> On the occasion of a banquet, December 3, 1935, sponsored by New York Armenians honoring Werfel, S. Panosian of Philadelphia, a native of YoghunOluk and a participant of the defense on Musa Dagh, showed Werfel a number of pictures of Musa Dagh and its vicinity. "This is Musa Dagh," Panosian said, "Of course you remember these heights?" "No, I don't remember because I have never seen Musa Dagh," answered Werfel. "But you have described everything so accurately in your book, how were you able to describe these places so accurately?" "I myself wonder at it as I now hear you say that my description has been so true." [32]

Werfel's most important *Musa Dagh* source at the Mekhitarist Library was a translation of the Reverend Dikran Andreasian's (Antreassian) eyewitness report of the events at Musa Dagh, *Zeituni Antsnadviutuin yev Suedia Inkabashbanatuin (The Surrender of Zeitun and the Self-Defense of Suedia)* and an article in *The Outlook* magazine, "A Red Cross Flag That Saved Four Thousand."[33] (Although the English spelling of Andreasian has many variations, Werfel had handwritten in his research notes, "Scenarios and Plans," "Past. Dikran Andreasian," just as it was spelled in *The Outlook* article of December 1, 1915.)[34] The evidence is conclusive that both sources provided Werfel the vital information for the basic structure of *The Forty Days of Musa Dagh* (Appendix IV, VI).

Because the French Navy was primarily responsible in relieving the siege at Musa Dagh, the official report of the event was contained in the French Ministry of War documents, which were made available to Werfel. The Mekhitarists, avid collectors of foreign language books and print media that related to anything Armenian, had on file *Souvenir de Guerre d'un Amiral, 1914-1916* (Paris, 1920), the memoirs of Vice-Admiral Dartige du Fournet, who commanded the Allied Naval Task Force that rescued the Musa Dagh survivors. Werfel's novel indicates it was one of his sources.

George Schulze-Behrend in his investigative report and analysis, "Sources and Background of Werfel's Novel," states that Werfel, in the course of his research, also relied on Paul Rohrbach's findings.[35] Rohrbach, an advocate of German penetration of the Near East (Drang nach Osten) via the Bagdad Railway, endorsed the relocation of the Armenians of Anatolia to Mesopotamia.[36] But Werfel depended more on the voluminous writings of the Armenophile German missionary Dr. Johannes Lepsius[37] (Lepsius' entreaties on behalf of the Armenians with the Ottoman Turkish triumvirate, the German diplomatic mission in Turkey, and the Foreign Office in Berlin had proved futile). These primary sources provided Werfel with a wide range of Armenian topics such as history, geography, political overviews, traditions, educational system, the Armenian church ... Werfel, intent on authenticity, even made his own sketches based on his research, for example:

- A penciled map locating Zeitun, Adana, Aintab, Urfa, Haleb (Aleppo), Iskenderun, and Musa Dagh, correctly marking the villages at its base with six dots.
- A sketch profiling the terrain from the plains of Antioch to the village of YoghunOluk (Werfel spelled it Yoghonolook) to the heights of Musa Dagh to the cliffs and the sea below.
- A sketch of the floor plan (cruciform) and a drawing of a traditional Armenian church (side and front views).[38]

Werfel's descriptions of the novel's battle scenes are reminiscent of his experiences as a front-line veteran in the Great War. In addition, Werfel demonstrates an extensive knowledge of regional flora and fauna, Turkish civil and military affairs, Armenian, Turkish, and Arabic expressions, religions of the region, and folklore.[39] Furthermore, Werfel's rigorous scholarship is evident in his grasp of ethnology, psychology, philosophy, and the Bible. The evidence is conclusive that Werfel received expert help at the Mekhitarist Library in Vienna.[40]

In a 1935 interview, the Reverend Harutiun Nokhudian, the exile of Bitias who survived the death march from Musa Dagh, complimented Werfel's depiction of the incident at Musa Dagh. Nokhudian told Avedis Derounian of *The Armenian Spectator* that Werfel must have thought him dead since his is the only true Armenian character he used in *The Forty Days of Musa Dagh*, the other characters being disguised by fictional names. Werfel incorporated Nokhudian and his Protestant congregation into his novel, and, following Andreasian's assumption, he concluded that Nokhudian and his people had perished during the deportation. Unknown to Werfel at the time he wrote the novel, Nokhudian was alive and working for Dan Akulian of the Grand Cash Markets in Albany, New York, in addition to carrying out his duties as the pastor of the United Armenian Congregational Church in Troy, New York.[41]

A few months after the Derounian interview, Nokhudian charged Werfel with using his name for his own purposes and threatened a lawsuit against him and Viking Press.[42] Nothing came of Nokhudian's threat. Had Nokhudian read Werfel's novel, he would have known that Werfel portrayed him as a hero because he bought time for those on Musa Dagh by informing the Turks that the Armenians:

> ... set out of their own accord into exile ... in every conceivable direction ... Pastor Nokhudian, whose mildness and Christian spirit of obedience had caused many to mistake him for a coward, revealed his heroism. This deception which he undertook to practice meant, at the least, death ... The instant the Turks discovered the stratagem, it would be all over with him. The fighters on the mountain had to gain time. This feint would postpone discovery several days and give them sufficient grace to complete the defenses.[43]

If Nokhudian had a legitimate complaint, he could have faulted Werfel for describing him as "the old pastor."[44]

The incident in Damascus had shocked Werfel's sensibilities. The Armenian children unable to operate the looms in the carpet factory never left his thoughts. He had the germ of an idea: he would describe Turkish anti-Armenian oppression by tapping the information he had gleaned since 1929 from various German, Austrian, French, English, and Armenian sources. He had also been struck by the similarity of the events of 1915 in Ottoman Turkey and the current miasma created by Adolf Hitler and his "brown shirts." It was as if Werfel had a premonition of the Jewish Holocaust to come.[46] To Werfel, there was a striking correlation between the Young Turks, represented by the oligarchy of Enver, Talaat, and Djemal, and the bigoted former Austrian corporal and the Nazis. Whereas the former were intent on destroying the Armenian nation, the latter were bent on ridding Germany of the Jews and all opposition.[47]

By July 1932, Werfel had amassed enough material to write his novel. Combining historical events and personalities, literary license, and reinforced with a creative genius, Werfel wrote *The Forty Days of Musa Dagh* in less than a year. During the writing process, he argued heatedly with Alma over Werfel's concept of a hero and heroism. Werfel rejected Alma's heroic ideal, which she had cultivated from her study of Wagner and Nietzsche. He was determined to portray an involuntary hero who has leadership thrust upon him.[48] In Gabriel Bagradian, the protagonist in *The Forty Days of Musa Dagh*, Werfel created a heroic figure who temporarily lost sight of his ancestral roots, and yet, because of his presence at a certain time and place, found himself taking on the responsibility of protecting his ethnic compatriots from their own government.

Warner Blumenthal, in his essay, "Father and Son in the East: A New Look at Werfel's *The Forty Days of Musa Dagh*," captures the essence of Werfel's involuntary hero, noting how Gabriel Bagradian rediscovered himself. Bagradian had lived in France for twenty-three years and was married to a sophisticated Parisian, Juliette. They are the parents of a thirteen-year-old son, Stephan. Being a non-Armenian, Juliette is looked upon as an outsider (the Armenian word is odar). On the death of his older brother, Gabriel is obligated to return to his birthplace to tidy up his family's affairs. In the process, he is caught up in a succession of events that cut off his escape to the peace and security he once knew in Paris. Gabriel wants to send his family out of danger to France. Stephan wants to stay. In a short time, Stephan has been bound to the land of his ancestors; he is more Armenian than French. Tragically he bears witness to his ancestry and faith like the biblical Stephen." The following passage in the novel emphasizes Werfel's point:

> Who so sees his father sees God. For the father is the last link in a long, unbroken chain of ancestors, binding all men to Adam, and hence to the origin of creation. And yet who so sees his son sees God. For this son is the next link, binding humans to The Last Judgment, the end of all things, the consummation.[49]

Gabriel, having returned to his native village of YoghunOluk, is torn between his ancestral heritage and the life he knew in Paris. As the Musa Daghians take to the heights of their protective mountain, Gabriel rejoins his people. His fate is to be the savior of his people in his moment of truth, the final meaning of his life. By sharing their fate, and by seeing the blood of his son spill onto his native soil, he becomes father to his people and witnesses their rescue. His purpose on earth has been fulfilled and his existence comes to an end. Werfel's piety comes forth in a particular passage:

> To the priest, Ter Haigasun, overcome with the euphoria of the miraculous rescue, the siege and deliverance of Musa Dagh have an eternal meaning: "The evil only happened ... to enable God to show us His goodness. [50]

Blumenthal goes on to say, the 'forty days' transformed Gabriel from the debonair, self-centered French-Armenian into the selfless, giving, sacrificial Christian Armenian. In parallels to the Old and New

Testaments, Gabriel fulfills his divine mission as father and as son, from Moses figure to Christ. Like Moses, Gabriel cannot share in his people's future. Nevertheless his leadership guarantees the survivors of Musa Dagh their salvation and the perpetuation of their faith and heritage. He envisions the promised land of the rescue, but is unable to enter it. He realizes that God has used him to fulfill a mission. His compatriots have evacuated Musa Dagh and are on their way to safe haven. Alone on Musa Dagh with the enemy stalking him, he comes upon the grave of his son. A Turkish sniper kills Gabriel. He falls on his son's grave; his son's cross lies upon his heart. As Christ died on the Cross for the sins of man and offered salvation, Gabriel Bagradian, the last martyr of Musa Dagh, is sacrificed so that his compatriots may live. In *The Forty Days of Musa Dagh*, Werfel succeeded in depicting the faith and the spirit of the Armenian people. The siege at Musa Dagh was a testing process, a "crucible that frees man from his temporal cross."[51]

It has been suggested that the novel "is not so much a historical novel as it is more of a metaphysically dramatized passion of the Armenian people."[52] Others may see it as an allegory on the Bible or of the 1930s in Germany and Palestine.

Although the actual siege atop Musa Dagh lasted fifty-three days, Werfel chose to phrase the title and theme of his novel in biblical terms.

Those who are versed in the Bible and the Christian religion should recognize the obvious references to the number forty in the Old and New Testaments, for example:

- It rained upon the earth for forty days in the story of Noah and the Ark.
- Christ's forty days of temptation and fasting in the wilderness.
- Ascension Day marking Christ's appearance before his Apostles forty days after his resurrection.

Among other Biblical references in the novel are:

- Gabriel's son, Stephan, who died of forty wounds in Werfel's novel, personifies Stephen, the first Christian martyr.
- The name Gabriel conjures up thoughts of the archangel, the messenger of God.
- In each of the novel's three books there are prefatory quotations from the *New Testament's Revelation of St. John the Divine.*

In November 1932, Werfel spent two weeks in Germany on a lecture tour. He read to his audiences the "Interlude of the Gods" chapter of his uncompleted novel, retelling the portentous historical confrontation between Enver, the Turkish minister of war, and the German missionary, Dr. Johannes Lepsius, the tireless champion of the Armenians. Werfel's presentation is intense and foreboding. Enver is the epitome of sartorial splendor and military correctness: inflexible, the personification of smooth, efficient cruelty and cold-blooded intransigence. He fends off the pleas of the awkward, disheveled, diabetic clergyman, a sincere man incapable of hate. Lepsius loses his argument. Werfel's choice of this chapter was calculated to show the correlation between Enver and Hitler.[53] Ironically, Enver was on record attesting to the bravery of Armenian soldiers in the Caucasus campaign. He even admitted that he owed his life to an Armenian.[54]

Werfel saw Hitler in Breslau on the last day of his lecture tour. On an earlier occasion, Heinrich Bruening, the former chancellor of the Weimar Republic, had told Werfel that Hitler would be victorious because he was infinitely patient and had a tremendous number of followers. The Werfels wanted to see for themselves this "new German" who had mesmerized 30 million people. One encounter was sufficient: Hitler was a man with "clutching eyes, frightened features ... an adolescent ... who would never mature ... would never reach wisdom."[55] What Werfel witnessed was enough to give him the final impetus to complete his task. He then focused on the completion of *The Forty Days of Musa Dagh*, isolating himself from Alma, family, and friends in Santa Margherita, Italy and Breitenstein am Semmering, Austria, for weeks. And then as Alma described it:

> *This afternoon Franz finished his great book,* The Forty Days of Musa Dagh. *The whole house waited breathlessly for his descent from his study. It is a titanic achievement for a Jew to write a work like this at this time, exposed to such animosities.*[56]

In November 1933, *Die Vierzig Tage Des Musa Dagh (The Forty Days of Musa Dagh)*, in two volumes, appeared in Vienna, Zurich, Leipzig, and Berlin bookstores[57] and immediately was hailed as Werfel's masterpiece. Despite his blacklisting and the loss of lecture engagements in Germany, Austria, and Switzerland, the novel was an overnight sensation in the opinion of critics and the literate public. The income realized from its sales afforded the Werfels temporary financial security.[58]

However, the ascendancy of the Nazis caused Werfel's fortunes to diminish. Raising one of the few voices against the "brown shirt" pestilence, he became a marked man in the Nazi periodical *Schwarze Korps*.[59] The same year his "Armenian" novel was published, he was expelled from the Prussian Academy of Art. In 1934, the Third Reich banned *The Forty Days of Musa Dagh* and eventually burned all his works.[60]

Meanwhile, the publicity surrounding *The Forty Days of Musa Dagh* had brought Werfel an invitation from the Mekhitarist fathers to speak to the Armenian community at St. Stebannos (Stephen) Church in Vienna. Werfel impressed the gathering with his knowledge of Armenian history and culture. He touched on the creation of the Armenian alphabet, the Armenian contribution to architecture, and the Armenians' great talent, mind, and soul. He was convinced that Armenia's geographic position made her the guardian of the crossroads between Europe and Asia and that the world owes the Armenians credit for exerting a decisive influence on the West. He extolled the Armenian will to survive despite the attempt by the Turkish government to exterminate an entire people. He emphasized in his closing statement that the Pilot of history selects martyred peoples like the Armenians for a special purpose.[61]

Chapter 8

THE POWER OF ART

It should make a magnificent movie

Before the publication of *The Forty Days of Musa Dagh* in Europe, Werfel had already found an American publisher. But the first English language edition appeared in London under the title *The Forty Days*, translated from the German by Geoffrey Dunlop, published by Jarrolds, and distributed in Canada about the same time by Ryerson Press, Toronto.[62] The Viking Press (New York) publication of Dunlop's translation was a single volume of 824 pages titled *The Forty Days of Musa Dagh*. It was in bookstores in the United States in December 1934.

As is so often said about translations from the original, something is lost. This was especially true with *The Forty Days of Musa Dagh*. A comparative analysis of the German and English language versions by Haigaz Kazarian reveals that Dunlop had deleted 312 passages totaling 1062 lines, about 11 percent of the original German language version. The deletions are equivalent to 90 missing pages in the Viking Press edition. Dunlop also made 53 errors in translation. A few examples of the deletions cited by Kazarian are:

- The omission of positive Armenian achievements in history (Vol. I of the original German edition, p. 87).
- The passage, "They had not fallen into the hands of an enemy

country, so that reciprocity of humane treatment as imposed by international law could have been respected. Alas, they had fallen into the hands of a ruthless, bloodthirsty foe, their own State — the Turkish Government." (Vol. I, p. 136)

- The absence of a discourse on the Armenian deportations (Vol. I, p. 206).

In addition, Kazarian points out the following substitutions:

- The phrase "to set out" is used as a euphemism for "deportation" (Vol. I, p. 135).
- In the German edition, the sentence, "The exile was enforced to the last letter." (Vol. II, p. 111), reads in the English translation, "The deportation law had already taken full effect." (p. 541). The change in the wording legalizes the murder and the looting that accompanied the deportations.
- In Volume I, page 546 of the original, Werfel speaks of the Turk who "only robs, kills, steals and rapes." In the English translation the same passage on page 380 reads "to loot."

Kazarian insists that the Dunlop version minimizes the toll of the Armenian Genocide.[63]

As in Europe, the book thrilled the literary world and stirred the reading public's imagination in the United States. It became the best seller of 1934-1935. More than 34,000 copies were sold in American bookstores in the first two weeks of December, surpassing any other book published in 1934. By the fall of 1935, it had been published in eighteen languages and had sold 200,000 copies in the United States alone.[64] Viking Press was so confident in *The Forty Days of Musa Dagh*'s appeal that it was uncompromising in its first commercial broadside,

THE POWER OF ART

claiming: "… it is the most magnificent combination of great literature and heroic story written in our time."[65]

The interest aroused by Werfel's novel was so momentous that Robert Hutchins, president of the University of Chicago, included it in his list of *100 Great Books*. *The Forty Days of Musa Dagh* also won Werfel consideration for the Nobel Prize in Literature.[66] It recognized him as the equal of Thomas Mann.

Commenting in the *Saturday Review*, Fresno's "man on the flying trapeze," William Saroyan wrote:

> … the timeless chronicle of … the good in man … at war with the evil in man … At a time of chaos and confusion, fear and madness, Franz Werfel reveals the naked heart of man, who is weak yet strong, sinful yet virtuous, mortal yet godly, evanescent yet timeless. His perception sinks deeply to qualities in man which do not end when men die, but go on forever in the living. This is a long novel, but in swiftness of movement it is all too short. Reading it, one hopes it might never end … The novel is written with that ease which gives writing and life inevitability. Franz Werfel's discipline, instead of repulsing, attracts freedom and power, and the consequence at times is prose of such beauty and strength that one is impelled, virtually, to stand and cheer … Here, at last, is a contemporary novel full of the breath, the flesh, blood, bone, and spirit of life.[67]

The *New York Times Book Review*, December 2, 1934, gave *The Forty Days of Musa Dagh* a full, front-page treatment, centered with a pensive portrait of Franz Werfel. Its editor, Louis Kronenberger, also heaped abundant praise:

> *A dramatic narrative that has stirring emotional forces*

... a story of men accepting the fate of heroes and the task of supermen ... If Hollywood does not mar and mishandle it, it should make a magnificent movie ... It is concerned with a moment in history still so close to us and with two races whose enmity has become such a byword—the subtler hate on the Turks' part for a race of superior culture ... It is a book that tells a story which is almost one's duty as an intelligent human being to read. And one's duty here becomes one's pleasure too![68]

Levon Garabed Baljian (the future Catholicos of the Church of Armenia) hailed:

Werfel's contribution to the Armenian people is unparalleled ... The Armenian nation will never be able to express sufficient gratitude ... We have nothing equivalent to this novel about the Armenian Genocide ... We have many memoirs, official documents, and foreign eyewitness accounts of the Genocide, but all these fade compared to Werfel's creation ... Franz Werfel's Armenians will live forever in the conscience of the world ... The power of art is great ... Because only art can immortalize an event, know the secret of eternity, and convey truth and reality more than reality itself ... Alas, if only the leaders of people and governments were cultivated by high understandings of art, probably our fate would have been different ... This day will come. Judging, humanly, it must come, for it is a human necessity.[69]

Elie Wiesel, Nobel Peace Prize Laureate and former Chairman of the United States Holocaust Commission, in an introduction to the new French edition wrote:

The novel is a masterpiece, both imaginative and historic.

I found in it the power of evocation and a troubled conscience which, in the past, had penetrated my innermost being. This Armenian village community became very close to me. Written before the coming of Hitler, this novel seems to foretell the future. How did Franz Werfel know the vocabulary and the mechanism of the Holocaust before the Holocaust — artistic intuition or historic memory? The novel is precisely about this memory. The besieged Armenians feared not death but being forgotten. The Turks should understand the pain and the anger of the Armenians who are denied the right to remember. Franz Werfel's great novel leads us to compassion, ... even to hope.[70]

More than seventy years have passed since the novel's appearance, and it still sparks comments. Yair Auron in his "*The Forty Days of Musa Dagh*: Its Impact on Jewish Youth in Palestine and Europe" hails Werfel's novel as more than a masterpiece. He credits him for bringing the Armenian Genocide to the attention of the world public and particularly influencing young Palestinian Jews. Auron goes on to say of World War II that the Warsaw uprising cannot be understood without reading *The Forty Days of Musa Dagh*. He cites Yitzhak Zuckerman, the deputy commander of the Jewish revolt in the Warsaw ghetto, as being inspired by Werfel's novel, for he appreciated the Armenian psyche. In Holland *The Forty Days of Musa Dagh* was a textbook passed from hand-to-hand by the Jewish underground. It was an example, a point of reference, and a model to be esteemed, admired, and imitated. It left the door open for at least a chance of survival.[71] David Shavit in *Hunger for the Printed World: Books and Libraries in the Jewish Ghettoes of Nazi-Occupied Europe* claims that Werfel's novel and Tolstoy's *War and Peace* were the most widely read books among adults.[72]

Ironically, Kronenberger's Hollywood comment proved prophetic.

The Forty Days of Musa Dagh became one of the most eagerly anticipated movies of the 1930s, and one of the most controversial.

Chapter 9

ICON

Werfel gave us a soul

The publicity accorded *The Forty Days of Musa Dagh* as a best-seller and potential motion picture, together with an invitation from Max Reinhardt, encouraged the Werfels to set sail for the United States in November 1935. It was Franz Werfel's first trip to America. Werfel had been commissioned by Reinhardt to write a libretto encompassing the Old Testament and European Jewish life into a biblical cavalcade called *The Eternal Road*. The stage production received tremendous advance publicity due to the involvement of Werfel, composer Kurt Weill, and set designer Norman Bel Geddes.[73] Werfel's reason for being part of the high-powered trio "in this age of paganism was to try to bring out the truth, the tolerance, the love, and the culture contained in the Bible. My political credo is to search for humanity everywhere and to avoid barbarism."[74]

Before embarking for America, Werfel had been warned by his editor, Ben Huebsch of Viking Press, that his "visit here would be punctuated by wearisome, entertaining delegations, and Armenians."[75] It was not an exaggeration. Werfel's novel had so swept the country that upon reaching New York he was deluged aboard ship by the press, among whom were representatives of the Armenian media. He told the journalists that he was aware of Turkish opposition to his novel and expressed his desire to see *The Forty Days of Musa Dagh* filmed. The Armenian reporters unanimously praised him for writing "the greatest monument of all dedicated to the Armenian cause."[76] Werfel responded, "The Armenian people are worthy of much more, and I, in acquainting myself with their heroic achievements and their glorious history, performed only my human duty and shall continue to perform."[77]

Werfel granted a private interview to Vartkes Aharonian of *The Hairenik Weekly*, an English language Armenian American newspaper. Aharonian described Werfel "… about forty-five, rather short and somewhat stout, with high forehead and curly hair, and a simple, affable and modest personality verging on shyness."[78] Werfel told Aharonian that the heartrending and terrifying stories he heard about the Armenian massacre inspired him to research and write *The Forty Days of Musa Dagh* as a permanent memorial to its victims. When asked if the events described in the novel were true, Werfel replied:

> *More than the truth; because an epic represents the truth colored by imagination. An epic written by a true poet contains more reality than a history written by a historian … The struggle of 5000 people on Musa Dagh had so fascinated me that I wished to aid the Armenian people by writing about it and bringing it to the world. Everything I have written is the truth.*[79]

While conducting research at the Mekhitarist Library, he was touched by the story of an Armenian who so loved his books that he carried them wherever he went. It gave him the inspiration for one of the characters in *Musa Dagh*, the apothecary Krikor of YoghunOluk.

In the novel, applying biblical symbolism, Krikor is described as "the fisher of men."[80] Werfel goes on to explain that to him, Krikor is:

> *A bibliophile whose library included books in Arabic, Hebrew, French, as well as Armenian. He was a man who contained within himself that deep Armenian love of culture, the secret of all ancient races which survive centuries. To Krikor, a book was the transformed sunbeam of a far higher sun than that whose beams we see with our eyes. He is the embodiment of the cultural aspirations of the Armenian people, while the novel's hero, Gabriel Bagradian, exemplifies the fighting spirit and the spirit of liberty and freedom.*[81]

Werfel emphasized that, more than anything else, the incident in Damascus was the catalyst that inspired him to write *The Forty Days of Musa Dagh*. He was the messenger. He told the press that the book was already in thirty-four languages but was banned in Germany. Aware of the Turkish opposition to the making of the film,[82] Werfel had nothing definite to add to the reporters' queries, other than to state that the Turks were trying to bring pressure upon the American film producers through the intervention of the French government. It was Alma who volunteered that her husband had received several threatening letters from Turks, which had alarmed her. The interview ended on a positive note when Werfel indicated, much to the delight of the Armenian press, that he would be willing to address local Armenians at a meeting.[83]

Basking in the adulation accorded him by the Armenians in America, the Werfels took time to acknowledge their outpouring of love, admiration, and gratitude. On December 3, 1935, at a testimonial banquet sponsored by the Armenian Revolutionary Federation in the Winter Garden, Hotel McAlpin, New York City, more than 500 Armenians paid tribute to the Werfels. As they entered the hall, the audience rose as one body and greeted them with a tumultuous and prolonged applause and cheers. Congratulatory letters and telegrams were read from New York Governor Herbert H. Lehman; Rabbi Stephen Wise, representing the Jewish community; Henry Morgenthau, Sr., the former American ambassador to Turkey (1913-1916); Cardinal Hayes; Bishop Manning; Col. Edward House (President Wilson's chief confidante and advisor); and James Gerard, former ambassador to Germany.

Werfel, in his address, acknowledged his indebtedness to the Armenian people and apologized for not being able to speak in Armenian or in English. "But whatever language I speak, it will be the language of my love for the Armenians."[84] He told the audience that *Musa Dagh* was a process by which his soul gained greatly and went on to explain that the process had four stages:

- During the World War, I heard about your great misfortunes and my sympathy and interest were aroused.
- During my sojourn in Damascus ... the sight of maimed children and stories of horror and heroism moved me, and I decided to write about Musa Dagh.
- As I researched and studied Armenian history and literature, my sympathy was transformed into admiration and made me want to know more.
- Acquainted with your ancient history and your cultural treasures, I knew why you had survived. I saw why the mighty nations that had once ruled over and oppressed you— Babylon, Rome, Byzantium, were dead and gone, but you were still alive. It was because you are a nation of book lovers, children of the spirit. The day Mesrob invented your alphabet, he laid the foundation of an immortal life for you. In spite of all your suffering you have

preserved your identity and have grown. You have produced valuable works of art and literature, and knowing you, I predict that you will produce still greater ones in the future. And this, my friends, is the part of you that cannot and will not be destroyed.[85]

From the audience came the voice of Mr. Amato, a Turkish Jew from Musa Dagh: "The real need of the Armenians is to unite for the common cause. You must patronize one another regardless of your political beliefs. You must do this by action and not words."[86] Jacob Banton, former New York district attorney, instilled hope in his audience when he said: "Perhaps forty years after Franz Werfel's book Armenia shall regain its freedom."[87]

In a parting note, Werfel brought the audience to its feet again when he told them that *The Forty Days of Musa Dagh* would be filmed and expressed his gratitude that he had won the battle to have the film made.[88] The master of ceremonies lauded Franz Werfel as "one of the foremost friends of the Armenians, a man Armenians respect, admire, love and cherish and to whom the Armenians will be forever grateful."[89]

However, the objections of the Turkish government were already making their way into the American press. Unknown to Werfel, that same week the trade journal *Motion Picture Herald* reported:

> *The objection of the Turkish government was based on the fact that the story,* Musa Dagh, *portrays Turkish persecution of the Armenian people—a historical fact which is about as plain as, say, the German invasion of Belgium in 1914. Yet the Turkish government, brushing aside the plain facts of history, ignoring the essential truth of the story, simply introduces arbitrary objection to which, of course, is added at least an intimation of exerting the full measure of its influence against*

*the producer in the event the story is produced ... It is to be
assumed that this (U.S.) government would accept the protest of
the Turkish government ... that the State Department would
forbid the picture in the United States ... The process is simply
one of arbitrary exclusion, based only on the selfish wish that a
skeleton which has long reposed in the closet of a nation shall
not be rattled.*[90]

On Christmas Eve, the Werfels were welcomed to participate in the
services of the Protestant Armenian Evangelical Church. In his sermon,
the pastor, the Reverend Antranik Bedikian, praised Franz Werfel, telling
the congregation, "We were a nation, but Franz Werfel gave us a soul."[91]
At the conclusion of the service, every member of the congregation
shook hands with the man who had rekindled their hopes in reminding
the world of the Armenian massacres in Turkey.[92]

Werfel consented to be the celebrant at several more gala banquets.
On Christmas Eve of the Armenian Apostolic Church, January 5, 1936,
the Werfels were feted at an immense banquet in the Hotel Pennsylvania,
hosted by the Rt. Rev. Mampre Calfayan, acting primate of the Armenian
Church in America. Once again he heard spirited speeches and received
six standing ovations. Among the speakers was former ambassador to
Turkey Henry Morgenthau, Sr.[93] At yet another banquet, the Jewish
Forum paid homage to Werfel at a testimonial attended by 2000 people
at the Hotel Astor featuring Albert Einstein as the speaker.[94]

In the meantime, Max Reinhardt's production of *The Eternal Road*
had not gone well. Half a million dollars was spent before there were
any sets or any costumes. Labor unions were a constant problem, and
the production was always threatened with closure. The producers had
to beg money from the wealthy. Many Eastern Jews invested in *The*

Eternal Road, but never saw a return on their investment. The experience put an extreme strain on Werfel.[95] Notwithstanding the powerful names involved in the production, *The Eternal Road* was tedious and a failure at the box office and with the critics. The Werfels never saw the pageant. Shortly thereafter, in February 1936, they returned to Europe where the tributes continued.[96]

In Paris a crowd of young Armenians sang a hymn as Werfel's train pulled into the station, as if some foreign dignitary were arriving. Another sumptuous banquet was sponsored by the various Parisian Armenian organizations. In attendance was Dartige du Fournet, vice admiral of the Allied fleet that had rescued the Musa Dagh survivors.[97] Werfel was pleased that unlike the Armenian community in New York, the Parisian Armenians were united. Ignorant of the ongoing machinations in Hollywood, Werfel reassured his audience that Metro-Goldwyn-Mayer was preparing to produce a film of *The Forty Days of Musa Dagh*.[98] In Armenian communities throughout the world, Werfel had become an icon permanently ensconced in the Armenian pantheon. He had given another boost to Armenians in their age-old struggle for justice.

In one generation the world had forgotten the Armenian Genocide of the Great War. Distracted by the Great Depression that had gripped the industrial nations and an isolationist attitude that had permeated American and European societies, many nations initially viewed the totalitarians with a combination of ridicule, contempt, and appeasement. The world of the 1930s had immunized itself from the lessons of history. But for Armenians, the year 1935 offered one real sign of hope. They were elated that Metro-Goldwyn-Mayer was preparing *The Forty Days of Musa Dagh* for production.[99]

NOTES - BOOK II

THE CATALYST AND THE MESSENGER

Chapter 5

THE PASSION OF FRANZ WERFEL

1. Alma Mahler Werfel, *And the Bridge Is Love, Memories of a Lifetime*, in collaboration with E. B. Ashton, New York: Harcourt, Brace, 1958, p. 279.

2. *New York Times*, "Franz Werfel, Noted Author Dies," 8/27/45, p. 19.

3. Mahler Werfel, *Bridge*, pp. 94-95.

4. Gottfried Reinhardt, *The Genius*, New York: Knopf, 1979, p. 166.

5. Mahler Werfel, *Bridge*, p. 95.

6. Alma's remarkable career was full of adventure, highlighted by her marriages to a trio of eminent masters of the arts: the renowned composer Gustav Mahler; the architectural giant Walter Gropius; and the gifted literary titan Franz Werfel. In the interim between Mahler's death, who dedicated his *Symphony No. 8* to her, and her marriage to Gropius, Alma enjoyed an intimate relationship with the prodigious expressionist artist Oskar Kokoschka, who painted her many times, most notably in *The Tempest*. Among her many other admirers was Alban Berg, who dedicated his opera *Wozzeck* to her.

7. Reinhardt, *The Genius*, p. 250.

8. Mahler Werfel, *Bridge*, p. 3.

9. Ibid., p. 93.

10. Karen Monson, *Alma Mahler, Muse to Genius: From Fin-de-Siecle Vienna to Hollywood's Heyday*, Boston: Houghton Mifflin, 1983, p. 185.

11. Ibid., p. 195.

12. Mahler Werfel, *Bridge*, p. 130.

13. Ibid., p. 135.

14. Reinhardt, *The Genius*, pp. 200-201; Mahler Werfel, *Bridge*, p. 93.

15. Monson, *Muse to Genius*, p. 218.

16. Mahler Werfel, *Bridge*, p. 166.

17. Ibid., p. 245.

18. Gottfried Reinhardt, son of the renowned theatrical producer Max Reinhardt, produced Greta Garbo's last film, *Two Faced Woman* ('41) and John Huston's *The Red Badge of Courage* ('51) at Metro-Goldwyn-Mayer.

19. Reinhardt, *The Genius*, p. 24.

20. Ibid., p. 250.

Chapter 6

APPOINTMENT IN DAMASCUS

21. In a prefatory note to his novel, Werfel says that the thought of writing *The Forty Days of Musa Dagh* occurred to him in March 1929, during a stay in Damascus. Alma Mahler Werfel states in her autobiography *And the Bridge is Love*, pp. 197-198, she and Werfel were married on July 6, 1929, and had taken their second Near Eastern trip earlier in the year. Werfel confirmed the wedding date in his American citizenship application, June 18, 1941.

22. Mahler Werfel, *Bridge*, p. 199.

23. University of California at Los Angeles, Research Library, Special Collections Library, *Franz Werfel Papers*, Collection 512, Box 5, *Scenarios and Plans*, June 1930. The file contains 108 unnumbered pages of original handwritten penciled notes consisting of Werfel's first ideas outlining his projected novel about Musa Dagh. The only notation of an individual in Damascus is that of a manufacturer, "George Messon, fabrike en Demeskus." Since his name does not appear in the novel, the author contends that Messon was the owner of the carpet-weaving factory where Werfel saw the Armenian children.

24. Mahler Werfel, *Bridge*, p. 200.

25. *Hairenik Weekly*, "Herr Werfel's Speech, at Recent N.Y. Banquet," 12 /13/35, p. 3. Werfel told his audience that during World War I he knew about the Armenians' misfortunes. He was so touched that he wanted to write about them long before his experience in Damascus.

26. Franz Werfel, *The Forty Days of Musa Dagh*, translated from the German by Geoffrey Dunlop, New York: Viking Press, 1934, prefatory note.

27. Mahler Werfel, *Bridge*, p. 201.

28. *Hairenik Weekly*, "Franz Werfel Feted by Armenians in New York," 12/13/35, pp. 1, 3.

Chapter 7

THE FORTY DAYS OF MUSA DAGH, THE NOVEL

29. Mahler Werfel, *Bridge*, p. 202.

30. George Schulz-Behrend, "Sources and Background of Werfel's Novel *Die Vierzig Tage des Musa Dagh,*" *The Germanic Review*, Vol. XXVI, No. 2, April 1951, p. 111, footnote 2.

31. *Hairenik Weekly*, "An Hour with Franz Werfel," ll/29/35, pp. 2-3. An article based on the interview of Franz Werfel by Vartkes Aharonian representing the Armenian Press Bureau, aboard the Ile de France, on the Werfels' arrival in New York, November 12, 1935.

32. Ibid., "Werfel Meets Survivor of Musa Dagh," 12/13/35, p. 5.

33. Dikran Andreasian, *Zeituni Antsnadviutuin yev Suedia Inkabashbanatuin (The Surrender of Zeitun and the Self-Defense of Suedia)*, Cairo, 1915, 68 pages. English translation by Knarik O. Meneshian, Armenian Missionary Association of America, 1993. Dikran Andreasian, "A Red Cross Flag That Saved Four Thousand," *The Outlook*, Translated by Stephen Trowbridge, CXI, 12/1/15; pp. 790, 799-803.

34. UCLA, *Werfel Papers*, Collection 512, Box 5.

35. Schulz-Behrend, "Sources and Background ... ," *The Germanic Review*, April 1951, pp. 111-123. Paul Rohrbach, *Armenien: Beitrage zur armenischen Landes-und Volkskunde, herausgegeben (Articles About Armenian Lands and the Armenian People)*, Stuttgart, 1919.

36. Vahakn N. Dadrian, *German Responsibility in the Armenian Genocide–*

A Review of the Historical Evidence of German Complicity, Watertown, Mass.: Blue Crane Books, 1996, p. 114.

37. Schulz-Behrend, "Sources…," *The Germanic Review*, April 1951, pp.12-123. Johannes Lepsius, "Suedije, eine Episode aus der Ziet der Armenierverfolgungen" (Suedia, an Episode During the Armenian Persecutions), 1919, No. 4-5, pp. 67-73.

_____, *Deutschland und Armenien* (Germany and Armenia), 1914-1918, Potsdam, 1919, pp. 457-67.

_____, "Mein Besuch in Konstantinopel (My Visit to Constantinople), Juli - August 1915," *Orient*, No. 1-3, pp. 21-33.

_____, *Bericht uber die Lage dis armenischen Volkes in der Turkei* (A Report of the Conditions of the Armenians in Turkey), Potsdam, 1916.

38. UCLA, *Werfel Papers*, "Scenarios and Plans, June 1930," Box 5, forty-nine unnumbered pages.

39. Schulz-Behrend, "Sources …," *Germanic Review*, April 1951, pp. 122-123.

40. Warner Blumenthal, "Father and Son in the East: A New Look at Werfel's *The Forty Days of Musa Dagh*," West Georgia College, *Interstate Foreign Language Conference*, Vol. 23, 1973, pp. 75-79.

41. UCLA, *Werfel Papers*, Box 9, New York Herald Tribune Books, "Werfel and *The Forty Days of Musa Dagh*, Comments by Survivors of the Tragedy on the Novel's Authenticity in Spirit and Fact," Interview of the Reverend Harutiun Nokhudian by Avedis Derounian of *The Armenian Spectator* (an English language weekly), 3/24/35, VII, p. 10.

42. *Hairenik Weekly*, "Minister of Mousa Dagh Fame to Bring Suit Against Werfel," 11/22/35, p. 5. Based on an article by Zoe B. Fales, *Albany Times Union*, 11/13/35.

43. Werfel, *The Forty Days of Musa Dagh*, pp. 276-277.

44. Ibid., p. 214.

45. Ibid.

46. *The California Courier*, "Elie Wiesel's Introduction to the French Edition of Werfel's *The Forty Days of Musa Dagh*," 5/21/87, pp. 1, 15.

47. Ironically, on the eve of the invasion of Poland, Hitler was reminded by his staff of the world's reaction. His reply: "Who, after all, speaks today of the annihilation of the Armenians?" Professor Kevork Bardakjian presents conclusive evidence of the authenticity of the quotation in *Hitler and Armenian Genocide*, Cambridge, Mass.: Zoryan Institute, Special Report No. 3, 1985, p. 43. Bardakjian cites Louis P. Lochner's *What About Germany?*, New York: Dodd, Mead & Co., 1942, pp. 1-4. Researching Hitler's statement of August 22, 1939, regarding the "Armenian quotation," Dr. William Mandel in a letter addressed to the author September 3, 1985, stated that the original German quotation, "Wer redet heute noch von der Vernichtung der Armenier?" was recorded by Admiral Canaris. Canaris gave his notes to his assistant, Colonel Oster, who gave them to Herman Maas for transmittal to Louis Lochner, Associated Press correspondent in Germany.

48. Mahler Werfel, *Bridge*, pp. 211-212.

49. Werfel, *The Forty Days of Musa Dagh*, p. 15. Blumenthal, "Father and Son ...," p. 76.

50. Werfel, *The Forty Days of Musa Dagh*, p. 785. Blumenthal, "Father and Son ...," p. 77.

51. Blumenthal, "Father and Son ... ," pp. 77-78.

52. Blumenthal, "Father and Son in the East ... ," *Interstate Foreign Language Conference*, Vol. 23, pp. 75-79.

53. Schulz-Behrend, "Sources ...," *The Germanic Review*, April 1951, pp. 118-119– Werfel's rendition of the Lepsius-Enver meeting is taken from Dr. Lepsius' "Mein Besuch in Konstantinopel, Juli-August 1915," *Orient* (1919), No. 1-3, pp. 21-33.

54. Ibid., p. 115.

55. Mahler Werfel, *Bridge*, p. 213.

56. Ibid., p. 217.

57. The German language publication consisted of two books: Vol. I, 557 pages and Vol. II, 584 pages, totaling 1141 pages; Paul Zsolnay Verlag, Berlin, Vienna, Leipzig, 1933.

58. Monson, *Muse to Genius*, p. 232.

59. Vahakn N, Dadrian, *The History of the Armenian Genocide: Ethnic Conflict from the Balkans to Anatolia to the Caucasus*, Providence, R. I.: Berghahn Books, 1997, p. 410.

60. *New York Times*, 8/27/45, p. 19.

61. *Hairenik Weekly*, "Franz Werfel's Speech at Mekhitarist Celebration of Bible in Vienna," 10/20/35, p. 6.

Chapter 8

THE POWER OF ART

62. *Metro-Goldwyn-Mayer, MGM Archives, Musa Dagh File*, Correspondence, Johnson & Tannenbaum, Attorneys-at-Law, to Metro-Goldwyn-Mayer (Samuel W. Tannenbaum to Mildred Basch), May 6, 1975.

63. Haigaz Kazarian, "*The Forty Days of Musa Dagh* and Its English Translation," *The Armenian Review*, Vol. XVI, September 1963, pp. 18-22. Originally published in *Hairenik*, Boston, June 1951.

64. Monson, *Muse to Genius*, pp. 244-245.

65. *New York Times Book Review*, Viking Press advertisement, 12/2/34, p. 19.

66. Monson, *Muse to Genius*, p. 230.

67. William Saroyan, "Forty Days of Good and Evil," *Saturday Review*, Vol XI, 12/8/34, p. 1.

68. Louis Kronenberger, "Franz Werfel's Heroic Novel," *New York Times Book Review*, 12/2/34, Section 5, p. 1.

69. Levon Garabed Baljian, *The Living Power of Art, The Musa Dagh Armenians in Franz Werfel's Novel, An Analysis of the Moving Story of a Heroic Episode in Armenian Life, 1940*. Translated from the Armenian by Joseph Matossian. Levon Garabed Baljian was ordained a celibate priest in 1943. Consecrated a bishop in 1951, he was then elected Supreme Patriarch and Catholicos of All Armenians in 1955 in Etchmiadzin, Armenia, taking the name Vasken I. He served in that capacity until his death in 1994.

70. *The California Courier*, "Elie Wiesel's Introduction to the French Edition of Werfel's *The Forty Days of Musa Dagh*," 5/21/87, pp. 1, 15.

71. Yair Auron, "*The Forty Days of Musa Dagh*: Its Impact on Jewish Youth in Palestine and Europe," in *Remembrance and Denial, The Case of the Armenian Genocide*, Richard G. Hovannisian, ed., Detroit: Wayne State University Press, 1998, pp. 147-164.

72. Yair Auron, *The Banality of Indifference, Zionism and the Armenian Genocide*, New Brunswick and London: Transaction Publishers, 2000, Chapter 7, "*The Forty Days of Musa Dagh*: Symbol and Parable," pp. 293-309.

Chapter 9

ICON

73. Reinhardt, *The Genius*, pp. 251-265.

74. *New York Times*, "Franz Werfel, Noted Author, Dies," 8/27/45, p. 19.

75. UCLA, *Werfel Papers*, Collection 512, Box 5, Letter: Ben Huebsch (Viking Press) to Franz Werfel, 12/1/35.

76. *Hairenik Weekly*, "Werfel Grants Interview to Armenian Press Bureau Representatives, Famous Author to Stay Three Months in U.S.," 11/22/35, p. 1.

77. Ibid.

78. Ibid., Vartkes Aharonian, "An Hour with Franz Werfel," 11/29/35, pp. 2-3.

79. Ibid.

80. Franz Werfel, *The Forty Days of Musa Dagh*, p. 629.

81. *Hairenik Weekly*, "A.R.F. Representative Extols Author of Musa Dagh," 12/13/35, p. 3.

82. Ibid., "Werfel Grants Interview," 11/22/35, p. 6.

83. Ibid., Aharonian, "An Hour with Franz Werfel," 11/29/35, pp. 2-3.

84. Ibid., "Franz Werfel Is Feted by Armenians in New York," 12/13/35, pp. 1, 3.

85. Ibid.

86. Ibid., "Herr Werfel's Speech, Delivered at New York Banquet," 12/13/35, pp. 1, 3.

87. Ibid.

88. Ibid., "M.G.M. Decides to Film *Musa Dagh*," 12/6/35, p. 1.

89. Ibid., "A.R.F. Representative Extols Author of *Musa Dagh*," 12/13/35, p. 3.

90. *U.S. Department of State, Division of Near Eastern Affairs*, Document 811.4061, Musa Dagh/44, 12/17/35. Attached article: *Motion Picture Herald*, "The Case of *Musa Dagh*," 12/7/35.

91. Mahler Werfel, *Bridge*, p. 229.

92. Ibid.

93. *New York Times*, "Armenians Fete Werfel," 1/6/36, p.15.

94. Monson, *Muse to Genius*, p. 246.

95. Mahler Werfel, *Bridge*, pp. 228-229.

96. *Hairenik Weekly*, "Franz Werfel Leaves U.S.," 2/28/36, p. 1.

97. Mahler Werfel, *Bridge*, p. 230.

98. *Hairenik Weekly*, "Werfel Arrives in Paris," 3/13/36, pp. 1, 3.

99. Of the documents in the *Musa Dagh File* (MGM archives at Culver City) provided to the author, no correspondence was discovered between Werfel and the studio after the contract to purchase the rights had been signed.

22 Franz Werfel, the sight of maimed Armenian children inspired him to write *The Forty Days of Musa Dagh*.

23 Franz and Alma Werfel, on their arrival on the *Ile de France* in New York, November 1935.

24 Rev. Dr. Johannes Lepsius, tireless champion of the Armenians, who dared to question the Young Turk Armenian policy.

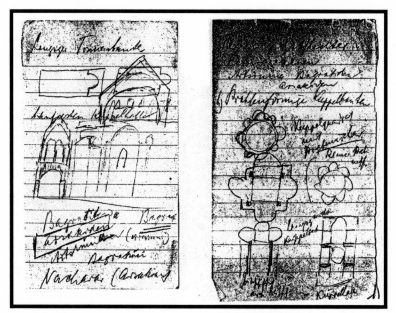

25 Werfel's sketches of an Armenian Apostolic Church.
Researched at the Mekhitarist Library, Vienna.

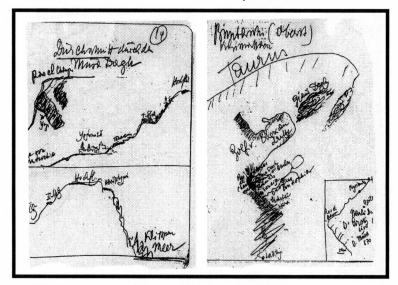

26 Werfel's sketches of Musa Dagh and environs.
Researched at the Mekhitarist Library, Vienna.

BOOK III

Babylon-On-The-Pacific
and
On-The-Potomac

... as when a lion roareth.
—The Revelation of St. John the Divine 10:3

Chapter 10

THE LION ROARS

No one at MGM expected any problem

While the literary world was in a flurry over Franz Werfel's *The Forty Days of Musa Dagh*, another drama was about to unfold in the tinseltown called Hollywood. Hollywood, the epitome of dream factories, a film colony akin to a never-never land of uppers and downers, great films and trash, nepotism and couch interviews, huge profits and monumental losses. Greer Garson branded it "Babylon-on-the-Pacific."[1] Geographically situated in the booming metropolis of Los Angeles, to fledging aspirants, Hollywood was the fantasy world where one found the stuff that dreams are made of. In reality it was a dichotomy.

On the basis of the world's public awareness of the Golden State in the 1930s, Hollywood was its capital and its movies were the great escape from the Great Depression. It was the motion picture capital and the social arbiter of the world. By the third decade of the twentieth century, Hollywood had become the world's most influential communications force through the art form of film.

The most powerful of the film capital's studios was Metro-Goldwyn-Mayer (a.k.a. Metro, Leo the lion, and the "studio that had more stars than in heaven") in Culver City.[2] Two moguls ruled Metro-Goldwyn-Mayer (MGM): Louis B. Mayer, first vice-president of Loew's Inc.

(MGM's corporate headquarters in New York City) and studio general manager; and Irving G. Thalberg, second vice-president, Loew's Inc., supervisor of production[3] and Hollywood's wunderkind. Without question, it was the largest movie company in the world and "the Cadillac of the Hollywood studios."[4] Mayer and Thalberg remain in the annals of screen legend as the epitome of eminently successful moviemakers who personified the studio's motto *Ars Gratia Artis* (Art for the sake of art). Fred Zinnemann, one of filmdom's respected directors and one-time MGM employee, described Mayer as probably the most powerful man in Hollywood.[5] Frances Marion, an MGM stalwart and one of Hollywood's highest paid screenwriters for thirty years, described Thalberg as her "rock of Gibraltar, a Renaissance man, a genius."[6] As late as 1992, columnist Gerald Nachman praised Mayer and Thalberg as the royalty of filmdom's mythical kingdom in the 1930s. "They made movies not merely for power, prestige, ego, and money (though clearly for all those worthy reasons too), nor even merely to amuse, but also for themselves and, thus, treated moviegoers as adults."[7]

When Franz Werfel began his *Musa Dagh* negotiations with MGM, he should have remembered his visit with his good friend, the venerable German playwright and essayist, Gerhard Hauptmann. When Werfel casually mentioned the word "Hollywood," he was challenged by one of the guests. "In Gerhard Hauptmann's presence, one does not speak of Hollywood. That's sacrilege."[8] It suggests that the literati, at least in Europe, held Hollywood in contempt for its corruption and distortion of literature and history. The well-intentioned Werfel could not know at the time how his dealings with MGM and Hollywood would make *The Forty Days of Musa Dagh* one of the most contentious projects in Hollywood history.[9]

In December 1933, twelve months before Werfel's novel was published in the United States, MGM had been alerted to the book's sweeping presence in the bookstores of Germany, Austria, and Switzerland. That same month, the Culver City studio was sent a synopsis of the book in the hope that somebody at MGM might be interested in buying the movie rights. The synopsis emphasized the actual incident of the heroic defense at Musa Dagh against an Ottoman government determined to cleanse itself of its Armenian subjects.[10] In February 1934, Mayer's perusal of the galley proofs, sent by Werfel's Viennese agent and publisher Paul Zsolnay, stirred him to set the wheels in motion, thus assuring MGM's acquisition of what was predicted to be a prime property.[11] Within a week the cables were humming between Vienna, MGM's corporate headquarters at Loew's in New York City, and the Culver City studio. At that time no one at MGM expected any problem from Werfel's book.[12]

J. Robert Rubin, Loew's/MGM legal counsel and a Loew's board director was instructed to get a price.[13] Rubin, one of the most astute attorneys in the movie business, immediately contacted Zsolnay. On Werfel's insistence, MGM made an offer. It was unacceptable. A cablegram from Ann Bernstein, MGM's representative in Europe, admonished Rubin that Werfel was adamant.[14] Rubin, fearing the deal would be lost, informed Mayer that Werfel and Zsolnay wanted $20,000 and MGM had to respond in three days.[15] The studio, in reality "the front office" at Loew's, acceded to Werfel's demand. What MGM bought was what Rubin soon received from Zsolnay: a two-volume, 1200-page copy of the original German language publication of Franz Werfel's *Die Vierzig Tage des Musa Dagh*.[16]

The contract was recorded in the United States Copyright Office on May 26, 1934.[17] On Zsolnay's request, $15,000 was paid to Werfel in Vienna and another $4500 was deposited in Werfel's account in Zurich, Switzerland.[18] The $500 discrepancy may have been Zsolnay's fee.

The contract gave MGM world motion picture rights for five years and stipulated that the dramatization of *Musa Dagh* be submitted to Werfel or his representative for the author's approval. It also gave the studio the right, but not the obligation, to make a stage production in English-speaking countries twelve months after the completion of the screenplay.[19] As an added incentive, Loew's/MGM agreed to pay Werfel for the stage play: 3½ percent of the first $5000 box office weekly receipts; 4½ percent of the following $2000; and 5½ percent of everything exceeding $10,000.[20]

In April of 1934, during contract negotiations, Rubin had alerted Mayer that the theme of Werfel's novel was so delicate that it could be dangerous. He advised that the filming of *The Forty Days of Musa Dagh* be approached with caution. Rubin felt that:

> *Mayer must understand that it is impossible to make a picture with the personalities involved and more particularly with the circumstances and conditions that form the frame without offending not only the Turks but other races. All the Turks mean very little to us. I still don't believe it is your purpose to offend any race even though the events may be historically exact and correct ... It is quite possible that the Turks will have the picture withdrawn in every territory ... unless your diplomatic and consular services in conjunction with the State Department use a vigorous attitude and use the same influence on other territories no matter how small in matters that concern their own nationalism ... I think you must be told of how dangerous this question of nationalism has become.[21]*

Rubin's concern was ignored for the time being.

So convinced was the studio hierarchy of the profits to be realized from MGM's rights to Werfel's novel that Rubin sounded out Broadway producer John Golden about the possibilities of a stage play following the film's production.[22] Golden informed Rubin of the great difficulty in transforming the book into a play and turned it down.[23] Golden's rejection may have been more influenced by Werfel's contractual condition that he have final approval of *Musa Dagh*'s stage dramatization in addition to a box office percentage.

In July 1934, before the American public was aware of the existence of Franz Werfel or *The Forty Days of Musa Dagh*, questions were raised by other satraps within the MGM empire, among whom was producer David O. Selznick, Hollywood's legendary memo writer and Mayer's son-in-law. Selznick recommended doing the picture with Clark Gable as Gabriel Bagradian, the novel's protagonist, under the direction of Fritz Lang. Picking up from Rubin's admonition so as not to offend the Motion Picture Producers and Distributors of America (MPPDA),[24] better known as the Hays Office,[25] and Kemal Ataturk's Turkish government,[26] Selznick thought of making one Turk the culprit rather than fault an entire nation. His intention was to make clear that most Turks opposed the Armenian atrocities. He believed that since the present Ataturk government had condemned the Young Turk regime of World War I, MGM could simply make the latter the villain and thus be on safe ground.[27] To protect the studio's interests, Selznick urged Rubin to "contact Major Frederick L. Herron, the foreign manager of the Hays Office in New York City and ask him to take up the *Musa Dagh* issue as a matter of courtesy with the Turkish ambassador in Washington."[28] Selznick's suggestion alerted the Kemalist government of Turkey.

Meanwhile, Marshall Best at Viking Press, Werfel's American publisher, in a letter addressed to Rubin, offered MGM the Geoffrey Dunlop translation of *The Forty Days of Musa Dagh* if MGM did not have a copy, noting that "It's a great book and we expect big things of it."[29] Within days of the book's availability to the American public, Viking Press and MGM had been deluged with scores of comments and suggestions to make *The Forty Days of Musa Dagh* into a great movie.[30] MGM's reaction was to ignore the unsolicited overtures. In the meantime, *Musa Dagh* had become a publisher's dream, selling 85,000 copies including Book-of-the-Month club sales, a record for 1934.[31] For the remainder of the year and into 1936, the book's sales were phenomenal.

The Hairenik Weekly, an English language Armenian newspaper, aroused its Armenian American readers with the following Page One comment:

> *Werfel has approached his subject with profound reverence*
> *… Werfel presents the Armenian people not as a mass to be the*
> *object of commiseration and pity "starving Armenians" but as*
> *fighting Armenians … Amazing that he was able to collect as*
> *much material as he did … What is outstanding is Werfel's*
> *love for the Armenian people … Being a Jew he knows suffering*
> *… he has a great heart and has approached the Armenian*
> *people with humanity, respect, and warm sympathy.*[32]

Armenians championed Hollywood's one and only Armenian director and recognized stage and screen craftsman, Rouben Mamoulian, as their choice to bring *Musa Dagh* to the screen.

A few weeks before Werfel's novel appeared in American bookstores, Will H. Hays, president of the Motion Pictures Producers and Distributors of America, received a communiqué from Wallace Murray, the State Department's chief of Near Eastern affairs, to inform Hays of the visit of Mehmet Munir Ertegun Bey, the Turkish ambassador to the United States.[33]

Chapter 11

COLLUSION IN DIPLOMACY

Warn MGM of the Turks' concerns

An erroneous news item stating that Paramount Pictures was to make a movie of *The Forty Days of Musa Dagh* had alarmed the Turkish Embassy in Washington. It provoked Ambassador Mehmet Munir Ertegun Bey[34] to meet with Wallace Murray, chief of Near Eastern affairs for the secretary of state, to express his concerns about Werfel, his novel, and the proposed movie of *The Forty Days of Musa Dagh*. The ambassador reminded Murray that the German government had suppressed the book, and he "earnestly hoped that Paramount would desist from presenting any such picture, which could only give a distorted version of the alleged massacres[35] and would almost certainly stir up anti-Turkish feelings in this country."[36] Murray relayed the gist of his conversation with Ertegun to Will Hays:

> *This Government was, of course, not in a position to prevent the presentation of a picture of this kind but ... saw no objection to bring Ertegun's views to the attention of ... Paramount. Judging from ... earlier experiences in dealing with moving picture organizations, they wished to avoid as far as possible any disputes with foreign governments ... and that ... Paramount ... would doubtlessly give due weight to the Ambassador's views in the present matter."* [37]

Hays shared Murray's concern with Major Frederick L. Herron, the Hays Office foreign manager in New York. From then on, Herron became the Hays Office *Musa Dagh* point man. Responding to Murray's communiqué, Herron claimed he had read the MGM *Musa Dagh* scenario and saw no reference to the Armenian massacres. (Soon after MGM's purchase of *Musa Dagh*, Thalberg had assigned the screenplay to Carey Wilson. If Herron read anything, it was Thalberg's outline.) He reassured Murray that the MPPDA/Hays Office had confidence, in MGM (not Paramount):

> *In reality, the whole story is built up around the private life of the leader of the Armenians, his trouble with his French wife, his son, and an Armenian girl who comes into his life ... and when the studio decides to put this story into production, I feel certain there will be nothing included in it that could offend the Turkish ambassador or his countrymen.*[38]

Within the week, Murray sent Herron's response to Ertegun,[39] who acknowledged Murray's letter "... with satisfaction that if the film is produced, there will be nothing in it which could alter the friendly feelings existing now between the Turkish and the American people. With my best thanks for your friendly action ..."[40] No matter that the Turkish ambassador had been informed and presumably placated, the issue continued to fester.

On December 19, 1934, Murray was advised of a conversation in Istanbul between Turkish Foreign Minister Tevfik Rustu Aras Bey and Chargé d'Affaires G. Howland Shaw at the American Embassy in Ankara:

> *Tevfik Rustu Bey spoke to me about an anti-Turkish film entitled "Mousadagh," which he greatly fears is about to be produced in the United States ... I understand that it is based*

upon a novel written by a German anti-Nazi, who is using the treatment of the Armenians by the Turks to excite sympathy with minorities in general. The Minister asked if the proper authorities at Washington could not intervene to prevent the production of the film in the United States ... I am passing the foregoing on to you in case you are able and think it wise to take some unofficial and informal action.[41]

Three weeks later, Secretary of State Cordell Hull received a message from Ambassador Robert P. Skinner in Istanbul informing him of his pleasure to learn that the Division of Near Eastern Affairs had been successful in preventing the exhibition of a film (*Musa Dagh*) that might be offensive to the Turkish government.[42] Skinner was misinformed.

On the contrary, the *Musa Dagh* issue had intensified, inciting the Turkish government and its representatives in the United States to launch a surveillance of the proposed film, now that Ankara's suspicions had been aroused. Some time later, on the basis of a newspaper article in the *Washington Herald*, Ertegun immediately contacted Murray:

I refer to your letter of November 26th, 1934, in which you informed me that, if a film would be produced from Werfel's book, "The Forty Days of Musa Dagh," there would be nothing in it which could give offense to Turkey.

I see now in a Washington paper that the production of the film is under way. You will see from the enclosed clipping that the story is referred to as a matter of religious conflict between Christians and Mohammedans, and mention is made of "Turkish massacres in Armenia."

Before the film is released, I think that it would be advisable to draw the attention of Mr. Herron to the interpretation given to the story by the press and to the fact that the production under such circumstances would be inopportune.

I am sure that you will appreciate how much importance I place on preventing the misleading of public opinion in America through erroneous features concerning the history of my country.[43]

The news item cited by Ertegun stated that *Musa Dagh* was to be filmed by MGM under the supervision of Irving Thalberg with Carey Wilson writing the screenplay, William Wellman to direct, and William Powell to play the lead. The article made no mention of a religious conflict between Christians and Muslims. In reality what aroused the ambassador's wrath was the reference the MGM press release made to "Christians who combined against the Turkish massacres in Armenia."[44]

Murray sent Ertegun's request to Herron, reiterating the State Department's cooperation with the Turkish Embassy and its willingness to relay Herron's response to Ertegun and so advised the Turkish ambassador.[45]

Herron immediately informed Hays' second-in-command, Joseph I. Breen, America's most powerful movie censor, that he was aware of the Turkish concern and that MGM's production was being closely watched.[46] Herron expressed his regrets "that someone who may or may not be connected with the studio gave out the supposed interview with Irving Thalberg."[47] He reassured Murray, on his own authority, that this type of interview would not be repeated.[48] That same day, on receipt of Herron's letter, Murray passed it on to Ertegun.[49] Herron then urged Breen to warn MGM of the Turks' concerns.[50]

While the *Musa Dagh* issue was smoldering, there was unbridled jubilation throughout the Armenian American community when they heard of MGM's official announcement that *The Forty Days of Musa Dagh* would be among its top-priority films for 1935 in company with

The Great Ziegfeld and Mutiny on the Bounty.[51] With Thalberg at the helm, it boded well for *Musa Dagh* and Armenian Americans, for it was the wunderkind's credo that "Idealism is profitable ... The quality production, which is more often than not the expensive production, is the one that pays the big returns;"[52] in other words, "Make it good, make it big, give it class!"[53]

In addition to Wilson, Thalberg thought of also assigning the screen adaptation of Werfel's novel to MGM's Frances Marion, one of Hollywood's pre-eminent screenwriters. She believed *Musa Dagh* was a masterpiece of dramatic writing. When she learned that Rouben Mamoulian was the director, she eagerly welcomed the challenge.[54]

The air of cautious optimism in 1935 was transposed, for the time being, into a euphoric reassurance for the movie proponents of Werfel's epic novel. However, *Musa Dagh* had already begun a process, that would establish an unenviable reputation.

Meanwhile, communications between Ankara, the Turkish Embassy in Washington, the United States Department of State, the American Embassy in Turkey, the Hays Office in Hollywood and New York City, MGM in Culver City, and Loew's in New York City increased in number and in heat.

Chapter 12

A CABAL OF CONSPIRATORS

A principle was at stake

The Metro-Goldwyn-Mayer Archives *Musa Dagh* file and State Department *Musa Dagh* documents provide incontrovertible evidence that there was collusion on the part of the Hays Office, the State Department, and the Turkish Embassy to apply pressure first to censor and then to abort the filming of *The Forty Days of Musa Dagh*. The major American participants were Wallace Murray of the State Department's Near Eastern affairs and Frederick L. Herron of the Hays Office. Their conduct was unprecedented in Hollywood history at the time and especially for a liberal administration in Washington in the 1930s.

In early May 1935, Murray once again relayed Herron's assurance to Ertegun that the Hays Office would see to it that *Musa Dagh* publicity in the press would not be repeated and advised him that the Hays Office in Hollywood was very closely watching the film.[55]

In an official communiqué alerting the American Embassy in Turkey on May 14, 1935, Murray informed the staff:

- The Hays Office foreign manager Frederick Herron had personally called on the Turkish Ambassador in Washington and had found him strongly opposed to the filming of Werfel's novel and had informed him that no scenario had yet been written. (In a letter to

Murray, November 20, 1934, Herron said he had read the scenario).

- Furthermore, Herron had assured the ambassador that, when the screenplay was completed, no offense would be given to the Turkish government and promised that the unabridged script would be sent to the ambassador for his scrutiny and approval.[56]

Murray reminded Herron of the remote possibility the film would ever be permitted in Turkey or in Germany. Nazi Germany at the time, intent on neutralizing the presence of Great Britain and France in the eastern Mediterranean and gaining favor with Turkey, had supported Turkey from the start on the *Musa Dagh* issue. Playing catch-up, the British government also supported Turkey to discourage Nazi influence there. Murray also mentioned the possibility of certain countries in the Balkans banning the picture on Turkey's request. Herron was not worried about the latter eventuality since the market in that part of the world was inconsequential. He was more concerned that France might also be induced to ban the picture out of friendship to Turkey.[57]

In the meantime, Rubin had already relayed to Thalberg "confidential information" that the Turkish government was so incensed at MGM's recalcitrance regarding *Musa Dagh* that, if the production was not canceled, all MGM films would be banned in Turkey, but even more alarming was the threat to ban all American movies as well. The reason for Rubin's concern was a document he had been shown, stamped "For Official Eyes," stating "the Turkish authorities were prepared to expend every effort all over the world to prohibit the picture from being screened."[58]

Among the first to protest in the United States was a Turkish student, Nihat Ferit, residing in North Carolina. In his letter to *Son Posta* (Istanbul) titled "We Labor Under the Impression That The Entire World Knows Us. This Is Not True: Especially America Does Not Know Us at

All," he complained, "Armenians in America indulge in hostile Turkish propaganda to which the American people lend with great naiveté a credulous ear."[59] Playing the racist card, Ferit claimed that Armenians had published the book that MGM had bought and were primarily instrumental in promoting the movie.[60]

In Turkey, Ferit's diatribe aroused press attacks against *Musa Dagh* that were limited initially to Istanbul journals such as *Son Posta* (Latest Mail) and *Haber* (News). Reacting to the Turkish press concerns, Ambassador Skinner sent a dispatch to Secretary Hull enclosing the translations of the articles in *Haber* and *Son Posta*. In essence, they were Ferit's letter, calling for a boycott of MGM films. Skinner expressed the hope that the film would be abandoned because it could be harmful to Armenians in Turkey. Skinner mentioned the only good American film to appear in Istanbul was *The House of Rothschild* ('34). The fact was, movies currently shown in Turkey were mainly of French and German origin, and the few American films were old and inferior and usually appeared in the smaller theaters.[61]

A week later Skinner let Murray know that he took exception to a recent cable sent by Attaché Gillespie of the U.S. Department of Commerce in Istanbul. Gillespie had expressed his concern to his superiors in Washington about the anti-*Musa Dagh* Turkish press reports. Skinner thought that Gillespie was overreacting to the *Son Posta* and *Haber* articles and downgraded both newspapers as having small circulations and an indifferent standing in the Turkish community. He reiterated what he had told Secretary Hull, that he "didn't see a boycott materializing against American movies."[62]

On the contrary, the Turks were serious and uncompromising. The MGM power brokers could not comprehend that a proposed movie could so incense a foreign government that it would work itself into a frenzy. Turkish ambassadors, consuls, and press representatives were alerted worldwide to convince them of the threat posed by *Musa Dagh*. Turkey was especially concerned over the news that Werfel's novel was already the literary rage in eighteen languages.[64]

From then on *The Forty Days of Musa Dagh* generated into a Turkish obsession warranting top priority by the Ankara government. The Turks marshaled their forces by alerting friendly governments to the machinations of the MGM hierarchy and, by implication, the United States government. Turkish professionals and businessmen wrote to their foreign counterparts expressing the concerns of their government and people that MGM's production of *Musa Dagh* would create a bad impression of Turkey. Eastern countries, in particular, were requested to ban American films and were told that it was absolutely certain that the Turkish government would find ways to prevent its release.[65]

Adding more fuel to the *Musa Dagh* fire, *Son Posta* launched an intensive campaign against the film, calling on Turkey's friends to advise America that such a film would bring about only hatred and misunderstanding. Along those lines, Fahir Epikci, MGM's Turkish distributor, had already followed through when he alerted his French counterpart in Paris and MGM's representative there that "… the film should be abandoned because it would be injurious to our business."[66] In the meantime, the State Department began to feel uneasy, and the Hays Office was increasingly apprehensive. Herron told Rubin that the State Department had convinced him of the seriousness of the issue because Turkey would do everything in its power to prevent the showing of the film in all European countries. He advised Rubin that MGM should realize that the revival of the "Armenian Question" could serve no useful purpose. Indicative of the Hays Office's power, he demanded Rubin's immediate response.[67]

About two weeks later, a worried Wallace Murray informed Ambassador Skinner that Ertegun had made a second visit to convince Murray of the urgency of the *Musa Dagh* matter, insisting that the film production be terminated. Murray again reminded Ertegun that under our system of government such action was impossible and that movie producers were making efforts not to displease foreign governments, and he was "hopeful that if the film is produced, there will be nothing in it which would offend the Turkish authorities."[68] Concurrently, the top echelon at the State Department continued to apply pressure on the Hays Office through Herron to convince MGM that the filming of *Musa Dagh* was creating a tempest in Turkey and would result in a ban on all its films.[69]

The *Musa Dagh* issue now took on such dimensions that it astonished MGM's managers. At first, MGM's hierarchy picked up the gauntlet and proposed to do battle for *Musa Dagh*. The word was already out in the trade papers and the national media. To back out now would not only sacrifice a financial investment and waste much favorable publicity but also lose a public already primed by Werfel's novel. For such stalwarts at MGM as production chief Irving Thalberg, story editor Samuel Marx, studio manager Eddie Mannix, and screenwriter Carey Wilson, a principle was at stake: A foreign government should not be allowed to intimidate or to exert such pressure and authority as to suppress the making of an American motion picture.[70]

In Washington, Ertegun, ever persistent, reiterated his concerns about *Musa Dagh*. He begged Murray to take the matter to Secretary of State Hull to prevent the production of the picture. Ertegun told Murray of his recent meeting with Loew's/MGM legal counsel, J. Robert Rubin, upon whom he had impressed the Turkish government's intention to ban all MGM pictures, insisting that it was unfair to treat a question of this kind, involving Turkish honor, when only one side of the story is being told. When Rubin offered to have the ambassador examine the script, Ertegun replied that it would be useless to ask any Turk to approve such a film. To placate the Turkish ambassador, Murray agreed to inform Secretary Hull of Ertegun's feelings. He repeated what he had previously told Ertegun, while certain states in this country maintain censorship boards that ban the showing of films, no such authority is vested in the federal government, and could not exercise such authority under the United States Constitution. In any case, the federal government was not in a legal position to forbid the production of this film in California, but he felt sure that MGM, once it had been informed of the misgivings of the Turkish government, would not produce a film offensive to the Turkish people. It was Murray's opinion "that by the time the novel was filmed, nothing much except the title would remain."[71] Once again, in the time worn "best" tradition of Foggy Bottom, Murray managed to calm the Turkish envoy with his diplomatic double talk, advising him not to take the matter too much to heart and to inform his government of the unquestionable desire of the United States government to accede as far as possible to any wishes of the Turkish government.[72]

Within three days of Rubin's offer, Ertegun changed his mind and agreed to accept the *Musa Dagh* screenplay for his government's perusal. The studio bosses responded immediately. Thalberg instructed Marx to have Mannix send Rubin two copies of Carey Wilson's *Musa Dagh* script.[73] It was promptly done that evening.[74] Mannix had already informed Loew's in New York that "Mayer had alerted all the parties involved and that the *Musa Dagh* issue was now being considered at the highest level."[75]

Rubin met again with Ertegun in Washington and, in an unprecedented and consequential act between an American movie studio and a foreign government, gave him two copies of Carey Wilson's *Musa Dagh* screenplay. One copy was for Ankara and the other for Ertegun, who agreed to examine the script and inform Rubin of his comments.[76]

Speaking for the Hays Office, Herron told Murray that Rubin was hoping to elicit from Ertegun a degree of cooperation and understanding that would be satisfactory to all parties. He reassured Murray that *Musa Dagh* would not have anything in it suggesting the Armenian massacres as MGM expected to meet the wishes of the Turkish government. He opined that the concerns expressed in Ankara and in the Turkish press were not only "unwarranted but extremely exaggerated."[77]

Simultaneously, to step up the pressure on MGM and give credence to the genuine concern of the Turkish government, Mayer received a translation of the article (via the State Department's Near Eastern Affairs Office and the Hays Office) that had appeared in the Turkish newspaper *Haber* entitled "They Will Be the Losers." In essence, it was the article based on Nihat Ferit's letter, highly critical of the studio "for making a film against us" and threatening a reprisal on MGM. To emphasize Turkey's displeasure, *Haber* informed its readers that Ankara was going to influence its friends to bring about a massive boycott of all MGM movies. The article's author stressed that the real culprits in stirring up the issue were Armenian propagandists, whose intentions were to seize upon the movie as a tool to arouse world public opinion against the government and the people of Turkey.[78]

The fact that MGM had bought the rights to Werfel's novel is what infuriated the Turkish government from the start. Attempting to arouse the Turkish public, *Haber* erroneously stated that production had already begun with MGM's star, Clark Gable, playing the novel's hero, Gabriel Bagradian. It castigated the proposed movie as a serious impediment to the maintenance and improvement of Turkish-American relations.

Haber predicted that the movie would be a box office failure due to the boycott brought on by Turkey and sympathetic countries such as France and those in the Balkans. While stirring up anti-*Musa Dagh* sentiments at home, *Haber* regretted the absence of a pro-Turkish organization in the United States.[79]

Musa Dagh had become a cause célèbre. The controversy expanded: letters, telegrams, cablegrams, phone calls, appointments, and meetings multiplied. From then on, MGM was deluged with constant reminders from the State Department, the Hays Office, the Turkish Embassy, the Turkish press, and *Musa Dagh* advocates. Some studio executives were now more concerned that the *Musa Dagh* production would be detrimental to the studio's bottom line.

Irving Thalberg, whose commitment to make the movie was well known, had pressure applied on him personally since he was the man in charge of production. He was warned that he should consider the ramifications of such a movie, which had already escalated into a volatile issue. Once again the opposition, led by the Hays Office, was reassured that the production would be launched only after the Turkish authorities approved the script. Some of the studio's managers thought the review was a waste of time and expected the Turks to disavow such approval once the film was distributed.[80] Thalberg was especially concerned that it would be extremely difficult to reopen the matter if the Turkish government rejected the script.[81] Continuing to apply pressure, Turkish officials in Washington contacted Loew's in New York as to MGM's intentions with *Musa Dagh* and whether the movie was to be made in Culver City or London. One of the weaknesses in the *Musa Dagh* case was the Loew's and MGM staffs. For the most part, they had not read Werfel's novel and were ignorant of its theme and its obvious arousal of Armenian interest and Turkish fury. To many of them, "the issue was making a mountain out of a molehill."[82]

Five weeks after receiving two copies of the screenplay, Ambassador Ertegun advised MGM that he had sent a copy to the foreign affairs office in Ankara and hoped to have an evaluation of the script soon.[83] As the weeks went by with no word from Ankara, each passing day caused the Loew's/MGM bosses to become increasingly worried. They seriously considered sending "a well-established diplomatic person" to Turkey before its ambassador in Washington received Ankara's response. Either because he gave in to the corporate heads or just to ward them off, Rubin became that "well-established diplomatic person." In early August 1935, he sailed for France to deal first hand with a situation that had expanded into an international affair.[84]

From Paris, Rubin wired Mayer and Thalberg of his difficulties with the Turkish representatives and recommended, in order to restore calm, that MGM stop all publicity about *Musa Dagh*. Indicative of his concern and commitment to the movie, Rubin intended to send Rudi Monta from Culver City to Istanbul to obtain Turkish authorization for the production.[85] Heretofore, governmental authorization pertained only to locating film production crews in foreign countries. Considering that *Musa Dagh* would be shot in Culver City, Rubin's gesture was a marked departure from common practice in Hollywood.[86]

The controversy distracted those involved in the project from other matters and began to take its toll. Some raised questions as to the value of the production. Others backed away from the project, not so much to appease the Hays Office and the State Department, or even the Turks, but because other studio concerns had been ignored and now had to be addressed.[87]

Joining the mounting opposition was MGM's Turkish distributor in Istanbul, the Epikci brothers. Fahir Epikci again warned MGM in August 1935:

MGM's business would be greatly harmed and that it was sheer folly for the studio to think that Turkey would ever give its approval to the movie, as it would be a contradiction since Werfel's book was already banned in Turkey. Negotiations were useless. The Turkish government would never accept the script, … the title would always be unacceptable. Publicity about Musa Dagh *is sowing hatred between Turkish and Armenian nationals. The best thing to do is to cancel this unfortunate production.*[88]

Epikci was determined to convince MGM that it was indulging in a harmful and futile exercise. The studio had to understand that the Turks were unrelenting in their anti-*Musa Dagh* position.

And yet the facts related to Werfel's novel were documented and irrefutable and still are. The story of a disadvantaged and oppressed Armenian minority who held off the Turkish army long enough to assure the survival of most of its defenders was a historic fact. The *Musa Dagh* issue next focused on the Istanbul Armenians.

Chapter 13

THE EXPEDIENCY OF
TURKISH ARMENIAN PATRIOTISM

The premise of self-preservation

Due to Turkish press coverage, the publicity that ensued from MGM's intention to film *The Forty Days of Musa Dagh* threatened to renew the ancient antagonisms between Turks and Armenians in Turkey. In the 1930s, the only large Armenian community in Turkey was centered in Istanbul, and it began to feel the barbs of the Turkish press and officialdom. Some Armenians feared that another storm was gathering and persecutions were to be resumed. How could a book written by an Austrian Jew about a fairly recent historic event have such impact? Could it stir a tempest into an international maelstrom? Could a film cause all this preoccupation by governments and corporations? It could and it did.

The objective of the Turkish press and government was to apply pressure on the Armenian community in Istanbul to appreciate the Turkish position. Some Istanbul Armenians soon joined in the protest against *Musa Dagh* and communicated their concerns to MGM and to their compatriots and the Armenian press in the United States.[89] A history of prejudice and persecution under Turkish rule had cowed the Armenians there into obedience on the premise of self-preservation. They demonstrated their loyalty, as reported in the Turkish newspaper *Cumhuriyet*:

Turkish Armenian intellectuals met in their churchyard at Pangalti and placed a photo of Werfel and his book on a pile of wood shavings before a large crowd of Armenians. Ashot Kecyan, the literary contributor to the newspapers Aztar *and* Norlur, *lighted a fire with a match ... the choir of the Pangalti church and students gathered there sang the Turkish national anthem.*

Aram Arslan, a member of the Beyoglu Body of Trustees, made this speech to the ever-increasing crowd:

"Citizens, the Turkish Armenians, who learned from the newspapers that a book had been written, full of slander against the noble Turkish nation, decided to strongly condemn the courage of this insolent man without a country and who has, for purely personal interests, capitalized on the name of the Armenians.

We wish to make it public to the world that the fate of those who try to create trouble among us is death, and this we did by burning the photo and the book, The Forty Days of Musa Dagh, *by the cursed Franz Werfel, who has plotted against our sacred country. By this action, the Turkish Armenians have actually proved their hearty attachment to this glorious country, which has been turned into a paradise by Ataturk, our great President of the Republic, and in which country they have lived a brotherly life for the first time in hundreds of years. Down with those who use their tongues and hands against Turkey."*

In the name of the Turkish Armenian intellectuals, Ashot Kecyan and Aram Arslan expressed these same sentiments in a telegram to the Ministry of the Interior.[90]

Commenting on the article to Secretary Hull, Ambassador Skinner observed that the Armenians in Istanbul were worried about the attention being focused on them. The Istanbul Armenians did not know that the book reflected honorably upon Armenians. Since the book had been banned in Turkey, whatever the Armenians there had learned of the book's contents came from Ashot Kecyan, Aram Arslan, and the Turkish press. Skinner characterized the book-burning scene as humiliating for the Turkish Armenians.[91]

The Turkish Armenian intervention had no impact on Armenians in America or on MGM.[92]

Chapter 14

PRESS AND PREJUDICE

A hopeful sign

The storms stirred by the Turkish government and its embassy in Washington led MGM's Paris office to ask Rubin if the studio was willing to make script alterations to satisfy the Turkish government.[93] About the same time, Ertegun informed Loew's in New York that, with some script changes, the Turkish government might revise its position— nothing definite, nothing official—just "a hopeful sign" awaiting the official communiqué from Ankara.[94] By September 1935, the "hopeful sign" proved to be a delaying tactic. MGM was beginning to understand that foreign diplomacy could be just as contentious as the studio games played in Hollywood.

Concurrently the anti-*Musa Dagh* campaign intensified in the Istanbul press on a daily basis. It became the front-page item in *Cumhuriyet* and its French edition, *La Republique*, as well as *Haber*, *Tan*, and *Son Posta*. Much of it was propaganda generated by journalistic rivalry and uniformly prejudicial in its blatant anti-Jewish and anti-Armenian harangues. According to the American Embassy in Istanbul,[95] the leading newspaper, *Cumhuriyet*, had the greater influence with a circulation of some 9000 (in a city of over a million). To comprehend the slant of the Turkish press in a span of just one week, a short excerpted review of its anti-*Musa Dagh* campaign is offered here:

Haber *(Turkish language), Istanbul, September 3, 1935*

We will have to take our own steps in case the Jewish people fail to bring this Jewish company (MGM) to reason ... The Forty Days of Musa Dagh *presents the Turco-Armenian struggle during the World War in a light hostile to the Turks. Its author is a Jew. This means that MGM, which is also a Jewish firm, utilizes for one of its films a work by one of its compatriots ... Declare a boycott against pictures by MGM ... Jewish firms which maintain commercial relations with our country will also suffer if they fail to stop this hostile propaganda.*

La Republique *(French language), Istanbul, September 3, 1935*

A German Jew has written ... a novel that is forged, contains extremely insulting passages ... it would be unjust to have a company which utilizes its funds for the filming of movies directed against us to benefit financially from us.

La Republique, *September 5, 1935*

A book written by a Jew and full of calumnies against us, MGM has entrusted the eventual production of the film to Rouben Mamoulian, an Armenian ...

Tan *(Turkish language), Istanbul, September 8, 1935*

The (U.S.) Secretaries of State and Commerce have wired the American Embassy in Istanbul that the Musa Dagh *picture will not be produced without the authorization of the Turkish Embassy ...* The Forty Days of Musa Dagh, *inaccurate and forged from beginning to end and saturated with animosity*

and hatred, which is aimed at renewing the propaganda of the
atrocities to which the Armenians were allegedly subjected at
the hands of Turks during the World War ... Our task is ... to
thank the American government for the friendship manifested
in preventing the production of this base work of propaganda
written in a really scandalous manner. (Appendix IX)

American embassy officials viewed the Turkish propaganda as pre-arranged for the specific purpose of embarrassing and denigrating the United States. The Turkish press relentlessly attacked Werfel, Jews, Diaspora Armenians, the State Department, MGM, and the American news media. Especially singled out were *The New York Times, Motion Picture Herald,* and a particular comment in the *New York Herald Tribune* which had asked:

Why should the American government authorize the Turks
to censure the film of The Forty Days of Musa Dagh *before its*
adaptation to the screen? What right has the Turkish government
to concern itself with our films? Is it for the Turks to say what
films Americans should see? [96]

The *Herald Tribune* statement was especially offensive to *La Republique*. In its September 8, 1935 issue, it challenged the *Herald Tribune* because it had taken exception to Ertegun's intervention in the *Musa Dagh* controversy.[97] MGM was rebuked for daring to make a film of a book written by "a shameless Jew [who] permits himself to describe the Turk as half savage, an enemy of honor, and a murderer of women and children."[98] Recognizing the power of film, *La Republique* alerted the reader to appreciate motion pictures:

As the most powerful modern means of propaganda because
taking advantage of a certain mysticism which obscurity exercises,

it magnetizes the eyes and spirit. Seated comfortably in our
own armchair we are doing more than reading, we are living,
in a way, without fatigue, in a short space of time of two hours,
… a subject which we could not know except by reading a
large volume …[99]

The Turkish press was virtually unanimous in calling for the making of a Turkish film about modern Turkey to counteract any distortions conveyed by the movie of *Musa Dagh*. Simultaneously the Turkish government aroused the populace through the media, "for our patience is at an end."[100] On September 10, 1935, *La Republique* informed its readers that MGM would not launch the production:

Without our approval, they will abstain from producing
the film … Everything liable to be construed against Turkey
has been excluded … and the subject to be filmed is entirely
different from that of the book … In addition (MGM) has
agreed, in submitting the new scenario to our Ambassador,
to have the film cast only with approval of our diplomatic
representative.[101]

From Washington, Wallace Murray had made it clear to the American embassy staff in Turkey that MGM had received repeated warnings from the State Department that the studio might lose money for any disregard of the Turkish government's wishes.[102] On the same day that Murray sent his communiqué to the embassy, Ertegun, dissatisfied with the efforts of the State Department's Near Eastern Affairs bureau, appealed directly to Secretary Hull, reiterating his disenchantment with MGM, Werfel's "fiction," and the influence of Armenian circles. He informed Hull that the Turkish government had received the draft scenario:

And found it utterly negative and any alteration would prove inefficient in erasing the original traits of the novel ... Kindly exert your high influence with a view to precluding the carrying out of this project ...[103]

Ertegun's plea impelled Secretary Hull to have Murray relay Ertegun's concern to Will Hays:

It is my duty to bring the matter again before you and to solicit such assistance as you may be able to render in disposing of a question which appears to be assuming very large proportions in the minds of the officials at Ankara. Anything that you can do to meet this problem will be greatly appreciated by the Department.[104]

Herron, speaking for Hays, assured Murray:

The Turkish Ambassador has nothing to worry about at the present time. If the Metro-Goldwyn-Mayer Company decides to make the picture, ... the scenario would again be submitted to the Turkish Ambassador in Washington before the picture went into production.[105]

Aware that the Department of Commerce had been alerted by its attaché in Turkey, Herron contacted N. D. Golden at the Specialties, Motion Picture Division of the Department of Commerce, informing him that J. R. Rubin of MGM had told him:

Under no circumstances would the picture go into production until the script had been taken up with the Turkish Ambassador and his objections had been met ... Tell Gillespie that he can answer every attack appearing out there with the statement that the Turkish Ambassador is fully informed on what is going on and until they hear from him that the picture has gone into production, there is nothing to worry about.[106]

A few days later, the secretary of state's office reassured Ertegun that his concern had been relayed to Will Hays. In turn, the Hays Office informed the State Department that the script would not go into production without the approval of the Turkish Ambassador.[107] To cover themselves, the State Department through the Division of Near Eastern Affairs in tandem with the Specialties and Motion Picture Division of the Bureau of Foreign and Domestic Commerce agreed to issue a disclaimer "in preparation for any representations that the Turkish Ambassador would doubtless make in the event that MGM does not live up entirely to its promise not to produce the picture without the approval of the Turkish ambassador."[108]

Underlining the seriousness of the situation, Chargé d'Affaires G. Howland Shaw in Istanbul apprised Secretary Hull of the establishment at Ankara of a General Directorate of the Press in the Ministry of the Interior with Vedat Nedim Tor, an energetic German-trained ex-communist in charge:

It has always been one of his cardinal policies that his organization should control and direct a positive type of propaganda to reach the Turkish people and the world at large ... Vedat Nedim, ... studied German propaganda technique under ... Goebbels. Is it a coincidence that Vedat Nedim's return to Turkey should coincide with references in the press to the Musa Dagh campaign? ... If modern Turkey is to be understood abroad, she must take steps to organize propaganda which brings out at least an undercurrent of anti-Semitism.[109]

As public fury in Turkey mounted, there came the Turkish govern-ment's demand that MGM issue an official declaration terminating the production. The affair had escalated into such an explosive issue that it threatened French-Turkish relations vis-à-vis Muslims in the French-administered territories in Syria and North Africa.[110]

In the meantime, the Armenian American community was heartened when it learned that Rouben Mamoulian had confirmed to the Armenian press that he had discussed directing *Musa Dagh* with Thalberg. He was aware of the Turkish government's protests and censorship endeavors and knew that the script had been submitted to the Turkish Ambassador for approval.[111]

The Armenian media kept its readers apprised of the mounting controversy surrounding *Musa Dagh*. Articles taken from Turkish newspapers were published in Armenian journals here and abroad emphasizing the anti-Jewish bias in the Turkish reports, for example:

> ... *Franz Werfel a "filthy Jew"* ... *MGM producers are money-mad usurers* ... *MGM is a Jewish company for whom money-making takes first rank* ... Musa Dagh *is the work of a Jew instigated by Armenian money* ... *Turkish government demands U.S. government stop film, if not, all MGM films will be banned in Turkey.*[112]

In spite of Turkish propaganda and threats, their ethnic newspapers reassured Armenians that the United States government could not prevent the filming of *Musa Dagh* without violating the First Amendment.[113]

From Istanbul, Chargé d'Affaires Shaw reported to Hull the gist of conversations he had in Ankara with Turkish officials about *Musa Dagh*. Shaw was told that Vedat Nedim Tor, who now had authority over motion pictures in Turkey, had said:

> *The script had been received and it was horrible anti-*
> *Turkish propaganda. It was not a question of cutting out a line*
> *here and a page there—the whole thing was highly offensive to*
> *the Ministry of Foreign Affairs ... the film will be forbidden in*
> *Turkey ... in the Balkan countries, in Germany and probably*
> *in France. Turkey will in addition forbid the showing of any*
> *MGM films.*[114]

Shaw reminded those same officials that the United States government had no legal authority to prohibit the showing of any film. Furthermore it was only as a diplomatic courtesy that the State Department had brought the Turkish concern to the attention of the interested parties. Shaw was convinced that "in true Turkish fashion (Ankara) firmly believes that, if the Department really wanted to do something, a way could be found."[115]

The official Turkish decision finally reached Loew's in New York City and the studio in Culver City on September 27, 1935. William Orr at Loew's informed Rubin that he had met with the Turkish ambassador in Washington again. Ertegun had told him that Ankara, having read the script, had responded with a terse message:

> *The script was so antagonistic to Turkey that she will*
> *do everything in her power to stop the movie. Furthermore,*
> *alterations and/or deletions could never be made satisfactory to*
> *Turkey. If the movie is made, Turkey will launch a worldwide*
> *campaign against it. It rekindles the Armenian question. The*
> *Armenian question is settled. How else would you explain the*
> *presence of Armenians in the Turkish Parliament? The movie*
> *will only stir up troubles about a situation that has been*
> *smoothed out.*[116]

The ever-mounting Turkish pressure persuaded Rubin that the project was more trouble than it was worth. As far as he was concerned, *Musa Dagh* had lost its glamour and was all aggravation. Admitting the wonderful possibilities for *Musa Dagh*, he preferred that another studio make the movie.[117] Furthermore, the Turkish threat regarding *Musa Dagh's* reception in Europe presented too many complications, rendering the situation impossible. Rubin advised the studio to not go ahead with the production, believing that MGM's *Musa Dagh* had stirred up such a hornet's nest that the Turks would doom the film because passions had been so aroused in Turkey.[118]

Even the Turks' ancient enemy, the Greeks, notified MGM that any contemplated production of the film in Greece would be prohibited. In any case, a Greek exhibition license for the movie would not be granted.[119] If Turkey's traditional enemy supported her, could her friends do less? Film censorship had become a diplomatic tool.

Chapter 15

THE POLITICS OF
FILM CENSORSHIP

We've lost our guts

Attempts to censor or ban movies outside the United States were not uncommon in the era of the Great Depression. In England, Alexander Korda, the pre-eminent British film producer, owned the rights to T.E. Lawrence's *Seven Pillars of Wisdom* but wanted to change the film title to *Lawrence of Arabia*. He had submitted Miles Malleson's script of the film to the Turkish government. Like the *Musa Dagh* screenplay, it, too, raised similar objections. The script's disparaging portrayal of Turks in "the blackest colors and shown in the most disparaging light"[120] disturbed both the British Colonial Office and the Foreign Office. The ensuing debate caused Lord Tyrell, president of the British Board of Censors, to deny Korda a Certificate of Approval.[121] None other than Winston Churchill, a Conservative member of the House of Commons, influenced Tyrell. The future World War II prime minister "was very worried because he felt it was important to have the Turks as allies when war came."[122] After trying to resurrect the project six times in a span of five years, Korda abandoned the production in 1939.

A similar situation confronted Paramount Pictures' *The Devil Is a Woman* ('35) starring Marlene Dietrich. The story line centered on a notorious Spanish seductress and her relationships with men. The film's police chief believed that arresting lawbreakers was a waste of time and preferred shooting them instead. To compound the matter, the Spanish Civil Guard was portrayed as full of drunks. It so antagonized the Spanish government that the studio withdrew the film from the world market.[123] *Variety*, the bible of the entertainment world, reported that Paramount's and MGM's experiences with foreign governments induced them to consult in the future with foreign sales executives in New York on all stories before production.[124]

The power of the foreign censor is simple, clear, and effective, then and now. If a film does not please the censor, he can adversely affect the studio's revenue by banning it or refusing to license it. It is a fact that the American market alone will not return a profit on an expensive movie. As a matter of business practicality, a movie is made for worldwide distribution. After MGM had bought Sinclair Lewis' *It Can't Happen Here* for $200,000, Lewis accused Will Hays of giving the order to suppress it at the insistence of Hitler and Mussolini. Similarly, France supported Turkey in protesting the filming of Werfel's *The Forty Days of Musa Dagh*.[125]

Fortunately, democratic institutions have withstood the intimidations of the "know-nothings" because times have changed. In 1981 there was a protest in the American Jewish community when Vanessa Redgrave, an avowed supporter of the Palestine Liberation Organization (PLO), was to play a Jewish inmate of Auschwitz in Fania Fenelon's autobiographical *Playing for Time*, a CBS television movie. Even Fenelon protested the casting. As a result, CBS lost $3,000,000 when many potential sponsors backed out.[126] In spite of the objections, the TV movie played on schedule and was a critical success, eventually winning awards.[127]

During the celebration of the thirty-third anniversary of the founding of Israel, Arab protests proved futile in preventing the world movie premiere of *The Chosen* ('81) in a thousand theaters in the United States and twenty foreign countries. The film had been financed by Jewish interests such as the Rapid American Corporation, made up of Schenley, McCrory Stores, Lerner Shops, Botany 500, et al. Similarly, thanks to the power brokers in Hollywood, Otto Preminger's 1960 movie production of Leon Uris' *Exodus* about Israel's fight for independence was an immediate box office hit, despite the protests of the Arab world.

Two other events serve as examples of the authority of modern filmmakers, as opposed to censors, studios, and governments. :

- African Americans rallied with donations of big money to help Spike Lee finish his film biography *Malcolm X* ('92) the way he wanted it made.[128]
- In 1993, the British Broadcasting Corp. (BBC) documentary *Chairman Mao—The Last Emperor* evoked a strong protest by the Chinese Communist government. Its appeal to the British Foreign Office was rejected.[129]

That such controversial productions were realized despite foreign protests while *Musa Dagh* languished on the shelf for forty years can be attributed to the demise of the Hays Office and the influence of big money and political clout. The Jewish community had the financial wherewithal and the Hollywood connections that Armenians lacked. From the 1930s to the 1960s, the power of the censor and the politics of the time worked against MGM's *Musa Dagh* project.

When one considers the history of anti-Jewish prejudice, it is astonishing that anti-*Musa Dagh* protests in Turkey had aroused Turkish Jews to repudiate Franz Werfel.[130] Ironically, fifty years later, the Jewish community in Turkey, egged on by Turkish officials, pressured American Jewish leaders not to recognize Armenians as fellow victims of genocide.

Turkish representatives implied that, if the American Jewish community recognized the Armenian Genocide, it could imperil the well-being of Turkish Jews.[131]

The single most dedicated force behind the *Musa Dagh* production from its inception was Irving Thalberg. His reputation as a movie producer had already won him accolades as "the boy wonder" of the movie world. He was a proven master, possessing a golden touch in the selection of properties and converting them into mega-hits for MGM in spite of the economic gloom of the 1930s.[132] A frail man in his thirties, Thalberg was a human dynamo who worked at fever pitch once he went into action. His commitment was unequivocal and inspiring.[133]

In November 1934, before *The Forty Days of Musa Dagh*'s American publication, Thalberg had assigned the screenplay to Carey Wilson, one of Hollywood's master screenwriters. Thalberg had given him a nine-page outline based on Arthur Hanko's translation of the original two-volume German language edition of *Die Vierzig Tage Des Musa Dagh (The Forty Days of Musa Dagh)*.[134] The following April, after many drafts, Wilson submitted a 193-page complete script, followed by several revised scripts by June 1935.[135] Thalberg believed that Wilson's script was the best ever written for a natural box office hit.[136] While Wilson had been busily engaged transposing Werfel's tome into a screenplay, MGM had also commissioned Talbot Jennings to work on a script. Of Jennings' four submissions, the most he produced was an incomplete script of twenty-nine pages in April 1935. That the studio gave *Musa Dagh* top priority is evident in the additional efforts of Frances Marion, Cortland Fitzsimmons, and Messrs. Harrison and Cannon, who made suggestions, notes, outlines; and also served as readers.[137] Counting Thalberg's outline, by 1936 seven writers had worked on the *Musa Dagh* screenplay in one form or other.[138]

Once Thalberg personally took over the production of *Musa Dagh*, he approached Rouben Mamoulian to direct it. Mamoulian, an Armenian native of Tiflis, Georgia, had made his mark on Broadway with the Heywood Broun stage play and George Gershwin folk opera, *Porgy and Bess*. He had gained stature in Hollywood for his motion picture innovations in such films as *Applause* ('29), *City Streets* ('31), the Rodgers and Hart musical *Love Me Tonight* ('32) starring Maurice Chevalier and Jeanette MacDonald, *Dr. Jekyll & Mr. Hyde* ('32), earning Fredric March his first best actor Academy Award, and Greta Garbo's *Queen Christina* ('33).[139]

Mamoulian welcomed Thalberg's offer with enthusiasm and began to make his own preparations to bring the novel to the screen. The Armenian community was ecstatic and confident that justice would be done to Werfel's novel in the hands of one of their own.[140]

In October 1935, Thalberg informed Mamoulian that the studio had run into trouble over *Musa Dagh* because Turkey had threatened to ban all MGM films unless production stopped. Thalberg's initial reaction to the Turkish threat had been a resounding, "To hell with the Turks, I'm going to make the picture anyway."[141] He assured Mamoulian that the picture would be made because he intended to contest the Turkish complaints. Both men proceeded with the project.

A few weeks later, Thalberg sent for Mamoulian and informed him regretfully that *Musa Dagh* had to be shelved. The Turkish government had convinced France to ban all MGM films there, but what was more distressing was the threat to ban all Hollywood movies. "I can't fight that," Thalberg told the equally dejected Mamoulian.[142] Thalberg told Samuel Marx that *Musa Dagh* would not have been called off without Turkey's support from friendly nations, especially France.[143] France at the time was more concerned about the Turkish Dardanelles, her occupation of Hatay (the former Turkish Sanjak of Alexandretta) and Syria, and Nazi Germany's influence in Turkey.

Frank Capra, ever alert and eager, made an attempt to convince MGM that he should direct *Musa Dagh*, but he, too, was rejected. Thalberg would have been willing to give Capra the job, but Mayer was still afraid of provoking the Turkish government.[144]

MGM, the most powerful movie studio in the world, Louis B. Mayer, the most powerful man in Hollywood, and Irving Thalberg, Hollywood's master producer, had met their match in the form of a foreign government and the U.S. State Department.[145] Relations between Thalberg and Mayer[146] had already become strained, partly due to *Musa Dagh*.[147] Ever the fighter, Thalberg tried to resurrect the production. In a one-on-one confrontation, he challenged Mayer: "What can the Turks do if we make *Musa Dagh*? Okay, let them keep us out of their thirty movie theaters."[148] When Mayer refused to carry the *Musa Dagh* fight to the State Department or appeal the Hays Office ruling on Sinclair Lewis' *It Can't Happen Here*, Thalberg snapped, "We've lost our guts, and when that happens to a studio, you can kiss it good-bye."[149] He told Frances Marion that the *Musa Dagh* production had been put on hold. "It was the same old story. Same old threats. Seems we can't afford to lose Turkey."[150] Marion was of the opinion that the studio would never be permitted to make *Musa Dagh*.

Quoting *The Morning Telegraph*, the Armenian American newspaper *The Hairenik Weekly* informed its readers that MGM stood to lose $50,000 a year if its pictures were banned in Turkey, whereas a boycott by Armenian Americans would mean a yearly loss of many times $50,000 to MGM. The article criticized:

> *The mighty American Republic, which had fought England*
> *rather than pay a tea tax, and which still ardently heeds George*

> *Washington's admonition to isolate itself from Europe, submitting*
> *to dictation from the murderous Turks. It is enough to make the*
> *signers of the Declaration of Independence turn in their graves.*[151]

Following MGM's decision to drop *Musa Dagh*, rumors abounded confusing the Armenian community and other *Musa Dagh* advocates. In November 1935, *The New York Evening Journal* reported that, in spite of the threat of a Turkish embargo on American films, "'Leo' (MGM) was going to make *Musa Dagh*, because the money it would lose in Turkey would make no great difference and *Musa Dagh* is a cinch to be an elegant picture."[152]

When reports reached the Armenian American community that MGM had definitely shelved the production of *Musa Dagh*, their reaction had no effect on the studio. The Armenian media called MGM's decision "pathetic," quoting Thalberg's press release:

> *We had to discard Musa Dagh because the Turkish gov-*
> *ernment wanted its history forgotten. Personally, I think it was*
> *a mistake. We all know about the Turkish atrocities against*
> *the Armenians. I think a picture giving a fair account of what*
> *really happened, even though it did not reflect entirely to the*
> *credit of Turkey, would be infinitely preferable. Truth is always*
> *better than propaganda.*[153]

In response to MGM's scuttling of *Musa Dagh*, in April 1936 the Armenian Revolutionary Federation Committee and the Armenian Theatrical Society of New York City presented an episodic play in the Armenian language based on the event itself and included scenes from Werfel's novel. Armenian patrons filled the 58th Street Theatre to capacity and responded with standing ovations and enthusiastic comments.[154]

The intent of the Armenian American community was to keep *Musa Dagh* alive, but neither the State Department, the Hays Office, or MGM were accommodating or attentive. Armenian Americans were absolutely convinced that the pressures exerted by the Turkish government were primarily responsible for terminating the production of *Musa Dagh*. But the greater disappointment was the stand taken by their own government. Armenians felt that U.S.-Turkish opposition to *Musa Dagh* had denied an ethnic minority and MGM their exercise of a basic constitutional right guaranteed in the First Amendment. The politics of film censorship had tilted the United States in favor of Turkey—the architect of the Armenian Genocide and perpetual promoter of its denial.

Chapter 16

THE CONSPIRATORIAL NATURE
OF CENSORSHIP

An agreeable duty

Uninformed as to the machinations in Washington, Ankara, Culver City, and Loew's in New York, Werfel and some *Musa Dagh* partisans were still under the illusion that MGM intended to make the movie. In reality the word was out when *Variety* carried the story in November 1935 that MGM had decided to shelve *Musa Dagh* because it might annoy Turkey.[155] The rumors and confusing press reports that had abounded since the book's publication contributed to the false impressions of *Musa Dagh*'s patrons.

In Turkey there was no let-up in the government's campaign against MGM and *Musa Dagh*. On September 5, 1935, Ambassador Ertegun in another official communiqué to Secretary Hull reiterated the Turkish government's position regarding *Musa Dagh*:

> *I have already had several occasions to discuss with the Department of State the projected filming of Franz Werfel's novel, "The Forty Days of Musa Dagh" by Metro-Goldwyn-Mayer Company of New York.*
>
> > *The representative of the said company upon the recommendations of the State Department came into contact with this Embassy to have the views of the Turkish Government*

on the matter. It was duly explained to them at that time that the fiction of Franz Werfel, presumably influenced by Armenian circles, is full of arbitrary calumnies and contempt against the Turkish people and that the filming of such a story, besides giving an utterly false conception of Turkey to the American public, would greatly hurt the Turkish nation …

The company, thereupon, had suggested to make some changes in the story with a view to neutralizing the objectionable features of the scenario … The Embassy has later on received the draft scenario, … However, the result of these attempts have been utterly negative, any alteration proving inefficient in erasing the original traits of the novel.

The Turkish Government … feels sure that it will not be looked upon sympathetically by the United States Government.

Having already communicated to the Metro-Goldwyn-Mayer Company the result, I have the honor of requesting your Excellency, upon the instruction of my Government, to kindly exert your high influence with a view to precluding the carrying out of this project which is so detrimental to the cordial feelings between the two peoples.

Accept, Excellency, the assurances of my highest consideration.

Mehmet Munir [156]

By going straight to the top, the Turks were confident that the United States government, being concerned about maintaining cordial relations with Turkey, would be more sympathetic and act accordingly.

Ertegun's second direct appeal to Hull reinforced the State Department's conviction that this was top priority to the Turks. Werfel's novel had incited the kind of fury in Turkey that Salmon Rushdie's *The Satanic Verses* did in Iran fifty years later. The Turkish government's request to stop the filming of *Musa Dagh* had evolved into an insistent demand that Washington exert its influence on MGM. To the Turks, *Musa Dagh* was a very sensitive issue, which they threatened to elevate to the level of a diplomatic blunder on the part of the United States. The Roosevelt administration was made to understand that MGM's film project threatened relations between the two countries. Hull once again relayed the Turkish concern to Wallace Murray and so informed Ertegun.[157] Murray promptly contacted Will Hays to clarify the State Department's position that Hays was to assist in "disposing of a question" that had assumed large proportions in Turkey.[158]

In its official response to the Turkish ambassador, the State Department again assumed no responsibility for MGM or the Hays Office actions, emphasizing that its role was merely to act in its diplomatic capacity as an intermediary to inform all involved parties of the Turkish concern. Herron let Murray know that the script was not finished and reiterated that it would not go into production without the approval of the Turkish ambassador.[159] Herron was mistaken. Carey Wilson's *Musa Dagh* screenplay was in Thalberg's hands in June 1935.

William Orr, representing Loew's and MGM, visited the Turkish ambassador to allay his fears and admitted that filming Werfel's novel would be harmful whatever the modifications and that it would be preferable to drop the project altogether. Ambassador Ertegun was so elated that he expressed his gratitude to the State Department in a handwritten letter to Wallace Murray:

Turkish Embassy, Washington, D.C.
October 4, 1935

My dear Mr. Murray

*A few days ago Mr. Orr of Metro-Goldwyn-Mayer called
on me at the Embassy to discuss the filming of* Musa Dagh. *As
a result of our conversation he joined us to admit that the filming
of this novel, whatever modifications it might be subjected to,
could not but be harmful from every standpoint.*

*Consequently he declared that they would rather drop this
scheme altogether.*

*I have already informed my government of the satisfactory
result reached through the kind support of the State Department.*

*In this connection it is an agreeable duty for me to extend
to you my best thanks and hearty appreciation for the efforts
you have been so kind to exert in this matter, without which
the happy conclusion which has created an excellent impression
in my country could not possibly have been attained.*

*Reiterating my gratitude I request you, dear Mr. Murray,
to believe me.*

Sincerely Yours,
M. Munir Ertegun[160]

Murray replied to the Turkish ambassador's letter by expressing
his great pleasure that the matter had been settled to the satisfaction
of Ertegun's government.[161] From Ankara came Ambassador Skinner's
communiqué informing the Secretary of State: "It is certainly the case
that the influence of the Department has been exerted with happy

effect in this matter," and of the Turkish government's satisfaction that the *Musa Dagh* production had been abandoned.[162]

Either the Turkish press was ignorant of these recent developments or chose to ignore the news that *Musa Dagh* had been shelved, because the Istanbul journals continued their tirades against MGM and *Musa Dagh*.[163] On request of Murray, Herron checked with Loew's and MGM again[164] and verified the "shelving" reports as facts.[165] In a memorandum briefly reviewing the *Musa Dagh* case, Murray noted the Turkish ambassador's "strenuous efforts to prevent the moving picture production of the popular novel depicting the heroic struggle of the Armenians against Turkey during the World War as a chapter in Turkish history which the present government is only too glad to soft-pedal."[166]

Never in Hollywood history had such a reaction to a film been witnessed. It astonished *Musa Dagh*'s advocates, and it still does. The full weight of a foreign nation had compelled the United States to lean on a movie studio not only to censor a movie but also to abort it, despite its heralded popularity and historic credibility.

To *Musa Dagh* devotees, the intervention of the State Department and the Hays Office was not only questionable but contemptible. To Armenians, the Hays Office's censorship powers had gone beyond judging the prurient content of movies to rendering a judgment on a proposed film because of its diplomatic ramifications. The Hays Office had cast itself in a supporting role as the partner of the State Department and the appeaser of the Turkish government. There was no doubting its awesome power in the 1930s. Although its victories at the time enhanced its prestige and authority, the Hays Office activities simultaneously aroused an understandable trepidation in the movie colony that one day would lead to its demise. American diplomacy, in this instance, had been designed to accommodate a foreign country by depriving American Musa Dagh proponents of their First Amendment rights. It was unconscionable that the United States had obliged the nation that had never honored the Treaty of Sevres, which would have guaranteed Armenian independence.[167] Twenty years after the removal of over 2,500,000 Armenians from the lands of their ancestors, the *Musa Dagh* case was effectively dismissed.

Both the American and Armenian press excoriated the parties responsible for shelving *Musa Dagh* and rebuked Turkey for threatening to ban all American films because it disliked *Musa Dagh*.[168] Concern was expressed that Hollywood movies offending foreign sensibilities were becoming so important that it looked like a matter for the League of Nations. Movie studios were finding that in every case of a story written about some foreign country, some objectionable angle would arise that might as well be eliminated immediately before foreign protests began. One cannot underestimate the power of governments whose diplomatic relations with other nations serve as a trigger when its national interests and pride are ruffled.[169]

Coming to the defense of *Musa Dagh*, Hollywood columnist Sheilah Graham said, "It was in the class of truth films that are in great demand and popular with movie fans."[170] *The Hairenik Weekly* focused on the Turkish government:

> *Why did the Turks do this incredible, unspeakable thing? … Was it because we were Christians? … Was it because the Turks were jealous of our economical and cultural superiority? … Was it because Armenians were people of shop-keepers and money-changers, exploiters of the honest Turk, as the clever, up-to-date Turkish propaganda is insinuating to a class-conscious world?*[171]

To Armenians ignorant of the details, the outcome was evidence of their individual helplessness and collective weakness. They simply lacked the political influence in the United States and abroad to counteract Turkish machinations. The Armenian American community was divided. There were too many spokesmen whose nationalistic rhetoric, while appealing to their captive ethnic audiences, did nothing in presenting a united front to effectively communicate Armenian concerns to non-Armenians here and abroad. Rather than choose and support respected, knowledgeable, and articulate representatives speaking for a united community above nationalistic politics to gain the attention of the power brokers, Armenians blundered into self-imposed quagmires that their enemies exploited. What semblance there was in the 1930s of unity was enveloped in the orbit of the Soviet Union, whose government had ignored the *Musa Dagh* controversy. The Comintern had its own agenda regarding Turkey, and *Musa Dagh* was not part of it.

On occasion, individual Armenian Americans who kept watch on the status of *Musa Dagh* compensated for the lack of unity within the Armenian community. A few years after the initial furor had died down, Warren Chiljan of Oakland, California, on request of some Bay Area Armenians, asked his congressman, John H. Tolan, to inquire at the State Department as to the facts terminating the filming of *Musa Dagh*. Congressman Tolan relayed the matter to Secretary of State Hull.[172] Hull, in turn, informed Tolan that the State Department was not in a position to comment upon a "privately concluded agreement" unless that agreement affected the interests of the United States government.[173] In his response to Tolan, Hull made no mention of the existence of the numerous documents regarding *Musa Dagh*. If he had, the State Department would never have been able to absolve itself of the pro-Turkish role it played in the *Musa Dagh* affair.

Ambassador Ertegun's letter of October 4, 1935, alone would have commanded Tolan's attention. The Chiljan and Tolan inquiries were forwarded to Wallace Murray, who in turn alerted Col. Frederick L. Herron.[174] In allaying Murray's concern, Herron responded:

> *We appreciate very much your handling this subject so splendidly. I think, of course, the less said about such things the better it is for everyone concerned and, unless something further is desired from us, I am going to bury the matter right where it stands.*[175]

Without the influence and pressure exerted by the State Department, as acknowledged by Ambassador Ertegun in his letter of October 4, 1935, the Turkish government would never have succeeded in terminating the film production of *The Forty Days of Musa Dagh*. The concern expressed by the *New York Times* was a timely reaction:

> *It is ironic that Hollywood, unable to make films of* It Can't Happen Here … or The Forty Days of Musa Dagh *through fear of treading on foreign sensibilities, is not restrained at all when it comes to pointing an accusing finger at certain unpalatable phases of our own national history. It would seem that the only toes we safely may tread upon are our own.*[176]

Even though Thalberg's production of Werfel's masterpiece was shelved, the determination to produce the film never diminished, and neither did the controversy surrounding *The Forty Days of Musa Dagh*.

Chapter 17

THE LION SQUEAKS

Continual repression had brought the motion picture pot to a boil

From the moment MGM secured its rights to Werfel's novel until the cancellation of the film production in late 1935, the *Musa Dagh* project had evolved into an unexpected corporate, political, and diplomatic fiasco. It had wasted the energies, talents, time, and money of all those involved, especially at the studio.

The film project had been magnified into a highly sensitive diplomatic issue threatening MGM's overseas markets. After the termination of *Musa Dagh*, the Turkish government made good on its earlier admonitions. Ankara authorized its customs officials to bar the release of MGM films to Turkish importers even though it had realized its objective.[177]

The shelving of *Musa Dagh* was of little consequence to the governments involved when measured against the maintenance of cordial relations with Turkey. The United States and Europe were concerned with Mussolini's invasion of Ethiopia and the threat posed by Hitler in central Europe. The world was gearing up for war, and the major powers were trying to curry favor with the unaligned nations, one of which was Turkey, owner of the Dardanelles and master of Asia Minor.

The storm created by *Musa Dagh* soon dissipated into a topic of conversation among some Armenians and a few partisans in Hollywood.

Several prominent players attempted to keep the project alive. One of the trade papers noted that Walter Wanger, aware of the pressures exerted by Turkey and her allies and MGM's unwillingness to see *Musa Dagh* through, had wanted to buy MGM's rights to the film. Wanger believed it was one of the finest, most dramatic novels he had ever read. Because it concerned the siege atop a mountain of determined Armenians defying the Turkish army, "Europe wouldn't let him make it."[178] Wanger was similarly embroiled in a controversy with the State Department and Franco's Spain over a film about the Spanish Civil War, *Blockade* ('38), starring Henry Fonda. To appease the opposition, Wanger toned down the film to the point that it blurred its anti-Fascist theme. It made no difference. It was still banned in some American cities and condemned by the Catholic Church.[179]

Soon after completing *Stella Dallas* ('37), King Vidor also expressed interest in making *Musa Dagh*. His efforts proved to be futile as well.[180] The number and caliber of prominent producers, directors, screenwriters, actors, et al, who wanted to make the *Musa Dagh* movie since 1935 would expand over the years.

The *Musa Dagh* propaganda war continued, much to the consternation of the Turks. Ambassador Ertegun took note of Hollywood columnist Louella Parsons' item in Hearst's *Boston Evening American* (November 22, 1938) that *Musa Dagh* was off the shelf and would star William Powell. Reacting to the gossip columnist's remarks, there was a resurgence of Turkish activity.[181] What ensued was a reprise with Herron and the Hays Office reassuring Ertegun that *Musa Dagh* would not be produced without his consent.[182] N. D. Golden, director, Motion Pictures Division, Bureau of Foreign and Domestic Commerce, dismissed Parsons' tidbit as having come from a "crackpot" West Coast film trade journal. Furthermore, if MGM were intent on making the movie, it would have launched a publicity campaign immediately. George V. Allen of the State Department's Division of Near Eastern Affairs was more concerned that if MGM revived *Musa Dagh* it would foment widespread anti-Americanism in Turkey, which might result in losses to Socony-Vacuum, General Motors, and Ford. Golden took exception to Allen's position. He felt that every business firm in the United States should stand on its own feet, that continual repression had brought the motion picture pot to a boil, and that the producers were determined to take the lid off. In defending big business, some parties in Washington were obviously applying a double standard where Hollywood was concerned.[183] It appears that U.S. corporations doing business in Turkey were privileged, whereas the Hollywood studios were not on an equal footing.

Parsons' *Musa Dagh* item stirred John Roy Carlson (a pseudonym of Avedis Derounian, author of the future best-seller *Under Cover*, the 1943 exposé of the Fascist totalitarians and their subversive activities in the United States), to make an inquiry of MGM. J. Robert Rubin told him there was no immediate prospect for *Musa Dagh*'s production.[184]

The Turkish government was under the impression that the report about MGM's decision to proceed with *Musa Dagh* was a reaction to the news of President Kemal Ataturk's death in November 1938. Ertegun was quick to inform Murray that the Turkish government's objections to the film had not changed in the least since the death of Ataturk.[185] The ever-vigilant Ertegun remained at his post until his death in 1944 and made sure that *Musa Dagh* never became a film while he was alive.[186]

It was déjà vu for the Hays Office east coast foreign manager, Colonel Frederick L. Herron. Acting on Murray's request, Herron checked on Parsons' report.[187] He dismissed it as "gossip originated without any foundation whatsoever."[188] The Turkish Embassy was reassured again (January 1939) that the State Department's position was unswerving in its support of Turkey and that "it could not approve *Musa Dagh* now, any more than when the picture was first brought up. Conditions had not changed."[189]

That same day, Murray brought the updated *Musa Dagh* developments to the attention of Under Secretary of State Sumner Welles, indicating that the Turkish Embassy, in addition to contacting Murray, had also appealed to Murray's superior,[190] Assistant Secretary of State George S. Messersmith. Messersmith was concerned that film companies not aggravate Turkey where our relationship "was on so good a basis," citing MGM's production of Robert Sherwood's *Idiot's Delight* ('39) as an example that had aggravated Italy. The issue was so important to Messersmith that he was going to arrange a meeting with Colonel Herron in Washington "so that what I say to him may be reinforced by other points of view from within the department."[191] Murray, bowing to Messersmith's position, agreed that the United States should:

> *Take every practicable step to cooperate in particular with the government of Turkey in matters of this kind, in view of the many marks of friendliness and cooperation that we have received during recent years from that government.*[192]

After making some inquiries on the West Coast, Herron had reason to believe that MGM was actually considering the production of the picture without the knowledge of Loew's. He knew that Loew's was distinctly opposed to filming the picture. The Hays Office was likewise opposed and could have prevented the picture from being made, as it did in 1935. Herron felt that if MGM had ignored the protests of Loew's and the Hays Office, it would have reached the State Department.

He suggested to Paul Alling at the State Department that "it would be sufficient to say to MGM that the death of Ataturk in no way lessened the objection which the Turkish government had to the production of this film." Alling assured him that the State Department would keep his suggestion in mind in the event that a direct approach was made by MGM.[193] Once again, the documents prove that the United States Department of State was still a major player, along with the Hays Office, in pressuring MGM to abort *Musa Dagh*'s production.

Although the *Musa Dagh* controversy centered in the United States, the British government also bolstered the Turkish position. In a communiqué dated June 5, 1939, Sam Eckman at MGM, Culver City, informed Arthur Loew at the corporate headquarters in New York City of a meeting he had in London with Lord Tyrell, president of the British Board of Censors, the same man who had rejected Alexander Korda's proposed film production of *Lawrence of Arabia*. Tyrell went to great lengths reviewing Great Britain's position in Europe, especially with Turkey and the Foreign Office's concern of Germany. (Hitler had already marched into Austria and the Sudetenland and was threatening Poland.) He was elated that his government had recently concluded a pact with Turkey. Tyrell saw it as "a great diplomatic victory." He had been very distressed by Germany's attempt to drive a wedge between London and Ankara. Tyrell was adamantly opposed to any film that would depict Turkish "excesses" (Eckman said Tyrell preferred "excesses" to "outrages"), as it would give the Nazis an opportunity to associate the British with such a movie and thus do harm to England's standing with the Turks. Tyrell was insistent that these "excesses" could not be attributed to the new Turkey but only to the regime of Abdul Hamid. He made no reference to the genocidal role played by the Young Turks in World War I. His defense was: "Were these normal times, no one on the British Board of Censors would ban a film of *The Forty Days of Musa Dagh*, but in consideration of the world situation in 1939, the times are different." In any case, he could not approve MGM's script. His parting comment to Eckman was: "When times are normal again, there'll be no objections on political grounds." Great Britain's intervention in the *Musa Dagh* case was not only requested by Ankara, but expected.[194]

Since the publication of Werfel's novel in 1933, the Turks were always on the alert whenever the buzzwords *Musa Dagh* came up. It was a sensitive issue constantly on the Turkish agenda and deserving priority attention. The Turkish response was always swift and formidable. Regarding Louella Parsons (William Randolph Hearst's favorite Hollywood reporter and employee), there was a germ of truth in her article reporting MGM's renewed interest in *Musa Dagh*.

The MGM hierarchy always opted for the bottom line that the movie business boiled down to a simple matter of debits and credits. The anti-*Musa Dagh* sentiment generated since 1934 only served to reinforce the opinion of its detractors that MGM had committed a rare blunder in picking up Werfel's book. As of August 31, 1938, in addition to its purchase price of $20,000, MGM had expended $29,800 for numerous scripts.[195] While the scripts sat on the shelf, the continuity costs of the film project brought the total to $77,000 by August 30, 1947, exclusive of the expenses incurred for travel, hotels, luncheon engagements, telephone calls, telegrams, and salaries. Hank Moonjean, Pandro Berman's MGM associate producer in the 1960s, believes that MGM spent hundreds of thousands of dollars by that time.[196] What was most confounding, despite the controversy, was MGM's refusal to give up its film rights. In August 1939, MGM renewed its rights to Franz Werfel's *The Forty Days of Musa Dagh*.[197] It reassured Turkey that the movie would never be made so long as MGM owned the rights.

In spite of these struggles, there were those in Hollywood whose determination to bring Werfel's novel to the screen never diminished. Their commitment kept the cause alive enough to result in its temporary resurrection from time to time as a possible motion picture, but not without the usual polemics. Controversy had become a permanent trait of *The Forty Days of Musa Dagh*. It would remain in the annals of movie history as one of the most contentious issues involving a foreign power (Turkey) and her supporters (France and Germany), an ethnic minority (Armenians), a democratic government's foreign service department (United States Department of State), the Motion Picture Producers and Distributors of America (MPPDA) and its censor the Hays Office, and a motion picture corporation and studio (Loew's/Metro-Goldwyn-Mayer).

As the 1930s came to a close, the Armenian American community saw the woes of the Great Depression compounded by the "cowardly lion's" suppression of their Armenian treasure. The most powerful movie studio in America had surrendered. "Leo's" roar had turned into a squeak or, more precisely, "Leo the lion" had turned into a mouse. From time to time there was a ray of hope evoked by news bulletins and rumors, false and real, that the film's production was to be resurrected for the umpteenth time. *The Forty Days of Musa Dagh* ordeal was not over. It was just beginning.

NOTES – BOOK III
BABYLON-ON-THE-PACIFIC AND ON-THE-POTOMAC

Chapter 10
THE LION ROARS

1. Doug McClelland, *Hollywood on Hollywood*, Tinsel Town Talks, Winchester, Mass.: Faber and Faber, 1985, p. 56.

2.   Fred Zinnemann, *An Autobiography, A Life in the Movies*, New York: A Robert Stewart book, Scribner's & Sons, Maxwell Macmillan International, 1992, pp. 45-46. MGM was required to make fifty-two films per year for its parent company, Loew's Inc. in New York City. Loew's in turn, screened first-run MGM movies in its own chain of theaters, prepared publicity, and set schedules and release dates.

3.   John Douglas Eames, *The MGM Story—The Complete History of Fifty Roaring Years*, New York: Crown Publishers, 1975, p. 8. In 1934, the MGM studio in Culver City consisted of 117 acres containing 27 sound stages and the world's largest film laboratory, which produced 150 million feet of release prints a year. Among its 4000 employees were 61 stars and featured players, 17 directors, and 51 writers.

4.   McClelland, *Hollywood*, p. 104.

5.   Zinnemann, *An Autobiography, A Life in the Movies*. Among Zinnemann's directorial triumphs were *High Noon* ('52), *From Here to Eternity* ('53), and *A Man For All Seasons* ('66).

6.   Cari Beauchamp, *Without Lying Down, Frances Marion and the Powerful Women of Early Hollywood*, New York: A Lisa Drew Book/Scribner's, 1997, p. 9 and book jacket. Marion wrote over two hundred scripts and was the first woman to win the Oscar twice for screenwriting.

7.   Gerald Nachman, "Roars, Rants and a Rave or Two," *San Francisco Chronicle*, Datebook, Show Business, 4/19/92, p. 7. Nachman castigates today's movies as being worse than ever and charges that the "Lion" did not just stop roaring; he turned into a mouse.

8.   Alma Mahler Werfel with E. B. Ashton, *And the Bridge Is Love*, New York: Harcourt, Brace, 1958, p. 177.

9.   *Variety*, 4/16/69.

10. *MGM Archives, Musa Dagh File*, Story 5807, Synopsis of *The Forty Days of Musa Dagh*, 12/34.

11. Ibid., Correspondence: Louis B. Mayer to J. Robert Rubin, 2/16/34.

12. Samuel Marx interview by the author, MGM Studio, Culver City, Calif., 1/28/81.

13. Ibid.

14. *MGM Archives, Musa Dagh File*, Story 5807, Correspondence: J. R. Rubin to L. B. Mayer, 2/23/34.

15. Ibid., Correspondence: Rubin to Mayer, 2/24/34.

16. Ibid., Cablegram: Paul Zsolnay Verlag, Vienna, Austria, to J. Robert Rubin, 2/27/34.

17. Ibid., Cablegram: L .L. Rosen, Paris, France, to J. Robert Rubin, New York City, 5/28/34. In the MGM archives is an impressive copy of the contract. It is embossed on heavy gray stock. Its Gothic lettering enhances its significance, which is highlighted with a grand seal. Along with Werfel's and Zsolnay's signatures is that of the American Consul in Vienna.

18. Ibid., Office Memo: Miss Browning to Mr. Krecke, 5/28/34.

19. Ibid., Letter: D. O. Decker to J. R. Rubin, 6/1/34.

20. Ibid., Memo: F. L. Hendrickson, 6/11/34.

21. Ibid., Letter: J. Robert Rubin to Louis B. Mayer, 4/7/34.

22. Ibid., Letter: J. R. Rubin to John Golden, 6/6/34.

23. Ibid., Letter: John Golden to J. R. Rubin, 6/11/34.

24. Gerald Gardner, *The Censorship Papers, Movie Censorship Letters from the Hays Office, 1934 to 1968*, New York: Dodd, Mead & Co., 1987, pp. xvi, xix. Hollywood scandals had caused the studio bosses in 1922 to hire Will H. Hays (a Republican politician and President Harding's former postmaster-general) to head the Motion Picture Producers and Distributors of America (MPPDA) to improve the movie colony's image. (The official name today is the Motion Picture Association of America [MPAA].) In 1934 the studio heads authorized the Hays Office to amend and enforce the Production Code of 1930 with the specific intent to censor motion pictures. The code was drawn up by a Jesuit priest, the Rev. Fr. Daniel Lord, S.J., and a prominent Catholic layman, Martin Quigley, publisher of the influential trade journal *Motion Picture Herald*, and enforced by Joseph I. Breen, a Catholic journalist. No movie could be shown unless Breen granted the Hays Office Seal of Approval.

25. John Stanley, "Hollywood's Daring Defiance of '30's Code," *San Francisco Chronicle*, Datebook, 7/31/88, p. 25. The guidelines required that "No picture shall be produced which would lower the moral standards of those who see it." Among scores of taboos: "…profanity, licentious or suggestive nudity, illegal traffic in drugs, sexual perversion, white slavery, miscegenation, sex hygiene and venereal diseases, scenes of childbirth, ridicule of the clergy and willful offense to any nation, race or creed." The intent of the MPPDA/Hays Office Production Code Administration was to go over scripts before filming began and then to preview the completed films. For three decades Hollywood's creativity was constricted.

26. The hero of the Dardanelles campaign, Mustapha Kemal, became the architect of post-World War I Turkey and its unchallenged leader, Kemal Ataturk, "Father of All Turks."

27. Selznick was informed by MGM representatives in Europe that Germany had appeased Turkey, her former World War I ally, by banning the publication and sale of Werfel's novel as of February 1934.

28. *MGM Archives, Musa Dagh File*, Story 5807, Memo: David O. Selznick to J. R. Rubin, 7/16/34.

29. Ibid., Letter: Marshall Best, Viking Press to J. R. Rubin, 8/9/34.

30. Ibid., Letters: Alexander Filian to L. B. Mayer, 12/26/34; Barney Glaser to Irving Thalberg, 3/17/35; Kennedy Nahas to MGM, 5/13/35; K. M. Baronian to MGM, 5/13/35; Sam Edelman to Viking Press, 5/31/35. They offered their services and expressed their concerns.

31. Ibid., Letter: Marshall Best, Viking Press to J. R. Rubin, 12/17/34.

32. V. Aharonian, Editorial: "The Forty Days of Musa Dagh," *Hairenik Weekly*, 1/18/35, p.1.

33. *U.S. Department of State, Division of Communications and Records, Division of Near Eastern Affairs*, Document 811.4061, Motion Pctures/142,143; Musa Dagh/ 1,2. Correspondence: Wallace Murray, Chief, Division of Near Eastern Affairs for the Secretary of State to The Honorable Will H. Hays, President, Motion Picture Producers and Distributors of America, 11/16,19/34.

Chapter 11

COLLUSION IN DIPLOMACY

34. Dorothy Wade and Justine Picardie, *Music Man, Ahmet Ertegun, Atlantic Records and the Triumph of Rock 'n' Roll*, W. W. Norton, New York: 1990, p. 28. A staunch supporter of Kemal Ataturk's revolution and a translator of his speeches, Mehmet Munir Ertegun had served as Turkish Ambassador to Switzerland and France before arriving in the United States with his family in 1934.

35. The Turkish government to this day refers to the Armenian Genocide as "alleged."

36. *U.S. Department of State, Division of Near Eastern Affairs*, Document 811.4061, Motion Pictures/142,143; Musa Dagh/1, 2. Correspondence: Wallace Murray, Chief, Division of Near Eastern Affairs for the Secretary of State to The Honorable Will H. Hays, President, Motion Picture Producers and Distributors of America, 11/16,19/34.

37. Ibid.

38. Ibid., Motion Pictures, Musa Dagh/3. Correspondence: Frederick L. Herron, Foreign Manager, Motion Picture Producers & Distributors of America, Inc., New York City, to Wallace Murray, Chief, Division of Near Eastern Affairs, Department of State, Washington, D. C., 11/20/34.

39. Ibid., Motion Pictures /146, Musa Dagh/5. Correspondence: Wallace Murray, Chief, Division of Near Eastern Affairs to Munir Bey, Turkish Ambassador to the United States, 11/26/34.

40. Ibid., Musa Dagh/4. Correspondence: Mehmet Munir, Turkish Embassy,

Washington, D.C., to Wallace Murray, Chief, Division of Near Eastern Affairs, Washington, D.C., 12/6/34.

41. Ibid., Musa Dagh/6. Correspondence: United States Embassy, Ankara, Turkey, Chargé d' Affaires G. Howland Shaw to Wallace Murray, Chief, Near Eastern Affairs, Washington D.C. 11/27/34.

42. Ibid., Embassy of the United States of America, Istanbul, Turkey, Musa Dagh/9. Correspondence: Robert P. Skinner, U.S. Embassy, Istanbul, to Secretary of State, Washington, D.C., 1/8/35.

43. Ibid., Musa Dagh/10. Correspondence: Turkish Embassy, Washington, D.C., Mehmet Munir Ertegun to Wallace Murray, Chief, Near Eastern Affairs, 4/22/35, and attachment of news clipping from the *Washington Herald*, 4/17/35.

44. *Washington Herald*, "Musa Dagh to be Filmed," 4/17/ 35.

45. *U.S. Department of State, Division of Near Eastern Affairs*, Document 811.4061, Musa Dagh/11,12. Letter: Wallace Murray, Chief, Near Eastern Affairs, to Frederick L. Herron, Foreign Manager, MPPDA, and to Mehmet Munir, Ambassador of Turkey, 4/27/35.

46. The MPPDA was created in March 1922. At an annual salary of $100,000, Will H. Hays was made the director by the movie moguls. In January 1927, a Studio Relations Committee (SRC) was set up to establish studio self-regulation. The Production Code came into being in March 1930. By October 1931, script submission was required. In 1934, SRC became the Production Code Administration with Joseph I. Breen the enforcer of a stricter code. From that time until 1968 the Code was enforced to the letter.

47. *MGM Archives, Musa Dagh File*, Story 5807, Letter: Frederick L. Herron to Joseph Breen, 4/29/35.

48. *U.S. Department of State*, Document 811.4061, Musa Dagh/13. Correspondence: Frederick L. Herron to Wallace Murray, 4/29/35.

49. Ibid., Musa Dagh/14. Correspondence: Wallace Murray to Mehmet Munir, 5/1/35.

50. *MGM Archives, Musa Dagh File*, Story 5807, Letter: Frederick L. Herron to Joseph Breen, 4/29/35.

51. The impressive MGM output in 1935 made it a banner year for the studio due to films such as *Naughty Marietta, A Night at the Opera, Anna Karenina, Rose Marie, A Tale of Two Cities. Mutiny on the Bounty* in 1935 and *The Great Ziegfeld* in 1936 won Best Picture Academy Awards and went on to become standard fare on television. If *Musa Dagh* had become a film then, one can imagine the size of the audiences of the screen, television, videocassette, and DVD versions since 1935. Perhaps a more educated public could have influenced the Turkish administrations that followed to profit from the example of the German Federal Republic in its acts of atonement since 1949 in acknowledging the history of the Third Reich, 1933-1945. (From the newsletter, *The Week in Germany*, "Kohl Sends Message to Holocaust Survivors," German Information Center, Newsletter, 7/22/88, p.7.) Chancellor Kohl's stand on the issue: "Germans were guilty as individuals for the crimes of the Holocaust and they are collectively liable for the injustice committed in their name ... The Holocaust must not be forgotten because the possibility that it could happen again cannot be ruled out ... It is not from forgetting but from remembering that we derive the courage to resist the forces of evil in history and to pave our common route into a better future."

52. Neal Gabler, *An Empire of Their Own—How the Jews Invented Hollywood*, New York: Anchor Books, Doubleday, 1988, p. 233.

53. Eames, *The MGM Story*, p. 9.

54. Cari Beauchamp, *Without Lying Down*, p. 300. Marion won her first Academy Award for her screenplay of King Vidor's *The Champ* ('31), starring Wallace Beery and Jackie Cooper.

Chapter 12

A CABAL OF CONSPIRATORS

55. *U.S. Department. of State, Division of Near Eastern Affairs*, Document 811.4061,

Musa Dagh/14. Correspondence: Wallace Murray, Chief, Near Eastern Affairs, to Mehmet Munir Bey, Ambassador of Turkey, 5/1/35.

56. Ibid., Musa Dagh/15. Correspondence: Wallace Murray to American Embassy, Istanbul, Turkey, 5/14/35.

57. Ibid., Musa Dagh/15. Correspondence: Wallace Murray to American Embassy, Istanbul, Turkey, 5/14/35.

58. *MGM Archives, Musa Dagh File*, Story 5807, Correspondence: J.R. Rubin to I. Thalberg, 5/9/35.

59. *U.S. Department of State, Division of Near Eastern Affairs*, Document 811.4061, Embassy of the U.S.A., Istanbul, Turkey. Musa Dagh/17. Enclosure No. 1, Despatch No. 665 of 6/4/35; Translation of *Son Posta* article of Nihat Ferit's letter of 5/29/35.

60. Ibid.

61. Ibid., Despatch No. 665, Musa Dagh/17. Robert P. Skinner to Secretary of State, 6/4/35; Translation of *Haber* article "They Themselves Will Be the Losers," 5/30/35.

62. Ibid., Musa Dagh/18. Correspondence: Robert P. Skinner to Wallace Murray, Chief, Division of Near Eastern Affairs, Washington, D. C., 6/6/35. Skinner retired from the Foreign Service in 1936.

63. *MGM Archives, Musa Dagh File*, Story 5807, Transcript of a telephone conversation: Frederick Herron (MPPDA) to J. R. Rubin, 6/9/35. Gillespie's given name is omitted.

64. *U. S. Department of State, Division of Near Eastern Affairs*, Embassy of U.S.A., Istanbul, Turkey, Document 811. 4061, Musa Dagh/35: Despatch No. 768, "Press Campaign Against MUSA DAGH Film," 9/10/35.

65. Ibid.

66. *MGM Archives, Musa Dagh File*, Story 5807, Correspondence: Fahir Epikci (MGM distributor in Istabul) to L. Lawrence (MGM representative in Paris), 3/29/35.

67. Ibid., Transcript of a telephone conversation: Frederick Herron (MPPDA) to J. R. Rubin, 6/9/35.

68. *U.S. Department of State*, Document 811.4061, Musa Dagh/19. Correspondence: Wallace Murray to The Honorable Robert P. Skinner, American Ambassador, Istanbul, Turkey. 6/ 20/35.

69. *MGM Archives, Musa Dagh File*, Story 5807, Transcript of a phone conversation, Frederick L. Herron to J. R. Rubin, 6/9/35.

70. Samuel Marx, *Mayer and Thalberg, The Make-Believe Saints*, New York: Random House, 1975, pp. 245-246.

71. *U.S. Department of State*, Document 811.4061, Musa Dagh/20. Memo: Wallace Murray, Chief, Division of Near Eastern Affairs; Copies to Secretary of State; Under Secretary of State; American Embassy, Istanbul; Col. Frederick L. Herron; 6/18/35.

72. Ibid.

73. *MGM Archives, Musa Dagh File*, Story 5807, Night Letter: Eddie Mannix (MGM Studio Manager) to J. R. Rubin, 6/21/35.

74. Ibid., Night Wire: Samuel Marx to J. R. Rubin, 6/21/35.

75. Ibid., Letter: Eddie Mannix to David Blum, 6/20/35.

76. *U.S. Department of State*, Document 811.4061, Musa Dagh/23. Correspondence: Frederick L. Herron, Foreign Manager, Motion Picture Producers & Distributors of America, Inc., to Wallace Murray, Chief, Division of Near Eastern Affairs, 6/24/35.

77. *MGM Archives, Musa Dagh File*, Story 5807, Copy of Col. Herron's letter to Murray, 6/24/35.

78. *U.S. Department of State, Division of Near Eastern Affairs*, Document 811.4061, Embassy of U.S.A., Istanbul, Turkey, Musa Dagh/35: Despatch No. 768, "Press Campaign Against MUSA DAGH Film," 9/10/35. Copy in MGM Archives, *Musa Dagh File*.

79. *MGM Archives, Musa Dagh File*, Story 5807, Copies of a translation of an article in Haber (Istanbul) sent to L. B. Mayer and J. R. Rubin from L. L. Lawrence, 6/26/35.

80. Ibid., Letter: L. R. (unidentified) to Sam Eckman, copies to Eddie Mannix and Irving Thalberg, 7/26/35.

81. Ibid., Correspondence: I. Thalberg to J. R. Rubin, 7/31/35.

82. Ibid., Letter: David Blum (NYC) to Eddie Mannix, 7/26/35.

83. Ibid., Letter: L. Browning to I. Thalberg, 7/30/35.

84. Ibid., Letter: J. Robert Rubin to Irving Thalberg, 7/31/35.

85. Ibid., Cablegram: J. R. Rubin (Paris) to L. B. Mayer and I. Thalberg, Culver City, 8/9/35.

86. *New York Times*, "Reich Bans Film Writer," 7/13/35, p. 16. In another example of foreign intervention in Hollywood, Hitler's propaganda minister, Josef Goebbels, had notified MGM that films carrying screenwriter Herman J. Mankiewicz's name (in 1940 he co-wrote the *Citizen Kane* screenplay with Orson Welles) would not be exhibited in Germany. Mankiewicz had contemplated making a movie called *The Mad Dog of Europe* but had abandoned the project due to the pleas of influential American Jews. They feared such a picture would have unfortunate consequences for the Jews in Nazi Germany.

87. Gene Brown, *Movie Time, A Chronology of Hollywood and the Movie Industry from Its Beginnings to the Present*, New York: Macmilllan, 1995, p. 140. In a similar instance, at the behest of the German consul in Los Angeles, the Hays Office censor, Joseph I. Breen, pressured MGM to water down F. Scott Fitzgerald's screenplay of Erich Maria Remarque's *Three Comrades* ('38) so that it was not overly anti-Nazi.

88. *MGM Archives, Musa Dagh File*, Story 5807, Translation of letter from Fahir Epikci to MGM Paris Office, 8/12/35.

Chapter 13

THE EXPEDIENCY OF TURKISH ARMENIAN PATRIOTISM

89. Donald E. Webster, *The Turkey of Ataturk*, Philadelphia: American Academy

of Political and Social Science, 1939, p. 193.

90. *U.S. Department of State, Division of Near Eastern Affairs*, Document 811.4061, Embassy of the U.S.A., Istanbul, Turkey, Musa Dagh/49. Enclosure No.1 to Despatch No. 874, dated 12/24/35. Translation of article in Turkish newspaper, *Cumhuriyet*, "The Answer of the Armenians of Istanbul to F. Werfel."

91. Ibid.

92. *The Armenian Observer*, "Captive Bolsahyes—Still Talking, This Time Denial," by Moorad Mooradian, Ph.D., 4/20/05, pp. 3,14. Some Turkish Armenians in the United States even today contend that any anti-Turkish propaganda or activity in the United States by Armenian Americans threatens the safety of Armenians in Turkey. In April 2005, several Istanbul Armenians spoke before the Turkish parliament to denounce the Armenian Diaspora for perpetuating the genocide issue. One speaker stated that the Ottoman Turkish government's response to the Armenian insurgency in World War I was justified. Another Armenian speaker said, "Armenians got what they deserved because (their) insurgency caused civil war."

Chapter 14
PRESS AND PREJUDICE

93. *MGM Archives, Musa Dagh File*, Story 5807, Confidential Letter: R. Monta (Paris) to J. R. Rubin, 8/19/35.

94. Ibid., Letter: William Orr to J. R. Rubin, 8/26/35.

95. Due to Istanbul's location and its population, the American Embassy maintained major offices there as well as at the official capital in Ankara.

96. Ibid.

97. Ibid.

98. Ibid., *La Republique*, "Our Patience Is at an End," 9/ 9/35.

99. Ibid.

100. Ibid.

101. Ibid., Enclosure No. 20 of Despatch No. 768, Source: *La Republique*, 9/10/35.

102. Ibid., Musa Dagh/26. Correspondence: Wallace Murray, Chief, Near Eastern Affairs to American Embassy, Istanbul, 9/5/35.

103. Ibid., Musa Dagh/25. Correspondence: Ambassador Mehmet Munir, Turkish Embassy, Washington, D.C. to Secretary of State Cordell Hull, 9/5/35.

104. Ibid., Musa Dagh/28. Letter: Wallace Murray, Chief, Division of Near Eastern Affairs, for the Secretary of State to Will H. Hays, President, Motion Picture Producers and Distributors of America, 9/7/35.

105. Ibid., Musa Dagh/29. Letter: Frederick L. Herron, Foreign Manager (MPPDA), to Wallace Murray, Chief, Division of Near Eastern Affairs, Dept. of State, 9/ 9/35.

106. Ibid., Letter: F. L. Herron (MPPDA), to N. D. Golden, Specialties, Motion Picture Division, Department of Commerce, 9/5/35.

107. Ibid., Musa Dagh/27. Letter: Wallace Murray on behalf of the Secretary of State to the Turkish Ambassador, Mehmet Munir Bey, 9/12/35.

108. Ibid., Musa Dagh/30. Memo, 9/12/35.

109. Ibid., Embassy of United States, Istanbul, Turkey, Musa Dagh/35. Despatch #768, Subject: Press Campaign against the Musa Dagh Film; Cover Letter, G. Howland Shaw, Chargé d'Affaires ad interim, to Secretary of State, 9/10/35. Handwritten across the first page of the document is a double underlined admonition: "Not for dissemination."

110. *MGM Archives, Musa Dagh File*, Story 5807, Correspondence: L. Lawrence to Arthur Loew, 9/24/35.

111. *Hairenik Weekly*, "Mamoulian Grants Interview to the 'Weekly' Reporter," 10/4/35, p. 3.

112. Ibid., "Turkey Alarmed Over Filming Of Musa Dagh," 10/4/35, p. 1.

113. Ibid.

114. *U.S. Department of State*, Embassy of the U.S.A., Istanbul, Document 811.4061, Musa Dagh/39. Despatch No. 783: G. Howland Shaw to the Secretary of State, 9/27/35.

115. Ibid.

116. *MGM Archives, Musa Dagh File*, Story 5807, Letter: William Orr to J. R. Rubin, 9/27/35. In reality, the so-called "presence of Armenians in the Turkish Parliament" was only a token representation of Istanbul Armenians having no political influence.

117. Ibid., Telegram: J. R. Rubin to I. Thalberg, Oct. 11, 1935.

118. Ibid., Correspondence: David Blum to J. R. Rubin, Oct. 27, 1935.

119. Ibid., Cablegram: R. Rosen (Athens) to J. R. Rubin, Dec. 27, 1935.

Chapter 15

THE POLITICS OF FILM CENSORSHIP

120. L. Robert Morris and Lawrence Raskin, *Lawrence of Arabia, The 30th Anniversary Pictorial History*, New York: Anchor Books, Doubleday, 1992, pp. 21-24.

121. Ibid.

122. Michael Korda, *Charmed Lives, A Family Romance*, New York: Random House, 1979, p. 340.

123. Homer Dickens, T*he Films of Marlene Dietrich*, Seacaucus, N. J.: Citadel Press, 1974, pp. 116-120.

124. *Variety*, 11/17/35.

125. *New York Times*, "Hollywood's Censor Is All the World, Should Turkey Ban American Films Because It Disliked *The Forty Days of Musa Dagh*?" 3/29/36, Sec. 7, p. 10.

126. *Oakland Tribune*, 3/26/81, Sec. D, p.1.

127. Ibid., In one of those numbing fatalistic ironies, Fenelon's story concerned her survival as a member of a Nazi concentration camp's all-women orchestra. The director of the orchestra was Gustav Mahler's niece. It was Mahler's widow, Alma Mahler Gropius, who married Franz Werfel.

128. *San Francisco Chronicle*, "Black Stars Help Spike Lee," Datebook, 5/20/92, Sec. E, p. 1.

129. Ibid., "BBC's Mao Film Fuels Battle with China," 12/18/93, Sec. E, p. 5.

130. *Hairenik Weekly*, "The Turkish Press Roused Against Franz Werfel," 1/3/36, p. 1.

131. Mark Arax, "Jews Pressured on Issue of Armenian Genocide," *Los Angeles Times*, 4/22/85, p. 1.

132. Marx interview, MGM Studio, Culver City, 1/28/81.

133. For more about Irving Thalberg, see Samuel Marx, *Mayer and Thalberg, The Make-Believe Saints*, New York: Random House, 1975 and Bob Thomas, *Thalberg, Life & Legend*, Garden City, N.Y.: Doubleday, 1969.

134. *MGM Archives, Musa Dagh File*, Story 5807, Memo to Saul Rittenberg, Chronological list of *Musa Dagh* screenwriters, Exhibit A, 9/3/70. MGM did not purchase the rights to the Viking Press edition of Geoffrey Dunlop's translation of *The Forty Days of Musa Dagh*. MGM had bought the original two-volume German language edition, which had been translated into English by Arthur Hanko.

135. American Film Institute, Louis B. Mayer Library, Los Angeles, Calif., *The Forty Days of Musa Dagh*, Special Collection No. 37, Register, Carey Wilson's screenplay, Wilson's opening scene begins with a narrator indicting the Turkish oppression of Armenians.

136. *Hollywood Reporter*, 7/11/40.

137. *MGM Archives, Musa Dagh File*, Story 5807, Memo to Saul Rittenberg, Chronology of *Musa Dagh* Writers, Exhibit A, 9/3/70.

138. In 1992 the *Musa Dagh* scripts were in the possession of the American Film Institute, Louis B. Mayer Library, Los Angeles, Calif.

139. Alexander Walker, *Garbo, A Portrait*, authorized by Metro-Goldwyn-Mayer, New York: MacMillan, 1980, p. 137. *Queen Christina* is remembered even today for the stunning photography of William Daniels. In the final scene, focusing on the incomparable beauty of a stoic Greta Garbo, it was director Rouben Mamoulian who elicited that shot, instructing her to "think of nothing." The result was a cinematographic "Mona Lisa."

140. *Hairenik Weekly*, "Mamoulian Grants Interview to the 'Weekly' Reporter", 10/4/35, p. 3.

141. Bob Thomas, *Thalberg: Life and Legend*, Garden City, N.Y.: Doubleday, 1969, p. 310.

142. Ibid. In 1935, soon after the *Musa Dagh* debacle, Mamoulian directed the first three-strip technicolor movie, *Becky Sharp*.

143. Marx interview, 1/28/81.

144. Joseph McBride, *Frank Capra, The Catastrophe of Success*, New York: Simon & Shuster, 1992, p. 284, footnote.

145. After completing *Romeo and Juliet* ('36) starring his wife Norma Shearer and Leslie Howard, he was preparing *Camille* ('36), *The Good Earth* ('37), *Maytime* ('37), *A Day At The Races* ('37), and *Marie Antoinette* ('38), and planning the productions of *Goodbye Mr. Chips* ('39) and *Pride And Prejudice* ('40). Unfortunately, Hollywood's "man of destiny" drove himself to an early grave in 1936 at the age of thirty-seven.

146. Cari Beauchamp, *Without Lying Down*, p. 300. Mayer often boasted that President Hoover had considered appointing him as ambassador to Turkey.

147. Marx interview, 1/28/81.

148. Marx, *Mayer & Thalberg*, p. 246.

149. Ibid.

150. Beauchamp, *Without Lying Down*. p. 330.

151. *Hairenik Weekly*, "Current Events by Politicus, His Master's Voice," 11/1/35, p. 1.

152. Ibid., "Rumor Says 40 Days Will Be Filmed," 11/1/35, p. 1. Information based on news report in *New York Evening Journal*, 10/25/35.

153. Ibid., "Apropos Musa Dagh," 4/3/36, p. 2. Excerpted from *Variety*, March 1936.

154. Ibid., "'Musa Dagh' Thrills Overflow House in New York," 4/24/36, p. 1.

Chapter 16

THE CONSPIRATORIAL NATURE OF CENSORSHIP

155. *Variety*, 11/17/35, p. 1.

156. *U. S. Department of State*, Document 811.4061, Musa Dagh/25. Correspondence: Turkish Embassy, Washington, D.C., Mehmet Munir to Cordell Hull,

Secretary of State, 9/5/35.

157. Ibid., Musa Dagh/27. Correspondence: Secretary of State to the Ambassador of Turkey, No date on letterhead.

158. Ibid., Musa Dagh/28. Correspondence: Wallace Murray to Will H. Hays, 9/7/35.

159. Ibid., Musa Dagh/29. Correspondence: Frederick L. Herron (MPPDA) to Wallace Murray, Chief, Division of Near Eastern Affairs, 9/9/35.

160. Ibid., Musa Dagh/36. Correspondence: Turkish Embassy, Washington, D.C., M. Munir Ertegun to Wallace Murray, Chief, Near Eastern Affairs, 10/4/35.

161. Ibid., Musa Dagh/37. Correspondence: Wallace Murray, Chief, Division of Near Eastern Affairs to Mehmet Munir Ertegun, Ambassador of the Turkish Republic; 10/8/35.

162. Ibid., Musa Dagh/41. Division of Near Eastern Affairs, Embassy of the U.S.A., Ankara, Turkey; Correspondence: Ambassador Robert P. Skinner to the Secretary of State; Subject: The Film "Forty Days of Musa Dagh." 10/5/35.

163. Ibid., Musa Dagh/42. Telegram received by Skinner (Ankara) from Gray (Istanbul) 12/12/35., Musa Dagh/48. Despatch No. 862, Subject: The Musa Dagh Film; Embassy of the U.S.A., Robert P. Skinner to the Secretary of State, 12/12/35.

164. Ibid., Musa Dagh/43. Correspondence: Wallace Murray, Chief, Division of Near Eastern Affairs, Washington, D.C. to Col. Frederick L. Herron, Foreign Manager, MPPDA, New York, N.Y., 12/14/35.

165. Ibid., Musa Dagh/45. Correspondence: Frederick L. Herron (MPPDA), New York, N.Y. to Wallace Murray, Chief, Near Eastern Affairs, Washington, D.C., 12/17/35.

166. Ibid., Musa Dagh/46. Memorandum for the Signing Officer: Wallace Murray, 12/19/35.

167. In the Treaty of Sevres (1920), Armenia's independence and President Woodrow Wilson's delineation of Armenia's boundaries were recognized by Turkey and the Allies. But Wilson's proposal for a U.S. Mandate for Armenia was doomed

when the U.S. Senate rejected the Treaty of Versailles. To appease Turkey, the Treaty of Lausanne gutted the Treaty of Sevres. The two-year old independent Armenia (1918–1920) was overwhelmed by Ataturk's Turkish forces from the west and the Bolsheviks from the east.

168. *New York Times*, "Hollywood's Censor Is All the World," 3/29/36, Sec. 7, p. 10.

169. *Hairenik Weekly*, "Apropos Musa Dagh," 4/3/36, p. 2, from *Variety*, March 1936.

170. Ibid.

171. Ibid., Vartouhie C. Nalbandian, "A Historic Crime and Its Motive," 4/24/36, pp. 1-2.

172. *U.S. Department of State*, Document 811.4061, Musa Dagh/50. Correspondence: Warren A. Chiljan to Congressman John H. Tolan, 6/30/37. Correspondence: Congressman John H. Tolan to Secretary of State, Cordell Hull, 7/2/37.

173. Ibid., Musa Dagh/51. Correspondence: Secretary of State, Cordell Hull to The Honorable John H. Tolan, House of Representatives, 7/14/37.

174. Ibid., Musa Dagh/52. Correspondence: Wallace Murray, Chief, Division of Near Eastern Affairs, Washington, D.C. to Col. Ferderick L. Herron, Foreign Manager (MPPDA), N.Y., N.Y., 6/10/37.

175. Ibid., Musa Dagh/53. Correspondence: Frederick L. Herron, Foreign Manager, Motion Picture Producers & Distributors of America, Inc., New York City, to Wallace Murray, Chief, Division of Near Eastern Affairs, Dept. of State, Washington, D.C., 7/13/37.

176. Roger Dooley, *From Scarface to Scarlett, American Films in the 1930s*, New York: Harcourt, Brace, Jovanovich, 1979, 1981, p. 150. Quotation taken from the New York Times, date unknown.

Chapter 17

THE LION SQUEAKS

177. *U.S Department of State*, Document 811.4061, Musa Dagh/49. Embassy of the U.S.A., Istanbul, Turkey; Despatch No. 874, Subject: The Musa Dagh Film;

Ambassador Robert P. Skinner to the Secretary of State, 12/24/35.

178. *MGM Archives, Musa Dagh File*, Story 5807, Correspondence: R. Rosen to J. R. Rubin, 1/23/36.

179. Tony Thomas, *The Films of Henry Fonda*, Secaucus, N.J.: Citadel Press, 1983, pp. 70-71.

180. *MGM Archives, Musa Dagh File*, Story 5807, Telegram: King Vidor to J. J. Cohen, 11/5/37. Among Vidor's directorial credits were *The Big Parade* ('25), *The Crowd* ('28), *The Champ* ('31), *Our Daily Bread* ('34).

181. *U.S. Department of State*, Document 811.4061, Musa Dagh/54. Correspondence: M. Munir Ertegun, Turkish Embassy, to Wallace Murray, Chief, Division of Near Eastern Affairs, Washington, D.C., 9/12/38. Re: Turkish inquiry of Louella Parsons' article of 11/22/38 in the *Boston Evening American*.

182. Ibid., Musa Dagh/63. Memorandum of Conversation: Col. Frederick L. Herron, Foreign Manager (MPPDA) and Paul Alling, Office of the Assistant Secretary of State, 1/11/39.

183. Ibid., Musa Dagh/57, Memorandum of Telephone Conversation, Participants: N. D. Golden and George V. Allen, 12/15/38.

184. *MGM Archives, Musa Dagh File*, Story 5807, Letter: J. R. Rubin to Avedis Derounian, 1/3/39.

185. *U.S. Department of State*, Document 811.4061, Musa Dagh/56. Correspondence: Wallace Murray, Chief, Division of Near Eastern Affairs to Turkish Ambassador Mehmet Munir Ertegun, 12/17/38.

186. Leslie Bennetts, "Ahmet Ertegun," *Vanity Fair*, 1/98, pp. 98-103,133; Dorothy Wade and Justine Picardie, *Music Man, Ahmet Ertegun, Atlantic Records, and the Triumph of Rock'n'Roll*, New York: Norton, 1990, pp. 31-33. Munir Ertegun's sons, Ahmet and Nesuhi, chose to remain in the United States. Ahmet (1923-2006) went on to found Atlantic Records in 1947 and became "the greatest Rock'n'Roll mogul in the world." He revered his father as a great statesman and patriot and funded an Ertegun Foundation for a Turkish Studies Chair at Princeton University in his name.

Ahmet, a multi-millionaire, also provided the funds to establish an Ertegun Chair in his brother's name at Georgetown University. Like his father, Ahmet Ertegun in January 1998, insisted that there was no planned Armenian Genocide. A few years ago, in a private interview with Harut Sassounian of *The California Courier*, aware of Turkey's application for membership in the European Union, Ahmet Ertegun said Turkey should recognize the Armenian Genocide. Sassounian made public Ertegun's change of heart after Ertegun died in December 2006. Their meeting was publicized in AZG, Armenian Daily, December 12, 2006.

187. *U.S. Department of State*, Document 811.4061, Musa Dagh/55. Correspondence: Wallace Murray, Chief, Division of Near Eastern Affairs, Washington, D. C., to Col. Frederick L. Herron, Foreign Manager (MPPDA), New York, New York, 12/17/38.

188. Ibid., Musa Dagh/59. Correspondence: Frederick L. Herron, Foreign Manager (MPPDA), New York City to Wallace Murray, Chief, Division of Near Eastern Affairs, Department of State, Washington, D. C., 12/19/38.

189. *MGM Archives, Musa Dagh File*, Story 5807, Record of telephone conversation: Will Hays' secretary to Loew's/MGM, 1/16/39.

190. *U.S. Department of State*, Document 811.4061, Musa Dagh/58. Correspondence: Wallace Murray, Chief, Division of Near Eastern Affairs to Sumner Welles, Under Secretary of State, 12/17/38.

191. Ibid., Musa Dagh/60. Correspondence: George S. Messersmith, Assistant Secretary of State to Mr. Murray and Mr. Burke, 12/20/38.

192. Ibid., Musa Dagh/62. Correspondence: Wallace Murray, Chief, Near Eastern Affairs to G. S. Messersmith, Assistant Secretary of State, 12/21/38.

193. Ibid., Musa Dagh/63. Memorandum of Conversation: Col. Frederick L. Herron, Foreign Manager (MPPDA) and Paul Alling, Office of the Assistant Secretary of State, 1/11/39.

194. *MGM Archives, Musa Dagh File*, Story 5807, Correspondence: Sam Eckman to Arthur Loew, 6/5/39.

195. Ibid., Memo: 8/30/38.

196. Interview of Hank Moonjean by the author, Los Angeles, Calif., 6/16/92.

197. *MGM Archives, Musa Dagh File*, Story 5807, Correspondence: Kathryn Barnes to Hendrickson, 8/26/39.

27 Louis B. Mayer, MGM General Manager, the most powerful man in Hollywood, 1924–1951.

28 Irving G. Thalberg, Hollywood's wunderkind and the single most dedicated force behind the *Musa Dagh* production in 1934–1935.

29 Rouben Mamoulian welcomed the opportunity to direct *Musa Dagh*.

30 Samuel Marx, MGM story editor. "A principle was at stake. A foreign government should not be allowed to suppress the making of an American motion picture."

31 Will H. Hays, "Czar" of the motion picture industry, 1922–1945.

32 Joseph I. Breen, Hays' office production code enforcer, 1934–1954.

33 Wallace Murray, Chief, Near Eastern Affairs. "The heroic struggle of the Armenians against Turkey during the World War is a chapter in Turkish history which the present government is only too glad to soft pedal." December 19, 1936.

34 G. Howland Shaw, Chargé d'Affaires, U.S. Embassy, Turkey. "If the State Dept. really wanted to do something (about *Musa Dagh*), a way could be found." September 27, 1935.

35 Cordell Hull, Secretary of State, claimed he was not in a position to comment upon Musa Dagh "A privately concluded agreement". June 10, 1937.

36 George V. Allen, Assistant Secretary of State for Public Affairs, was concerned that *Musa Dagh* would revive anti-Americanism in Turkey which night result in losses to Socony-Vacuum, General Motors and Ford. December 15, 1938.

37 Arthur Richards, U.S. State Department. "The Turkish people are particularly sensitive to this period of their history and are trying desperately to cover it up." August 17, 1953.

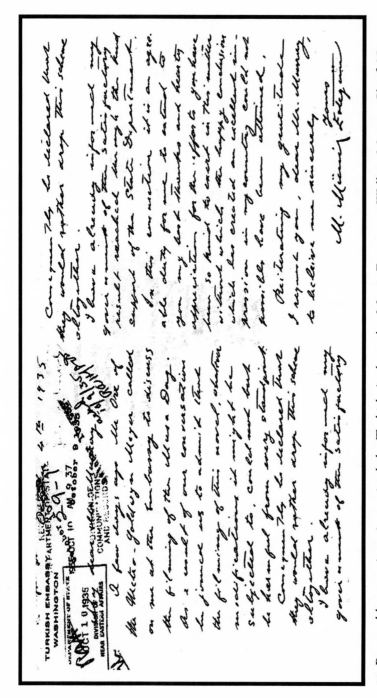

38 Personal letter written in gratitude by Turkish Ambassador Munir Ertegun to Wallace Murray, Chief, Near Eastern Affairs, U. S. State Department, for his efforts in terminating the *Musa Dagh* movie. October 4, 1935.

BOOK IV

The Quest
For Sanctuary

Here is wisdom.
—The Revelation of St. John the Divine 13:18

Chapter 18

CITIZEN WERFEL

Unflagging in optimism as to the dignity and destiny of man

In July 1940, an item in *The Hollywood Reporter* that MGM was reviving *The Forty Days of Musa Dagh*[1] must have been most welcome news to the Werfels, considering their current situation in Europe. After the German annexation of Austria in 1938, the Werfels were constantly on the run from the Nazis: Milan, Zurich, London, Amsterdam, Paris, Lourdes, Marseille, Barcelona, Madrid, and Lisbon. In Marseille, then under Vichy rule,[2] Werfel had heard that Hitler himself had put a price on his head, and British radio had announced that he had been murdered by the Nazis.[3]

In the course of his involuntary odyssey, Werfel's celebrity as the author of *The Forty Days of Musa Dagh* preceded him. Werfel had only to autograph the Portuguese edition for the consul in Marseille to expedite the granting of Portuguese transit visas for Alma and him.[4] This gesture proved to be a godsend in Lisbon.

Through the efforts of Thomas Mann, President Roosevelt granted special emergency visas to the Werfels.[5] They picked up their visas and a personal letter from Secretary of State Cordell Hull at the U.S. consulate in Marseille emphasizing that Werfel was a prominent Catholic writer. The strategy was designed to enlist the support of the hierarchs of the

Roman Catholic Church. The documents enabled Werfel, a native of Prague, to secure Czech passports for him and Alma.[6] At the same time, the Vichy government, to appease its Nazi masters, was rounding up Germans and Austrians wanted by the Nazis to prevent their departure to French territorial possessions or to foreign countries.

In the United States, the concern for the plight of European refugees, particularly stateless intellectuals, had resulted in the creation of such organizations as the League of American Writers, American Friends of German Freedom, and the Emergency Rescue Committee.[7] The latter, under the cover of the World Committee of the Young Men's Christian Association (YMCA), sent a veritable American "Scarlet Pimpernel,"— Varian Fry,[8] to Marseille to assist prominent refugees out of unoccupied France. In Fry's possession was a list of names of prominent émigrés drawn up by the Emergency Rescue Committee in New York, the American Federation of Labor, and the Museum of Modern Art. His instructions were to help only the eminent refugees. On the day he arrived in Marseille, he immediately contacted the Werfels. At first Alma thought he might be a Nazi agent. Werfel soon realized that Fry was anything but a Nazi and placed their fate in his hands.[9]

In spite of the documents in their possession, the Werfels also needed French exit visas. The resourceful Fry, through the YMCA in France, always had access to the necessary documents simply because they were counterfeit. The "French exit visas" were rejected. The only recourse was a harrowing trek on foot over the Pyrenees for the Werfels and their group. Favoring a game leg from a World War I disability and suffering from the effects of a heart attack in 1938, Werfel's physical condition was permanently and adversely affected by the journey. Led by another intrepid American, Fry's lieutenant, Dick Bell, they made it to the Spanish border. Fry was waiting for them, and so was the

Werfels' luggage. One suitcase contained all of the original manuscripts of Mahler's symphonies, Bruckner's *Third Symphony*, and an outline of what was to become *The Song of Bernadette*. Fry accompanied them by rail to Barcelona and then to Madrid.[10] Using their Portuguese transit visas in Madrid, they took their chances and flew to Lisbon—ironically, on the German airline *Lufthansa*.[11]

After two weeks of what seemed an interminable wait, they secured passage on the Greek liner *Nea Hellas*, which proved to be the last passenger vessel to make a regular run to New York. After eight years of relentless hounding since leaving Vienna, the Werfels arrived in New York City on October 13, 1940.[12] In the meantime, Werfel's editor and translator, Dr. Gustave O. Arlt, a professor at the University of California at Los Angeles (UCLA), had already made arrangements[13] for the Werfels to settle among many of their fellow émigrés[14] in Los Angeles, where nothing could penetrate their unique coterie.[15] Los Angeles was the center for the European intelligentsia in the 1930s and 1940s. Commenting on their presence there, S.M. Behrman said, "It was as crowded with artists as Renaissance Florence. It was a golden era. It had never happened before. It will never happen again."[16] Remembering their *Musa Dagh* experience with MGM, to Alma, Hollywood was the center of film jackals, where routine ruled.[17]

Soon after their arrival in California, Rabbi Stephen Wise, president of the American Jewish Congress, urged Werfel to file for American citizenship and make himself available to appear on the NBC *I'm an American* radio program in Los Angeles. Wise believed that Werfel's recent experience would make him an excellent guest.[18] On March 16, 1941, he appeared on the show and expressed his desire to become an American citizen. He told the interviewer that, when he saw the Statue of Liberty, she appeared to him as an angel of paradise. Overwhelmed by America's greatness, freedom, and way of life, he believed that Americans were a lucky people. He was convinced that America was destined to defend the eternal Christian values against the blitzkrieg of Satan and observed that it was easy to take freedom for granted if one had never experienced tyranny. To Franz Werfel, "America was more than a country and more than a people. It is a unique amalgam of strong races."[19] The situation in Europe convinced Werfel to take out "first papers" (citizenship application) on June 18, 1941.[20]

During their quest for sanctuary in the summer of 1940, the Werfels had made a short stay in Lourdes, France. In front of the Virgin Mary's shrine at the Grotto of Lourdes, Werfel had vowed, "If I escaped the surrounding perils and reached the sanctuary of America, I would lay all other work aside to sing the song of Bernadette."[21] Inspired by the moving experience he had there and in honor of the peasant girl, Bernadette Soubirous, whose vision of the Virgin was responsible for the shrine, within a few months of his arrival in California, Werfel had written his first "American" novel. *The Song of Bernadette* fulfilled his pledge. When Werfel showed his original *Bernadette* manuscript to Gottfried Reinhardt, Reinhardt was astounded to see that "not a single handwritten word or letter had been marred by a correction. 'I did not write this. I was just an instrument transmitting divine dictation,' said Werfel."[22]

When *The Song of Bernadette* became a best seller (350,000 copies), 20th Century Fox purchased the film rights for $100,000.[23] By December 1943, the movie was playing in theaters. It eventually won four Academy Awards, including a Best Actress Oscar for Jennifer Jones, who played Bernadette.

Werfel loved the movies, concerts, and to entertain. He reveled in the company of friends and fellow artists and especially in the freedom he found to pursue his writing in security and comfort. To get away from the urban din and distractions of Los Angeles, he had a favorite hideaway at the Hotel Mirasol in Santa Barbara, where he worked on *Jacobowsky and the Colonel.*[24]

In 1942, *Bernadette* made possible the purchase of an enchanting cottage, formerly built and owned by actress May Robson.[25] Their home on North Bedford Drive in Beverly Hills became a favorite rendezvous for their fellow German-speaking émigrés.[26] During the war years, movements of refugees were restricted, which contributed to their forming close-knit groups. Werfel begged Attorney General Francis Biddle in Washington to lift the ban on his colleagues who were refugees here, that "they were among the first and foremost fighters against the pest of National Socialism."[27] During the (Senator Joseph) McCarthy era, some of them became self-imposed exiles again.[28]

In time, colleagues and academia honored Werfel. In January 1943, the Authors' League of America informed him of his election to the Authors Guild and the Dramatists Guild.[29] On June 9, 1943, at UCLA, Werfel was awarded an honorary doctor of laws. His citation read:

> *Novelist, Playwright, Lyric Poet, fertile in imagination and skilled in the use of language, tolerant and understanding of human nature, unflagging in optimism as to the dignity and destiny of man. An author whose writings passing over the confines of geography are today widely read in England, France and the United States and someday will be prized in Germany.*[30]

In 1944, the National Conference of Christians and Jews also recognized his achievements. Their citation commended Werfel "for the promotion of unity, understanding and cooperation among the varied cultural groups that compose the population of the United States."[31]

An earlier heart attack in France, the grueling hike over the Pyrenees, and his addiction to tobacco and coffee caused Werfel to suffer another heart attack in September 1944.[32] He died at home on August 26, 1945, fourteen days short of his fifty-sixth birthday. In his wallet were medals of the Virgin Mary.[33]

All who had come to know "the little giant" responded with an outpouring of sorrow. Armenians everywhere were profoundly grieved. The Armenian media and clergy expressed their eternal gratitude to the Austrian Jew who reminded the world of the first genocide of the twentieth century in *The Forty Days of Musa Dagh*. *The Hairenik Weekly* acclaimed Werfel as the only man in the world who effectually projected to the world the most heinous crime of the century. An editorial asserted that no amount of Armenian expenditures, propaganda, and personal persuasion had done as much for the revival of the Armenian cause as that of *The Forty Days of Musa Dagh*. "The Armenian people are grateful to the Jewish race for such a noble son, and mourn his loss, no less deeply than the loss of a beloved Armenian author."[34] Commenting on his great volume of work, *The New York Times* noted, "Werfel instilled his faith in a Divine Being and in the spiritual union of mankind."[35]

Knowing Werfel did not wish a religious burial, Alma made sure there was no ritual. Alma had Werfel prepared as he described it in *A Star of the Unborn*, his futuristic autobiography and his last publication. He was dressed in a tuxedo, a new silk shirt, his glasses in the breast pocket; a spare silk shirt and several handkerchiefs were in the coffin. His funeral took place the morning of August 29, 1945, at the Pierce Brothers Mortuary in Beverly Hills. Among those in attendance were Arnold Schoenberg and his wife, Otto Preminger, Thomas Mann and his wife, Otto Klemperer, and Igor Stravinsky. A Franciscan priest delivered the eulogy.[36] Bruno Walter played the organ and Lotte Lehmann sang Schubert's *Sunset*.[37] The following day at Rosedale cemetery[38] in a unique and touching ecumenical gesture for an unbaptized Jew, Werfel's remains were blessed by the same Franciscan priest with special permission of the archbishop.[39]

In July 1975, Armenian Americans raised the necessary funds to re-inter the mortal remains of Franz Werfel in his beloved Vienna.[40] A Werfel memorial sculpted by Anna Mahler marks his grave there today.

Alma presented Werfel's papers containing his original Musa Dagh research notes to the UCLA Special Collections Library. She offered to sell the *Musa Dagh* manuscript to the Armenian Evangelical Church in New York City, but they could not meet her asking price.[41]

Rectifying the intolerance of the totalitarians, in July 1988, on the occasion of the sixty-sixth Salzburg Festival, the opening program paid tribute to three eminent Austrian writers who had been banned after Nazi Germany's annexation of Austria fifty years before. The vast audience listened to readings of Stefan Zweig, Franz Kafka, and Franz Werfel.[42] In appreciation of Werfel's *The Forty Days of Musa Dagh*, the Armenian government in 1990 marked the centennial of his birth by issuing commemorative medals and buttons. A tribute was offered by the Armenian Writers Union, and plans were made to erect a bust of Franz Werfel in Yerevan, the capital of Armenia.[43] Concurrently, the Armenian Ministry of Education named a school after him.[44]

Werfel's writings had been forbidden in the aftermath of the Communist takeover of Czechoslovakia following World War II. In 1991, the new democratic Czech government lifted the ban. Some of his writings were published in the first postwar textbook, *What Was Missing in the Textbooks*,[45] containing the German language literature of Bohemia and Moravia. In May 1993, actors and writers gathered in Berlin to observe the 60th anniversary of the Nazi book burning. In a triumph over state censorship, they read selections from a long list of writers, including Werfel, whose writings had been condemned.[46]

On April 23, 1998, in an event held in Yerevan at the Genocide Museum, Institute of the National Academy of Sciences of the Republic of Armenia, near the Martyrs Monument in Dzidzernagaberd, there was the deposition of urns with earth from the graves of Johannes Lepsius, James Bryce, and Franz Werfel. Plaques were also unveiled in honor of these three great friends of Armenia at the Genocide Monument complex.[47] The honors bestowed on Werfel are evidence of the high esteem Armenians had for Werfel and *The Forty Days of Musa Dagh*.

At the time of Werfel's death, *Musa Dagh*'s status as a film project had not changed. It was still languishing on the shelf at MGM.

NOTES – BOOK IV
THE QUEST FOR SANCTUARY

Chapter 18
CITIZEN WERFEL

1.   *The Hollywood Reporter*, 7/11/40, p. 3.

2.   After the fall of France in 1940, a puppet state subservient to Nazi Germany was set up under Marshal Henri Petain and Pierre Laval at Vichy, France.

3.   University of California, Los Angeles, Research Library, Special Collections Library, *Werfel Papers*, Collection 512, Box 19, *New York Post*, 7/16/40, p. 1.

4.   Mahler Werfel, *Bridge*, p. 264.

5.   Mary Jayne Gold, *Crossroads Marseille, A Memoir, 1940*, Garden City, N.Y.: Doubleday, 1980, p. 180.

6.   Ibid., p. 190.

7.   Ibid., Prologue. The National Committee of the Emergency Rescue Committee included in its membership: Elmer Davis (columnist and radio commentator), Dr.

Robert Hutchins (president, University of Chicago), Dorothy Thompson (lecturer and commentator), Dr. Charles Seymour (president, Yale University), Thomas Mann, and John Dewey. The chairman was Frank Kingdon, president, Newark University.

8. Ibid., p. 397, Varian Fry, Harvard graduate, deserter of the French Foreign Legion, editor of *Common Sense*, on the editorial staff of *The New Republic* and the Foreign Policy Association, member of the Liberal Party of New York, enabled hundreds of anti-Nazi refugees to escape from France legally and illegally. In 1940, Mary Jayne Gold joined Fry's Emergency Rescue Committee.

9. Ibid., p. 173.

10. Ibid., pp. 150, 155, 192-195.

11. John Russell Taylor, *Stangers in Paradise, The Hollywood Émigrés, 1933-1950*, New York: Holt, Rinehart and Winston, 1983, p. 145.

12. Mahler Werfel, *Bridge*, pp. 268-270.

13. Taylor, *Hollywood Émigrés,* p. 163.

14. Mahler Werfel, *Bridge*, pp.270-285. The Werfels' circle included such luminaries as Erich Korngold, the composer of many of the great scores in the Warner Bros. movies; the symphony conductor Bruno Walter; Ludwig Bemelmans, the incisive humorist and novelist; the poet Bruno Frank; Thomas Mann and son Golo; composer Arnold Schoenberg; queen of German light opera Fritzi Massary; opera star Lotte Lehmann; novelist Erich Maria Remarque; actor Oskar Homolka; and director/producer Max Reinhardt, among others. They were all escapees from Hitler's Europe.

15. Ibid., p. 218.

16. Doug McClelland, *Hollywood on Hollywood, Tinsel Town Talks,* Boston: Faber and Faber, 1985, p. 7. A comment by S. M. Behrman.

17. Mahler Werfel, *Bridge*, p. 275.

18. UCLA, *Werfel Papers*, Box 3, Letter: Stephen S. Wise, President, American Jewish Congress to Franz Werfel, 12/10/40.

19. Ibid., Box 9, *I'm an American* radio program, Script No. 44, Conversation:

Franz Werfel with William A. Carmichael of the Immigration and Naturalization Service, NBC, Station KECA, Los Angeles, Calif., Sunday, 3/16/41.

20. Ibid., Box 37, *Declaration of Intention, USA*, No. *108819*, 6/18/41. In his Declaration of Intention Werfel gave a Hollywood address and described himself: blue eyes, brown hair, 5'7", 150 lbs., Race: Hebrew, Nationality: Czech, and stated that he had married Alma Mahler on July 6, 1929.

21. Franz Werfel, "A Personal Preface," *The Song of Bernadette*, New York: Viking Press, 1942, pp. 5-7.

22. Reinhardt, *The Genius*, p. 201.

23. Taylor, *Hollywood Émigrés*, p. 163.

24. Ibid.

25. Mahler Werfel, *Bridge*, p. 280.

26. Taylor, *Hollywood Émigrés*, p. 163.

27. UCLA, *Werfel Papers*, Box 3, Letter: Franz Werfel to Francis Biddle, attorney general of the United States, 9/10/42.

28. Taylor, *Hollywood Émigrés*, p. 10.

29. UCLA, *Werfel Papers*, Box 4, Letter: *Authors' League of America* to Franz Werfel, 1/15/43.

30. Ibid., Box 38, Franz Werfel, honorary doctor of laws diploma, Regents of the University of California, 6/9/43.

31. *New York Times*, 8/27/45, p. 19.

32. Mahler Werfel, *Bridge*, p. 282.

33. Ibid., pp. 292-294. The official judgment was heart failure brought on by a coronary occlusion caused by arteriosclerosis (County Recorder, Los Angeles, Calif., *Certificate of Death*, Filed September 25, 1945. Copy furnished by Dr. William Mandel).

34. *Hairenik Weekly*, Editorial: "Franz Werfel," 9/6/45, p. 2.

35. *New York Times*, "Franz Werfel, 54, Noted Author, Dies," 8/27/45, p. 19.

36. Monson, *Muse to Genius,* p. 297.

37. Mahler Werfel, *Bridge*, p. 295.

38. Monson, *Muse to Genius,* p. 298.

39. Mahler Werfel, *Bridge*, p. 295.

40. Professor Richard Hovannisian, UCLA, says that Vartan Gregorian (former president of Brown University, currently president of the Carnegie Corporation of New York) and other Armenians were responsible for moving the remains of Franz Werfel from Los Angeles to Vienna.

41. Monson, *Muse to Genius*, p. 306.

42. *San Francisco Chronicle*, "Kurt Waldheim Opens Festival at Salzburg," 7/29/88, Sec. E, p.7.

43. At the entrance of the huge Musa Dagh monument in Musa Ler, Armenia, near Etchmiadzin, stands a large white bust of Franz Werfel.

44. *Armenian Mirror-Spectator*, "News From Armenia," 7/28/90, p. 5.

45. *The Week in Germany,* "Moravian, Bohemian Writers Featured in New German-Language Textbook," German Information Center, New York, 10/18/91, p. 6.

46. Ibid., "Numerous Events Mark the 60th Anniversary of Nazi Book Burning," German Information Center, New York, 5/14/93, p. 7.

47. *Armenian Observer*, "Ceremony in Honor of Three Great Friends of Armenia: Dr. Johannes Lepsius, Viscount James Bryce, and Franz Werfel," 4/15/98, p. 13.

BOOK V

Babylon Redux

... the habitation of devils.
—The Revelation of St. John the Divine 18:2

Chapter 19

MUSA DAGH INCOGNITO

It's a Rolls Royce

Despite *Musa Dagh's* track record as a film denied, MGM made certain that the studio retained its film rights to Werfel's novel through World War II. Very much aware that the Hollywood studios had a patriotic duty to boost morale at home and with our armed forces, the dream factories turned out almost one hundred films related to the war. MGM produced more than twenty World War II films ranging from William Wyler's *Mrs. Miniver* ('42) to John Ford's *They Were Expendable* ('45). At the Culver City studio, *Musa Dagh* loyalists such as Rudi Monta, Sam Marx, and Al Block knew from the day MGM purchased the film rights to *Musa Dagh* that MGM had been sitting on another war film, albeit World War I vintage, that deserved reconsideration—*The Forty Days of Musa Dagh*.

Shortly after the end of World War II, Louis B. Mayer was advised "that this may be our only chance with this famous property to take advantage of the prevalent diplomatic disarray and reconsider *The Forty Days of Musa Dagh* production."[1] Mindful of Turkey's opposition in 1934 and 1935, Mayer was told that Ankara's objection would not carry much weight, especially in light of its diplomatic straddle during the war vis-à-vis the Allies and the Axis.[2] Mayer was reminded that *Musa Dagh* was still a great story, and it could be made without offending the Turks.[3]

By October 1945, MGM had already assigned Henry Bellous to prepare a treatment of Werfel's novel. Before his contract ran out in January 1946, Bellous had submitted seventy-four pages. Even though it was shelved,[4] *Musa* Dagh's advocates continued to urge MGM to make *Musa Dagh*, only to be rebuffed by production chief Robert Vogel.

Based on advice from Daniel Blum at Loew's in New York, Vogel predicted dire consequences for MGM, despite the fact that the studio was among the most prestigious and powerful motion picture companies in the world. It was 1934 and 1935 revisited. He contended MGM's international business would be thrown back twenty years, injuring all of Hollywood because the story concerned minorities and religion and was political dynamite involving Turkey, Syria, Russia, England, and France. All the old arguments to keep *Musa Dagh* on the shelf were re-employed by Vogel, who told his colleagues that he had never expressed himself so strongly about a prospective movie. He insisted that the facts warranted his fears and recalled Turkey's earlier threats that Ankara would exhort friendly countries to ban all MGM films. He was convinced that Turkey's admonition was not an idle threat. Vogel's parting shot was, "Unless there's a change in the title, story, and locale, and it becomes a movie about a mythical kingdom, *Musa Dagh* will never materialize into a movie."[5]

Regardless of Vogel's stance, *Musa Dagh*'s advocates pushed on, and the conflict was renewed. The publicity that came out of Hollywood's rumor mill about *Musa Dagh*'s possible resurrection rekindled the spirit of Armenian Americans. Several factions within the Armenian American community solidified their forces under the banner of The American Church Committee for Armenia. Through Secretary Charles Vertanes, they informed studio manager Eddie Mannix at MGM of their interest in *Musa Dagh*. Their underlying message was that the movie would be a timely gesture in acquainting the American public and the world at large with what Turkey had done to the Armenians. It was also intended as a warning of Turkey's capabilities to repeat the horrors of the past if it became obvious that she could again defy world opinion.[6]

Simultaneously, at the prodding of the Soviet Union, a concerted effort was being made by the Armenian National Council of America and other Armenian organizations and individuals to pressure Turkey to return the historic eastern Asia Minor (Anatolia) Armenian provinces of Kars, Ardahan, and Erzerum to Soviet Armenia.[7] This campaign was in conjunction with a worldwide drive by the Soviet Union exhorting Armenians in the Diaspora to repatriate to Soviet Armenia.[8] But the passage of the Truman Doctrine in March 1947, guaranteeing billions of dollars in American military and economic aid to Greece and Turkey to curb Soviet influence and threats there, eventually caused the Soviet Union to drop its demand for the cession. The ensuing publicity had an adverse effect on any immediate prospects for a *Musa Dagh* movie.

As usual, whenever the buzzwords *Musa Dagh* appeared in the media, MGM, the Turkish government, and the State Department reacted. The *Los Angeles Times* carried the story that screenwriter Aleen Leslie and her husband Jack Leslie wanted to produce *The Forty Days of Musa Dagh* if MGM was not willing.[9] The MGM legal department, in its response to the Leslies, insisted on retaining MGM's rights. As on every similar occasion, MGM made sure to mention the intervention of our State Department and Turkish opposition and the hopelessness of ever getting *Musa Dagh* on the screen.[10] These sporadic manifestations of interest in *Musa Dagh* kept the project alive in the media and in the public mind.

In November 1951, *The Hollywood Reporter* alerted its readers that MGM had been sitting on one of the greatest scripts ever written (Carey

Wilson's *Musa Dagh* screenplay), but it couldn't be filmed because of U.S. relations with Turkey. In its enthusiasm to reopen the issue, the trade journal suggested switching the locale to a mythical country with a new title and thereby handing the industry a great picture.[11] The news item conveyed the same message, as Vogel's critique—*Musa Dagh* was still a controversial issue.

Foreign interest in *Musa Dagh* had not diminished, either. In December 1952, Comedia Films of Rome asked for MGM's conditions for releasing *Musa Dagh*'s rights.[12] Based on these numerous inquiries alone, MGM's studio executives knew all along they had a valuable property. It suggests that MGM was hesitant to sell limited foreign language rights because it might jeopardize its future plans. Consequently, convinced that a foreign production would be a minor effort, MGM retained its *Musa Dagh* monopoly.[13] MGM also had reservations about a stage production despite the continued interest expressed by Elia Kazan, one of Broadway and Hollywood's most celebrated directors. The corporate heads at Loew's in New York still feared that the Turks would complain again and demand that the State Department re-apply pressure to abort a *Musa Dagh* production.[14] *The Forty Days of Musa Dagh* film/stage production had developed into a case of damned if we do and double damned if we don't.

It was no surprise when, on the barest information, the Turkish Embassy in Washington reacted to the news about *Musa Dagh*. It was an echo of its past performances. Arthur Richards, on top of Greek/Turkish/Armenian issues in the State Department, responding to the Turkish concern in August 1953, reminded Loew's/MGM that the United States government had not changed its mind about the film. He told Loew's that, while the State Department was not a censoring agency and could not prevent MGM from making *Musa Dagh*, he hoped "that the book would never be made into a play or a movie because the Turkish people are particularly sensitive to this period of their history and are trying desperately to cover it up."[15] Richards stressed that Turkey, being a friendly ally, would lodge the usual official objections and protests with other governments.[16]

For some time the Turkish government had been exerting every effort to foster favorable newspaper stories about Turkey and the Turks in the American press. The Turks were so sensitive to adverse publicity resulting from the *Musa Dagh* issue that they had recently protested over a small candy bar wrapper showing a Turk wearing a fez. They took exception to the caricature because Ataturk had banned the fez. The Turks had even lodged a complaint about a wrestler named Ali Pasha, the Terrible Turk. They did not want him to give the impression that the Turkish people fit the description. If these minor matters could trigger Turkish resentment, where would that leave other matters of a greater import, such as allowing *Musa Dagh* to reach stage or screen?[17] The Truman Doctrine (1947) had a beneficial side effect for Turkey; it assured Ankara of U.S. support on those issues that troubled the Turkish government, such as *Musa Dagh* and a congressional resolution recognizing the Armenian Genocide.

Another element had already been added to the ongoing controversy when in January 1947, MGM's legal department received a request from Werfel's widow, Alma Mahler Werfel, asking for a copy of *The Forty Days of Musa Dagh* contract her husband had signed with MGM. As the legal heir of Werfel's estate, she was establishing her claim to the contract.[18] For thirteen years, Alma Werfel had been well aware of the State Department's role and the Turkish government's objections to *Musa Dagh*. She was temporarily pacified when MGM, regardless of the pressures and the consequences, decided to pursue the possibilities of a *Musa Dagh* stage production. Having been assured of royalties and approval of the stage adaptation, Alma was agreeable, especially with the possibility of re-involving Rouben Mamoulian in the project along with screenwriter George Seaton.[19] Her hopes were dashed when the project failed to materialize.

Even the sudden departure in 1951 of Louis B. Mayer from the studio he had built did not deter his successor, Dore Schary, from indicating his strong interest in *Musa Dagh*. Schary believed "it was one of the few great books written since *War and Peace*"[20] and dreamed of making the movie. He was even willing to send a personal agent to Turkey if he could have some guarantee that his emissary would return with the written approval of the Turkish government.[21]

In May 1955, tired of MGM's vacillations, Alma, through her attorney, Felix Guggenheim, wanted to know MGM's true intentions regarding *Musa Dagh*. She suspected the studio did not plan to ever produce the film or stage play and that the hierarchs in New York and Culver City meant to sit on it indefinitely, thus denying the opportunity to interested parties to buy the rights. Knowing that the studio was under no legal obligation to make the film, Alma contended that was not the understanding of her late husband when he sold the rights in 1934. Certainly one of the "great novels of our time" should not be intentionally and indefinitely kept from the moviegoing public. She wanted to know under what conditions MGM would consider returning the rights to *Musa Dagh* to her, provided that no one else (Anna Mahler's ex-husband Paul Zsolnay) would have any claim once MGM agreed to release it to Alma Werfel.[22]

A whole year passed before MGM took a position in the matter, and that did not happen with a courteous response to Alma Werfel, but rather was initiated by Elia Kazan's renewed inquiry. After completing *A Face in the*

Crowd ('57), Kazan, ever persistent, made another effort to convince MGM of his sincerity in taking on *Musa Dagh*. He hoped that his undiminished interest and reputation would finally persuade the studio heads enough to result in a meeting of the minds, thus making at least the stage production a reality.[23] MGM turned him down again, reasoning that it still wished to explore the possibility of the studio making the movie.[24]

Kazan's inquiries and the continued interest expressed by the trade papers spurred MGM to reconsider *Musa Dagh*'s prospects.[25] Aware of Turkey's past successes in thwarting *Musa Dagh* through the State Department and the positions taken heretofore by France and England, MGM's strategy was to nourish the project under a disguised title set in a different locale to throw off its opponents.[26]

In the spring of 1957, Jan Lustig submitted a *Musa Dagh* treatment of 67 pages under the working title *From Every Mountain Side*[27] for studio boss "Sol Siegel's eyes only."[28] The title was lifted out of the lyrics of an unofficial national anthem, *America,* suggesting a flag-waving all-American story.

The "new breed" at MGM, like their predecessors, underestimated their foreign adversary. Once again MGM proved to be no match for the Turks. In the forty years that had elapsed since the Armenian Genocide and the incident at Musa Dagh, the Turkish government had refined its strategy and tactics into an exact science of denial. As to MGM's resurrection of the *Musa Dagh* project, the Turkish government saw through MGM's diversionary tactic of a new title and let it be known that Ankara had not modified its position despite the passage of time.[29] In spite of this warning, it was still MGM's position to hold on to the property and continue to ride out the storms and the offers.[30]

In midsummer 1958, Siegel received several more offers to buy MGM's rights to *Musa Dagh*. The bids ranged from $75,000 to $150,000.

Siegel insisted on a bottom line of $250,000, knowing that one of the interested parties was film auteur Stanley Kubrick.[31] At the studio there was a question of caveat emptor: whether to sell it to Kubrick to cut their losses and let him deal with the Turkish government and the State Department or to go ahead themselves regardless of the pressures. The consensus was that the State Department was highly unlikely to give MGM or Kubrick an official go-ahead anyway. Kubrick was turned down, but due to his inquiry, MGM decided to reconsider *Musa Dagh*'s film potential again.[32]

The studio assigned Elick Moll to write a new screenplay. To counter Turkish interference, he was instructed to bowderlize the locale, characters, and the main theme into a new working title, *The Hills of Home*. Since the title was linked with an earlier MGM release in 1948 for a Lassie movie, it was later changed to *Days of Wrath* (a one-letter difference from a classic 1943 Danish film, *Day of Wrath*). Between December 1958 and July 1959, Moll turned in twenty-six assignments, including notes, outlines, treatments, five complete screenplays ranging from 192 to 263 pages, and several sets of revisions. It was a new record for *Musa Dagh*.[33] They were all disapproved.[34] A positive aspect to this dilemma was the employment generated for seventy years to some of Hollywood's top wordsmiths.[35]

A quarter of a century after MGM's purchase of Werfel's novel, the prospective film continued to have its ardent advocates. Most outstanding in the 1950s was Leonard Fields. In August 1958, he was instrumental in arousing the interest of studio boss Sol Siegel. He purposely delayed his *Musa Dagh* proposal, timing it for a slow period so Siegel could give it his undivided attention. Fields extolled Werfel's book as a masterpiece. It was his opinion that it could be the best piece of material ever owned by any studio. He was firm in his belief that

Musa Dagh could be made into "the greatest picture of our time," both at the box office and as film art. But it had to be an all-out project that demanded and deserved the ultimate in producer, director, script, cast, and production values. "It's a Rolls Royce." Fields insisted that *Musa Dagh* be approached from that point of view or not be considered at all.[36]

Fields' memo went on to praise Werfel's novel as a complete story with a beginning, a middle, and an end involving about as pungent and picturesque a cast of characters as he had read in years, each created, explored, and developed so that he could lift it bodily from book to script. To Fields, the book offered such an embarrassment of riches that the job of assigning a producer and a writer would be essentially a matter of selecting those with a sense for creativity. He reviewed for Siegel the history of the Armenian Genocide and the Turkish attempt to remove a whole nation from the face of the earth. The event to him was so important that its implications had tremendous dramatic possibilities as a film masterpiece. He saw it as a universal theme overlapping national boundaries or limitations of time. To get the present Turkish government to back off, Fields suggested putting the onus of that tragic period of history on the Turkish government of 1915 in order to rid MGM of the obstacle that had blocked *Musa Dagh* in the past. Fields thought that the present Turkish government should be patted on the back for never permitting a recurrence of those events and be duly recognized as currently offering protection and security to all minorities and races.[37] But Fields was either ignorant or had forgotten that in September 1955 anti-Greek riots had broken out in Istanbul and Izmir over the Cyprus issue. Later, during the Menderes regime, riots erupted again in Turkey, particularly in Istanbul, resulting in Turkish attacks on Greeks and Armenians.

Fields admitted to Siegel that his approach was "a thousand-to-one shot" but worth taking. He suggested the project should be set up as an independent production financed through MGM. Above all, he urged that the property never be sold. He was a rock in his conviction that the movie would make huge profits for the studio. Fields insisted that the project involve the current luminaries of the film world, such as Sam Spiegel, David Lean, and Alec Guinness. He believed this combination would do better with *Musa Dagh* than even their Academy Award winning *The Bridge on the River Kwai* (Best Picture '57). To Fields, it was "worth every effort to tread through the political and corporate mine fields, so that *Musa Dagh* could be brought to realization with Metro's fingers very strongly in the pie."[38]

Fields' forceful presentation proved to be the factor in October 1958 in passing the *Musa Dagh* gauntlet to Julian Blaustein to produce the controversial movie and four other productions while under contract.[39] In Blaustein's efforts to avoid a confrontation with the Turkish government, the script was laundered and the title was changed to *Days of Wrath*. Blaustein decided to treat the Ottoman Turk versus Armenian theme by focusing on the triumvirate of Enver, Talaat, and Djemal and the Young Turks as the particular villains exhibiting the same pattern as the Nazis under Hitler. He accepted Siegel's admonition to stress that the present Turkish government and people did not perpetrate the Armenian Genocide.[40] Hoping to further defuse Turkish concerns then and in the future, MGM invited Suidem Koljecum at the Turkish Embassy in Washington to act as the official negotiator in conferring with the studio on *Musa Dagh*. Ankara rejected the offer.[41] In October 1959, the Turkish government had agreed to the establishment of an American intermediate ballistic missile base in Turkey. From then on Ankara had leverage on issues that alarmed the government, such as *Musa Dagh*.

The ultimate decision to proceed with *Musa Dagh* rested in the heart and mind of MGM boss Sol Siegel. Eight months after Blaustein was authorized to start the production, and unmoved by the news that Ingrid Bergman was considering playing in Blaustein's production,[42] Siegel, in an about-face, denigrated Werfel, his novel, its characters, and its movie potential:

> *Why make this story? I'm told it's a great love story. I fail to see it. The characters … speak in the same manner. Gabriel's (the hero) love for Karoun (Iskouhi in the book)[43] is so antiseptic that there is no relationship. Personal stories don't measure up to important values. The story of* Musa Dagh *is not worth the money or attention to bring it to the screen.*[44]

And yet, in July 1959 when MGM heard that Luther Davis, representing the American Entertainment Corp., planned to make *Musa Dagh* into a spectacular on television, stage, or film and that he was willing to buy MGM's rights,[45] Rudi Monta, defending the studio's copyright, admonished Davis that MGM:

> *Will take all necessary steps to enforce its rights which are all inclusive, namely ownership of the book, world production rights to the motion picture, broadcasting rights, stage production, and television rights, with no limitations or restrictions whatsoever.*[46]

To Davis' contention that the event itself was historic and free to research, Monta retorted that Werfel's theme, title, and plot were original and that it was a creative work recognized in "giving the events meaning and soul through his characters."[47] And so another *Musa Dagh* bid to beat MGM to the screen was defeated.

In the meantime, MGM's rights to *Musa Dagh* were due to expire. Ever alert, Rudi Monta informed the studio heads that the deadline was November 15, 1961, with renewal application to begin as early as

November 17, 1960.[48] Aware of the many offers to buy MGM's rights, Monta urged his superiors that, if MGM were ever to relinquish its rights to *Musa Dagh*, Alma Werfel should be given priority to claim ownership of her late husband's novel. Monta felt it was the ethical thing to do since she had been so cooperative when the question of renewal had come up in the past.[49] As much as Siegel questioned the filming of *Musa Dagh*, it was he who agreed to offer Alma Werfel an extension to the contract, thus locking in MGM's rights.[50]

Eighty years old, in poor health and in financial straits, Alma Werfel was amenable to renewing MGM's rights to *Musa Dagh*. In September 1960, realizing its twenty-five-year investment would be lost by November 17, 1961, MGM agreed to her demands.[51] In addition to a payment of $20,000, there was the stipulation that if MGM did not make the movie within ten years of the renewal date, she had the option to buy the property for $42,000 before MGM offered it to anyone else. Furthermore, she would be entitled to exercise her rights between September 1970 and September 1971.[52] If she did not purchase the book's rights at that time, then she would forfeit her rights to reclaim the property forever.[53] The contract was recorded in the Copyright Office on October 24, 1960, and a certificate to that effect was dated November 17, 1960. A renewal confirmation executed by Alma's daughter, Anna Mahler, was recorded January 12, 1961.[54] As of November 9, 1960, Anna had become the administrator of Franz Werfel's will and estate. Through her mother's attorney, Felix Guggenheim, Anna acted as intermediary and finalizer of all accounts. It was Anna who signed the new agreement with MGM.[55]

At the age of eighty-five, Alma Mahler Werfel died on December 11, 1964, in New York City, but not before she saw her autobiography, *And the Bridge Is Love,* published. Alma epitomized her attachment to

Werfel in the title, which was inspired by a passage from Thornton Wilder's *The Bridge of San Luis Rey*:

> *There is a land of the living*
> *and a land of the dead,*
> *and the bridge is love,*
> *the only survival, the only meaning.*[56]

Alma's autobiography is her version of a romantic adventure of love and devotion between two human beings who witnessed some of the major events of their times and came into contact with many of the twentieth century's luminaries. Alma believed that in Franz Werfel everything she might have wished for on Earth had been fulfilled.[57] While the bridge that joined Franz Werfel and Alma Mahler Werfel may have been love, ironically they were buried in separate cemeteries in their beloved Vienna. Anna Mahler arranged to have her mother buried alongside her father, Gustav Mahler, and her half-sister Manon Gropius.[58] The two people who had been most involved with *The Forty Days of Musa Dagh* from its inception did not live to see the novel translated to the screen.

It had been a thirty-year ordeal for Alma Werfel. It was common knowledge among their friends that the Werfels bitterly resented the fact that MGM had bought the rights to *Musa Dagh* but had never made the film. Franz and Alma Werfel had always considered *The Forty Days of Musa Dagh* to be Franz Werfel's masterpiece.[59]

The publicity about *Musa Dagh*'s renewal rights engendered additional offers to buy out MGM. When John Barry Knorp indicated his interest to buy the book outright, it too was to no avail.[60] While Siegel was panning the book as a film, he had simultaneously given the "green light" in October 1958 to Julian Blaustein's production.

Tenacious as ever, Elia Kazan again offered to make *Musa Dagh*, only to be put off. Siegel informed Kazan that MGM was developing a screenplay (Blaustein's production) that would be before the cameras in two years.[61] What kind of production would *Musa Dagh* have been in the hands of an honored craftsman such as Elia Kazan? On the merits of his direction of Tennessee Williams' stage and screen productions of *A Streetcar Named Desire* ('51), "Gadge" Kazan had conquered Hollywood with *Gentleman's Agreement* ('47), *Viva Zapata*, ('52), *On the Waterfront* ('54), and *East of Eden* ('55).[62] One can only imagine what Kazan could have done with *The Forty Days of Musa Dagh*.

And yet, wherever or whenever a staunch advocate of *Musa Dagh* dropped out due to death or retirement or resignation or defeat, someone was always there fanning the embers. Whether it was a topic of conversation, a letter, memo, news article, studio agenda item, or rumor, somehow it managed to remain current. Then, during the post World War II era, there appeared a new ray of hope.

At the studio Rudi Monta had never given up on *Musa Dagh*. In 1960 he reminded Daniel Melnick at Loew's of the greatness of Werfel's book and its huge post-World War II success in Europe and again throughout the world.[63] Like hundreds of writers whose works had been banned by the Axis powers, Werfel's *The Forty Days of Musa Dagh* rose out of the book burning ashes of the 1930s like a phoenix in the 1960s to become an immediate best seller for the second time, particularly in the German-speaking nations and the former occupied countries. Its international appeal was demonstrated on another occasion. Learning of a German film company's intention to film the story, Monta protested and threatened a lawsuit, countering the German argument that the event itself was a historical fact and therefore was in the public domain.[64]

Without warning, Julian Blaustein was next to suffer the dubious distinction of the *Musa Dagh* challenge, good intentions notwithstanding. Having been admonished to treat the production with extreme delicacy so as not to offend the Turks, he was expected to work simultaneously on five productions, including *Musa Dagh*. Blaustein had been on the *Musa Dagh* project since October 1958.[65] While Metro and Anna Mahler were negotiating the renewal of *Musa Dagh*'s rights, he had lost six months to a year by the time the settlement was finalized. The pressure increased. Two and a half years remained on Blaustein's contract. He had two pictures in the works and two others to go. Blaustein was dumbfounded to read in the trade papers on March 3, 1961, that MGM had stopped his *Musa Dagh* production at the request of the State Department.[66] Compounding his perplexity was an earlier announcement that Siegel had turned over the project to Carl Foreman.[67] The press releases strained credulity and logic in reporting that Foreman[68] was confident he could film it in Turkey.[69] As usual, *Musa Dagh* made good copy and continued to confound its detractors and ardent supporters.

Blaustein's commitment to Werfel's masterpiece was such a personal priority that he had sounded out Stefan Zweig to write the screenplay. Of his five assigned productions, Blaustein had envisioned *Musa Dagh* as his crowning achievement,[70] but MGM bought him out with a $58,000 settlement to compensate him for his time, and by December 1961, Julian Blaustein was officially off *Musa Dagh*.[71]

Once again *Musa Dagh* died aborning. How a contemplated movie could command so much attention and conflict for such a long time must have been baffling even to the most jaded movie bosses in or out of Hollywood. Nevertheless, on the sidelines were those who saw opportunity in adversity and were willing to risk the gamble.

Chapter 20

"OPERATION ROXBURY"

This project was announced by MGM forty times in forty years

As Julian Blaustein's *Musa Dagh* fortunes were fading away, the word was out that MGM was still determined to see *Musa Dagh* on the screen. The clincher was the studio's appointment of one of Hollywood's pre-eminent and most successful producers. It was not Carl Foreman.

The *Musa Dagh* challenge next fell to producer Pandro S. Berman, an experienced and intelligent moviemaker of impeccable taste.[72] Berman had started his movie career at RKO in 1923 at the age of seventeen. After compiling a long string of hits there, he signed up with MGM in 1940, where he remained for 27 years.[73] By the time he retired in 1970, he had produced 115 movies,[74] an enviable record even today by Hollywood standards.

A producer of the stature of Pandro Berman gave great comfort and confidence to *Musa Dagh* advocates. Werfel's Armenian treasure had found another worthy proponent and a new life. Rudi Monta, knowing of Alma Werfel's interest, communicated the good news about *Musa Dagh*'s resurrection.[75] Berman had been rewarded for his twenty-two years of service at MGM with another long-term contract in 1962. He was expected to produce five pictures in four years at a weekly salary of $3000.[76] The new studio boss, Robert M. Weitman, the third since

Louis B. Mayer's retirement, made it official with an emphatic and uncompromising commitment that "Franz Werfel's *The Forty Days of Musa Dagh* would be the first picture produced under terms of Berman's new contract."[77]

Initially, Weitman's statement was somewhat confusing and contradictory in light of Blaustein's abrupt removal from the project by Siegel and MGM's earlier pronouncement that the studio was not committed to *Musa Dagh*.[78] To add to the confusion, the official studio release mentioned, "The famous novel was set in the Far East."[79] Once again *Musa Dagh* took on the aura of clandestine intrigue. It was so hush-hush that a code name "Roxbury Productions" was temporarily applied to Berman's production[80] (Roxbury Drive was the Bermans' street address in Beverly Hills). While it was common practice in Hollywood to disguise a production to prevent others from knowing your business, it was often done for tax purposes, too.[81]

In the tradition of many of his predecessors and consistent with his track record, Berman gave *The Forty Days of Musa Dagh* his personal attention and went at it with genuine enthusiasm and aplomb. Among the incentives for Berman was the opportunity to participate in *Musa Dagh*'s net profits: one-third of the first $2,000,000 and one-half the sum over $2,000,000.[82]

Berman's initial determination for quality and prestige was evident in his quest of a top-notch director. Among the highly respected directors on Berman's list were some of filmdom's heavyweights: William Wyler, Fred Zinnemann, Elia Kazan, David Lean, and Robert Wise. And Wyler was willing.[83]

Having been at the Culver City studio for more than twenty years, Berman was well aware of *Musa Dagh*'s stormy career and especially of its leading adversaries: the Turkish government, the Hays Office, and the U.S. State Department. As expected, he was subjected to a barrage of opinions both solicited and volunteered. He was convinced that, if MGM avoided foreign entanglements, there would be nothing to fear. Taking on *Musa Dagh*'s opponents and reinforcing his *Musa Dagh* commitment to Weitman, Berman cited an article, "Portrait of a President" by William Manchester in the June 1962 *Holiday* magazine. While aboard a naval transport bound for the South Pacific during World War II, John F. Kennedy had encouraged his shipmates to read from his current list of favorite books, among which was *The Forty Days of Musa Dagh*. Tightening the development of his thesis, Berman was convinced that, with Kennedy in the White House, "I'm sure that if such a thing happened, I would get the backing of the President of the United States. There's nothing anyone can do to prevent making this picture or exhibiting it."[84] Berman was astute enough to know that a courtesy meeting with the Turks or the State Department would be a waste of time and only invite a repeat performance of 1934 and 1935. "This project was announced by MGM forty times in forty years and each and every time aroused Turkish indignation to the point it had become routine."[85]

Berman doubted that the government in Ankara would go beyond this standard procedure once it was certain that MGM intended to make the film. In any case, by the time the Turks were alerted, the project would have gone too far to turn back, even if the State Department pressured Loew's to abort the production. He cited the case of *The Caine Mutiny* ('54). When MGM had refused to make it because of the Navy Department's protest, producer Stanley Kramer decided to do it on his own. Kramer had told Berman that General Walter Bedell Smith had assured him that President Kennedy would overrule the Navy Department if Kramer wished to make the movie. The picture was successfully made by Columbia.[86]

While Berman was preparing *Musa Dagh*, he won a most powerful ally in Joseph R. Vogel, president of Loew's Inc., who communicated his thoughts on the subject to studio head Robert Weitman:[87]

> *The Turkish Ambassador had been called in and had been given a three-hour parley with Irving Thalberg [Thalberg never met the ambassador; it was J. R. Rubin and William Orr] and had refused to admit that there had ever been an Armenian massacre. Every time the project was introduced in the 1950s, MGM was subjected to pressure by our own State Department … The present Ankara government would not admit to a black page of its history because the Turks had a blind spot about it … not hopeful about the State Department, either … once you alerted the Turks and the State Department to the project, they would insist that you desist and the studio would be placed in an awkward position. Frankly … not overly concerned about the loss of fourteen piasters in Turkey. MGM would not be hurt by the Turks any more than the studios that made* Advise and Consent, Exodus, *and* The Ugly American.[88]

The publicity in the media about *Musa Dagh*'s resurrection once again elicited scores of letters from alert Armenian Americans. Collectively they were concerned that the screenplay should be true to the letter and spirit of Werfel's novel and MGM should not be threatened by the Turkish government or the State Department.[89] Yervant Hadidian of the Armenian Memorial Church, Watertown, Massachusetts, offered a 16-mm. film of the Musa Dagh region. He had shot the film in 1937 before the Sanjak of Hatay (formerly the Sanjak of Alexandretta) was transferred from French to Turkish rule and before most of the Armenians from the local villages were transplanted to Lebanon. His film included scenes of the graves of the heroes, the fog that protected the defenders from the enemy, the huge memorial built by the French, village customs. Hadidian's closing comment: "If you send your photographers there now, the place has been destroyed, people are not there, the monument has been destroyed, and graves have been wiped out. My film is valuable and historic because it has scenes which cannot be reproduced."[90]

Another offer came from one of the Armenian community's well-known personalities in southern California. Leon Surmelian, a professor of English and author of *I Ask, You, Ladies and Gentlemen* (an account of his experiences during World War I in Turkey and post-war America) volunteered as the eyewitness Berman needed as a writer and consultant.[91] Surmelian's offer was politely declined.[92] When the news about Berman's *Musa Dagh* production reached Europe, the Italian film producer, Carlo Ponti, expressed interest in the project and informed Metro and Berman of Sophia Loren's availability.[93]

While Berman was laying out his master plan for *Musa Dagh*, the studio decided to conduct a survey of the movie-going public. On February 19, 1963, MGM's Research Department, in cooperation with the Screen Directors Guild Theater in Hollywood, polled the movie audience. The studio wanted to determine the current appeal of Franz Werfel's *The Forty Days of Musa Dagh* and the impression the title had on that day's patrons (Appendix VIII).[94] To Berman's relief, the survey's tally was not detrimental to the production's progress in spite of *Musa Dagh*'s thirty-year hiatus.

MGM's commitment to produce *Musa Dagh* was coincidentally in tandem with Pocket Books' decision to publish Werfel's novel in paperback.[95] For the moment, the timing seemed to be right. A new generation was on the scene that was ignorant of the Armenian Genocide of World War I and of the novel's publication in the United States in 1934. Furthermore, books that had been banned in Europe during the Nazi occupation were being republished after World War II. Conversely, the 1960s generation had other things on its mind. The paperback *Musa Dagh* did not go beyond two printings. Nevertheless, between the studio and the publisher, the American public was being prepared to expect Werfel's long-overdue classic on the screen.

As excellent as the original 1935 screenplay by Carey Wilson had been in Thalberg's opinion, on this occasion MGM went outside the studio to retain the services of the British screenwriter Neil Paterson for a $100,000 fee.[96] Paterson had won an Academy Award for his screenplay of *Room At The Top* ('58) and plaudits for *The Little Kidnappers* ('54).[97] In January 1964, Weitman reviewed *Musa Dagh*'s cost estimates based on Neil Paterson's new screenplay. While it was overwhelming for that time, it was a pittance compared to today's blockbuster productions. It had the makings of a first-class motion picture.

Initially, Paterson's *Musa Dagh* screenplay was projected to cost about $14,500,000 by the time it reached the movie-going public. In reality, it would have gone over $17 million considering cost omissions, publicity, and salaries, making it one of the most expensive films in Hollywood history to that date. The immediate reaction was a command to Berman from Loew's/MGM to cut costs by 50 percent to $7 million. To achieve this goal, the directive called for such drastic changes in the film's concept as:

- A five-hour screenplay to be cut by 1 1/2 hours.
- Major action sequences to be eliminated from eight to four.
- The number of defenders to be reduced to seventy-five, with a minimum number of children (historically there were over 4000 Armenians on the mountain).[98]

It was estimated that shooting the picture abroad would save $400,000 in California state taxes alone.[99] In spite of this extreme and disappointing cutback, hopes remained high that MGM's most controversial project was finally going to make it to the screen because of Berman's leadership.[100]

The *Musa Dagh* project was soon to include another Britisher. In early 1964, cost cutting forced MGM and Berman to consider turning over the directorial reins to Guy Green.[101] Green now had the inside track to an enviable plum that had eluded many of Hollywood's top directors. In spite of MGM's tacit agreement with Green, Elia Kazan and Fred Zinnemann were still being discussed as possibilities. [102]

There is no doubt as to the preeminence of Fred Zinnemann and Elia Kazan. But due to the reputation both of these men had in shooting excessive film footage, it was felt that the costs would go much higher than budgeted and would lengthen the time each man would take to make the movie. In addition, the higher salaries and percentages that each would demand canceled them out. Berman held both directors in high esteem, but he wanted to be practical and realistic in light of the 50 percent budget cut. He was convinced that Guy Green was ready for a big picture because he was:

- Known to be a thoroughly disciplined director whose standards were high.
- An excellent former cinematographer: *In Which We Serve* ('42); Academy Award for *Great Expectations* ('46) who knew production techniques.
- Berman had talked to Sidney Buchman, for whom Green had directed *The Mark* ('61) and thought highly of him. Other Green pictures were *Light in the Piazza* ('62), *The Angry Silence* ('60), and *Diamond Head* ('62), which was commercially successful.[103]

On Berman's recommendation to Weitman, Green got the contract. The documents in the MGM archives at Culver City clearly indicate the studio's commitment to *Musa Dagh* at that time and the studio bosses' faith in Berman's guidance and his choice of Green. Because of Green's British citizenship, arrangements had to be made with the Department of Immigration and Naturalization to allow him to enter the United States outside of quota restrictions (a common practice for foreigners legally working temporarily in the United States).

An agreement was finally hammered out between Berman and Weitman to get the show on the road. The fact that both Berman and Green were sincerely committed to film *Musa Dagh* was evident in their meticulous planning, which called for a thorough and complete survey of all the productions' needs.[104] They now had the responsibility to work out the entire concept and scope of the picture, arrange for a new screenplay, undertake a location search and determine under what conditions it could be made for $7 million.[105]

In February 1964, Berman assigned Walter C. Strohm, one of the studio's production chiefs, to check out possible foreign locations and evaluate their potential. Among the selected shooting sites were Yugoslavia and Spain, which were estimated to save 75 percent of the cost of an American production. The consensus was that eight months would be needed at a minimum for preparation of a Technicolor picture. It was agreed that the best time to start would be April 1966. It offered a period of four to six of the best months of the year for actual shooting.

By early 1964, Berman, Green, Strohm, and assistant producer Hank Moonjean (Henry Moomjian) composed the management team as well as the auditing and financial control departments.[106] Moonjean had worked for Berman on a score of movies before the *Musa Dagh* project and would be on the project for more than a year.

He had input on the budget, scheduling, location sites, and preparing the production boards. His production boards display the meticulous detail and the kind of organization and planning that is required before a film production can be launched. He contends that *Musa Dagh* was to be an MGM/British production. In his opinion, MGM had spent millions since 1934 and a budget of $5 million to $7 million in 1964 for such a movie was far too low.[107] At the studio, MGM's bosses were encouraged with *Musa Dagh*'s progress and were elated to learn that Berman was "tremendously pleased with Guy Green, who was making superb contributions to both script and production plans."[108]

Encouraged by the surprising absence of Turkish protests during the preliminary production period, the studio thought seriously of sending someone to Turkey to check out location sites in eastern Asia Minor. On second thought, fearing that an MGM research team in the area would only stir up the Turks, who most certainly would file protests again with the State Department, cooler heads prevailed, and that particular mission was scrubbed. Furthermore, to avoid tipping their hand to the Turks, MGM and Berman opted to do the basic research at home.[109] The studio's art department was instructed to prepare photographs and a bibliography of books relating to Turkey. By April 1964, the Culver City studio had sent several books on Turkey to Arvid Griffen, MGM's British production head at Borehamwood, England (outside London), along with a *Musa Dagh* production portfolio that included eighty-five mounted pictures.[110] The Borehamwood facility was to provide the interior scenes.

Despite the positive attitude permeating the fledgling production, the fear of Turkish threats influenced the choice of location sites. The studio rejected the idea of filming in Cyprus because of the ancient feud between Greeks and Turks there and the likely opposition from Ankara.

To avoid this particular diplomatic complication, Malta was added to the list temporarily.[111]

Pre-production planning progressed due to the dedication of Berman and Green. Berman was convinced that *Musa Dagh* was going to be a great film.[112] Like Blaustein before him, he believed *Musa Dagh* was to be his crowning achievement.[113]

Even though Neil Paterson had already turned in four complete scripts before Green came on the project,[114] the production budget canceled them out. The scaled-down budget made it possible for Green to write his own screenplay. It offered him the chance to make *Musa Dagh* his tour de force. For the second time an Armenian, Hank Moonjean, read a *Musa Dagh* screenplay (Mamoulian was the first, having read Carey Wilson's screenplay). Green accepted Moonjean's comments, particularly the Armenian aspects of the screenplay.[115]

By mid June 1964, the search had been narrowed to four sites: Greece, Yugoslavia, Spain, and Majorca.[116] Moonjean secured year-round weather reports, including minimum and maximum temperatures for every potential location. He remembered the horrendous cost overruns incurred by the 1962 Brando remake of *Mutiny on the Bounty* due to unexpected torrential rains in Tahiti. Shooting at the wrong time of the year there had cost MGM $3 million over estimates.[117] On that basis, Yugoslavia was reported as a potential nightmare, with Greece and Majorca as the best sites.[118] Moonjean preferred Greece, for the similarity between Greek and Armenian physical characteristics, enabling MGM to hire local Greeks for the minor roles, and for the exteriors.[119]

Moonjean was supported by one of MGM's production managers and another *Musa Dagh* stalwart, William Kaplan. He, too, had checked out locations in Greece and passed the word to Culver City that many Greeks welcomed the production. The location site would be three and a half hours from Athens. The cast and crew would be housed in Delphi. The costs in Greece and all the post-production work at MGM's Borehamwood studio were estimated at $2,380,000.[120]

Among the items in the *Musa Dagh* production schedule that confirm the rationale for shooting Hollywood films abroad was the projected expenditure of $2 per man per day for Greek army soldiers who would serve as extras and be housed in tents. Compared with hiring extras in Hollywood, this was a huge savings. As of July 1964, the screenplay had been broken down to 183 scenes, calling for about 17,000 feet of film with a running time of three hours and fifteen minutes.[121] The budget was re-set at $5,715,000.[122] But shooting in Greece also had its drawbacks: Nine Greek holidays required work stoppages.[123]

At this stage the production had been fine-tuned due to Berman's expertise, Green's dedication, and Moonjean's thorough production boards. Because weather conditions could delay filming a Technicolor film in Panavision, it was hoped that shooting on location would begin in April and be completed in four months as scheduled.[124]

Moonjean's production charts noted the change in the code name of Berman's production to "Operation Roxbury." They consisted of two boards, 18 inches x 25 inches each. In long titled columns appear forty-two speaking parts, six lists of extras, a list of animals, ammunition, and explosives, and an exact schedule for 128 principal photography exterior scenes in Greece and 51 interior scenes in the London (Borehamwood) studio. Each scene was precisely drawn as a day or night sequence, whether on a studio set or on location, the actors involved, setting, time allotted for each scene, shooting dates, travel days, rehearsal, prerecording, props, equipment. Scenes and sets such as Damlayik (the environs atop Musa Dagh), YoghunOluk square and church, the Bagradian villa, and Krikor's apothecary storeroom were taken directly from the novel. In all, there were 179 scenes descriptively detailed, beginning with Scene 1: "Introduction of Gabriel and Stephan leaving the Bagradian villa en route to the village of YoghunOluk as background to the titles" and ending with Scene No. 179: Gabriel on the French armored cruiser as the camera pulls back. Preferring an upbeat ending, in the Berman production, the hero, Gabriel, does not die as depicted in the novel. The length of the film called for an intermission after Scene No. 100.[125] Once casting was finalized, the production would be ready to roll. At last, after thirty long and exasperating years, *The Forty Days of Musa Dagh* motion picture was approaching reality.[126]

The budget included salaries ranging from $750,000 for an American actor in the lead role of Gabriel, $300,000 for a French actress as Gabriel's wife, Juliette, $75,000 for the part of the priest, Ter Haigasun, $75,000 to $150,000 for a European actress in the role of Iskouhi, and on down to $1200 for a French cook's assistant. Shooting interiors in England were estimated at $370,000 as compared with $515,000 in Culver City. The revised schedule called for a twelve-week planning period, twelve weeks for a building period, seventeen weeks for travel, rehearsals, holidays and shooting, one week for wrap-up in Greece, and a sixteen-week editing period in England. The completed film was to be edited to run for a little over three hours.[127]

Mindful of the work poured into *Musa Dagh* and the dedication of those involved, the older Hollywood hands were not surprised when rumors spread within the movie colony that the picture had hit the same familiar snag—the Turkish government filing protests from its embassy in Washington. Guy Green was "horrified" at the thought of not doing the movie because everyone involved had been so "very keen on it and ready to go."[128] To abandon the production now was nonsensical, considering the expenditures already incurred. Production plans made at Culver City and Borehamwood had gone as far as making the necessary arrangements and comparing cost estimates for location, filming, lab work, director, cast, and music.

To compound the mounting difficulties, the project unexpectedly began to encounter obstacles with the Greek authorities. Projected expenses began to mount for local and government taxes for labor, health, and social insurance, and government requirements to hire Greek technicians on the crew. In addition, there were the expenses for using Greek cameras, sound and electrical equipment, transportation, and catering services. It was becoming a runaway production as the costs mounted (Appendix X). At the moment there were no cost breakdowns for the necessary property men, laborers, electricians, wardrobe master and assistant. In the offing were such expenses as the rental from the Greek navy of a suitable naval cruiser and a transport, plus exasperating negotiations with the wardrobe designer who had done Kazan's *America, America* ('63).[129]

In September 1964, Moonjean, keeping to his task despite the rumors of Turkish government protests, sent Berman a tentative Greek location final schedule of 130 days, even though a request for an official permit had not been filed with the Greek government.[130]

A separate work schedule was prepared for each of the script's major characters.[131] Moonjean had already mapped out a general plan for the battle scenes and the construction of the defense positions on Musa Dagh.[132] Moonjean still felt that the schedule he submitted was more than adequate.[133]

To assure the authenticity of the *Musa Dagh* sets, MGM had access to a 900 ft., 16-mm. home movie of Musa Dagh and the surrounding region. Most likely it was Yervant Hadidian's film. Moonjean says the home movie greatly enhanced the design of the sets and the selection of the location sites.[134]

Meanwhile, MGM's new President, Robert H. O'Brien, expressed doubts about the Greek location. He suggested that it might be better to shoot *Musa Dagh* in Spain since *Doctor Zhivago* ('65) had been filmed there. To O'Brien, a businessman who was more concerned with cost-cutting and box office receipts, it made sense to take advantage of the equipment, costumes, and sets left there and pay a percentage to the *Doctor Zhivago* producers for their use. It was common knowledge that Spain had served as a location for many recent films. Spanish soldiers were already experienced extras, and the Spanish navy would be able to provide the necessary ships. More importantly, Francisco Franco's Spain had an excellent track record with foreign filmmakers.[135]

The Berman team's reaction to O'Brien's recommendation was a swift rebuttal. Moonjean, in particular, defended the Greek location, noting that Spain and Majorca had already been scouted and that Greece would be the least expensive location in all of Europe.[136]

Recognizing O'Brien's power base, the experienced and practical Berman reconsidered Spain as a fallback position to maintain his support for *Musa Dagh*. *El Cid* ('61), *Lawrence of Arabia* ('62), and *The Fall of the Roman Empire* ('64) had been partially shot there. "Besides, Spanish extras resemble the people we have in mind."[137] Historically, Spain had an ethnic mix of Phoenicians, Romans, Visigoths, Greeks, and Moors. Mediterraneans may differ in language and dress, but their physical features are similar to each other. For Moonjean, his ancestral heritage turned the movie into a mission.[138] To keep the production alive, Moonjean began to lean in favor of Spain, even though his professional sense still favored Greece, because the Greek authorities were proving more and more difficult.[139]

Despite the diversions and the rumors, the pace was quickening. The pieces of the *Musa Daugh* puzzle were gradually coming together.

Still pending was the matter of finalizing the cast, getting the necessary government permits, securing rental agreements with hotels, and preparing the sets and costumes. Berman reminded the studio execs that because of weather and seasonal considerations the project was at a critical juncture if MGM wanted the film ready for distribution in 1966.[140]

In July 1965, a consensus was reached between the corporate headquarters in New York and Culver City to give the official "go" in March 1966.[141] Simultaneously the announcement of *Musa Dagh's* possible movie stars gave the project the cachet it needed: Omar Sharif as Gabriel, Audrey Hepburn or Leslie Caron as Juliette, Dahlia Lavi or Julie Christie as Iskouhi, and Ralph Richardson or Alec Guinness as Ter Haigasun. Other possibilities were Alain Delon, Warren Beatty, Anne Bancroft, Laurence Harvey, and Claudia Cardinale.[142]

Hank Moonjean recalls casting the role of Juliette was a problem, especially after Audrey Hepburn turned it down. She felt that the part was not as prominent as that of Iskouhi. He maintains to this day that one of the major stumbling blocks in casting the movie proved to be Omar Sharif. As Moonjean recalls, Sharif was willing to play Gabriel, but he backed out when he learned that Dahlia Lavi was to play Iskouhi. It wasn't because she was Jewish or that he was supposed to be anti-Jewish, but that he believed she was an Israeli who would be unacceptable in Sharif's homeland, Egypt, where he had family and property. In Moonjean's opinion, Sharif would have been the strength of the movie. He is convinced that Berman would have accommodated him in the Lavi matter. Sharif's rejection threatened to shut down *Musa Dagh*. And yet, Sharif had no problem later on playing opposite Barbra Streisand in *Funny Girl* ('68) and *Funny Lady* ('75). Both movies were based on the stage, screen, and radio career of Fanny Brice, who was Jewish. The difference was that Streisand was an American Jew and Lavi to Sharif was an Israeli, so Moonjean thought.[143]

By the end of July 1965, Berman, Green, and Spanish art director Gil Pirando, who had worked on *Doctor Zhivago,* had made their decision about the sets. The Greek location had apparently fallen through again because the three of them were in Majorca checking it as a possible location. In October, both Berman and Green approved the Majorca site and selected additional shooting sites in Spain. Pirando was so enthusiastic about *Musa Dagh* that he had already scouted sites near Madrid and San Juan. He was so determined to see that the movie was made in Spain that "he specified a location depicting the slopes of Musa Dagh near Escorial and Manzanares."[144]

Meanwhile, Berman was on the defensive again in justifying *Musa Dagh*'s fluid budget to O'Brien. He acknowledged that it was twice as much as the two pictures he had recently produced, but he insisted that *Musa Dagh* required more of his time and effort, especially now that preparations were approaching cast selection.[145]

Back at Culver City, Berman's production began to unravel. A script evaluation had convinced O'Brien that *Musa Dagh* was a perennial and universal curse that would turn off an audience that cared nothing about the Turkish persecution of the Armenians. As far as he was concerned, *Musa Dagh* did not warrant a $5 million investment.[146] In an unsigned, confidential memo dated October 5, 1965, Berman's production of *Musa Dagh* was abruptly canceled. The project was to be offered to another studio.[147]

To Moonjean, Berman's *Musa Dagh* problems were the enormous costs required to make it a first-class production, the inability to cast the leading lady (Juliette) with a top star, Sharif's "Israeli problem," inability to get France to loan vintage warships, the physical nature of the exterior shots, and padding of the payroll to get the job done. The $5,000,000 proposed budget was simply inadequate. "*Musa Dagh* should have been at least a $14,000,000 production."[148]

The project had come closer to realization than at any other time since 1934 and had aroused renewed interest in the *Musa Dagh* movie. It was a rare experience, especially for Pandro Berman, to have come so close to making a motion picture, only to see it aborted. Based on the numerous inquiries, memos, cablegrams, telegrams, and transcripts of phone calls and meetings between 1965 and 1967, Musa Dagh had bogged down into a state of confusion. Two weeks after Berman's *Musa Dagh* project was shut down, Stanley Goldsmith was still scouting locations in Spain and preparing a detailed budget for clearance by October 30, 1965.[149] As late as January 27, 1967, Robert Vogel reported that the Turks were still protesting Berman's *Musa Dagh*.[150]

An office memo dated January 18, 1966 notes that MGM had spent over $600,000 on *The Forty Days of Musa Dagh* during the stewardship of Pandro Berman. A later memo, August 22, 1966, states that the studio had spent about $400,000.[151] Moonjean insists, "these figures are the tip of the *Musa Dagh* iceberg."[152]

By April 1966, the MGM studio heads were pondering the fate of Berman's production. Who had the rights to film *Musa Dagh*, MGM or Berman? The studio contemplated paying Berman off for his investment in time, creativity, experience, and percentage of the net profits in order to establish *Musa Dagh* as abandoned property.[153] Compounding the studio's frustration was the embarrassment of turning the property over to another producer or studio. MGM was also concerned about the disposition of Berman's (Green) last script. Could it be used, or would another version be better? Berman's detractors, led by O'Brien, were determined to take *Musa Dagh* from him.[154] An inter-office memo Ray Klune sent to O'Brien in July 1964 suggests that the relationship between O'Brien and Berman[155] had begun to sour.[156] Moonjean was unaware at the time that there had been a problem between the MGM bosses and Berman. "When you are an associate producer, it's kind of like being a freshman congressman trying to talk to the President of the United States. Because you are new and lack access to the top, to get along, you go along. You say nothing."[157]

It was MGM's opinion that it could retain control of the picture once Berman's contract expired on January 27, 1967.[158] If the picture had begun before that date, it was believed that Berman could claim it. Moonjean says another ploy was designed to disengage Berman by casting a certain unidentified actress who so distressed him that he would let MGM take the picture away from him.[159] In the end, the studio decided to wait until Berman's contract expired.[160]

In the movie colony, rumors had Paramount negotiating for *Musa Dagh*, knowing that MGM's rights would expire in November 1970. Adolph Zukor's studio believed it could complete *Musa Dagh* by that date despite the trials and tribulations the project had endured the last thirty years. It certainly suggests that Paramount had the courage to see it through. There was even an Italian proposal to serialize *Musa Dagh* on the radio.[161]

Just before Berman's *Musa Dagh* production was called off, a documented inventory was ordered tracing the history of *Musa Dagh* from MGM's purchase of the film rights in 1934 through 1966. As of June 1966, at least twelve screenwriters had worked full time on preparing scripts, outlines, synopses, and various other treatments and had turned in over one hundred submissions. Somebody at MGM appropriately noted in an office memo, "This book has been worked on and reworked more than a cadaver in an anatomy class."[162]

Unknown to Moonjean, Pandro Berman tried to take his project to Universal, but O'Brien demanded as much as $750,000 for the rights and property.[163] Berman's attempt to salvage himself and the project was his undoing. He was informed that MGM was canceling all *Musa Dagh* indebtedness to the studio by Berman's company and was re-vesting its rights to the various screenplays.[164] Several weeks later, in a follow-up letter, MGM reiterated its position: "As you know we have elected to not let you proceed with *Musa Dagh* ... It is abandoned property within the meaning of ... the Agreement of October 1, 1962."[165] To his credit, Berman did not willingly abandon *Musa Dagh*, but was compelled to bow to the Loew's/MGM hierarchy on a legal technicality. Like Thalberg and Blaustein before him, Berman failed to bring *Musa Dagh* to the screen. Moonjean contends that if the Loew's/MGM executives had backed Berman "to the hilt," he would have produced not only an outstanding film but also a box office hit and a critical success.[166]

Despite the *Musa Dagh* debacle, the Berman-Green relationship remained professional and cordial, resulting in another kind of movie, *A Patch of Blue* ('65). Berman, fulfilling his contract, was the producer, Green was writer and director, and Moonjean was the assistant director. The film won four Academy Award nominations and an Oscar for Shelley Winters for Best Supporting Actress.

The studio finalized the *Musa Dagh* matter officially on October 31, 1966. MGM's costs of Berman's "Operation Roxbury" were "readjusted" to $381,000,[167] a figure Moonjean vehemently faults. Moonjean called it "creative accounting."[168] Unbelievably, the studio was ready to assign "the cadaver" to another producer post-haste.[169]

In retrospect, Hank Moonjean does not regret his *Musa Dagh* experience. He was absolutely euphoric and unequivocal in singing the praises of Pandro Berman. "He was the best." His recollection of Guy Green was that of a gentleman: well liked, receptive to Berman's ideas, an excellent director, economical, and a professional. But Moonjean was not sure if Green was the right director for *Musa Dagh*. He thought that Richard Brooks would have been a better choice.[170]

When the word got out that Berman was officially off *Musa Dagh*, MGM was again besieged by a myriad of proposals, offers, claims, and rumors. *The Hollywood Reporter* carried an item that Carlo Ponti was going to produce the movie in Italy in a multiple deal in conjunction with MGM in 1967.[171] Another proposal came from the French-Russian-Armenian author Henri Troyat (Levon Tarasseff-Torossian), who wanted an executive agreement to write yet another screenplay with the French-Armenian Henri Verneuil (Ashod Malakian)[172] as the director and Omar Sharif as Gabriel Bagradian.[173] The publicity that had been accorded to *Musa Dagh* since 1934 had alerted the Turkish government to keep a constant watch on *Musa Dagh*. In 1966, two inquiries were made of MGM.[174] On one occasion, the Turkish information officer Ulus, attached to the embassy in Washington, made a personal phone call to Ray Klune asking about the status of *Musa Dagh*.[175]

The bids, sincere and frivolous, still came in. Producer Elliott Kastner offered his "eye teeth to do *The Forty Days*."[176] Producer Mark Robson indicated his interest in directing, too.[177] Producer-director Robert Wise spoke to Carlo Ponti, who had sounded out Edward Dmytryk, and so it went, on and on. It had been reported in a bit of media hyperbole and then refuted that Ponti had possession of *Musa Dagh*.[178] Irrespective of the rumor mills and the media flurry, MGM was still in control of *Musa Dagh* and supposedly still interested in making the movie. It was Berman the studio (O'Brien) wanted out.

Recognizing the excellence of one of Hollywood's best directors, who had made *Bad Day at Black Rock* ('54), a hit for MGM, and *The Great Escape* ('63), a box office bonanza for United Artists, MGM then approached John Sturges. He was assured that another writer acceptable to him would be assigned to write a new screenplay. Although Sturges thought highly of the property, he wanted to read the material before committing himself. The offer was withdrawn.[179]

Despite its adversities, *Musa Dagh* still demonstrated amazing staying power. The interest in making the movie never let up. *Variety* carried an item in June 1968 that Franco Venturini in Italy was adapting Franz Werfel's *The Forty Days of Musa Dagh* for RAI radio's third channel.[180] And then, out of the blue, the following November, Gina Productions, headed by Jerry Gershwin and Elliott Kastner, struck an agreement with MGM to refinance the photoplay of *Musa Dagh*.[181] In March 1969, the ensuing publicity brought forth an inquiry from an Armenian American. George Juskalian, a retired U. S. Army colonel and decorated World War II and Vietnam veteran, offered his services as a technical advisor.[182] Lindsay Parsons, executive production manager at MGM, informed him that rumors regarding the filming of *Musa Dagh* were raised periodically but that the studio had no plans at that time to make the picture.[183] That same week of Juskalian's inquiry, both *The Hollywood Reporter*[184] and *Variety*[185] announced that Kastner and Gershwin were to film the controversial property—with *The Hollywood Reporter* noting "*Musa Dagh* as one of the film world's lost projects."[186] Amazingly, *Musa Dagh* was resurrected again, this time with Howard Clewes taking his turn at a new screenplay in the Kastner and Gershwin production.[187]

As soon as *Musa Dagh* reappeared as a news item, there was the inevitable Turkish response. Experienced hands were not surprised. Parsons was informed that the assistant secretary for Near Eastern affairs, Stewart Rockwell, had made two inquiries within a span of two weeks at the request of the Turkish ambassador. It was the familiar threat—if the film was made, the studio and the United States would invite Turkish wrath. Once again *Musa Dagh* aroused the Turks to actively campaign against the movie.[188] Now they had a trump card— American military bases on their soil.

The Armenian community reacted as well. In June 1969, on behalf of the Eastern Diocese of the Armenian Apostolic Church in America, the Armenian General Benevolent Union, and other concerned parties, the Diocesan Primate, Archbishop Torkom Manoogian, sent a telegram to Lindsay Parsons, offering the support of the Diocesan Office and Armenian organizations in the United States to counter Turkish opposition. He reminded Parsons: "If the movie had been made as planned in the 1930s, who knows, it may have deterred Hitler and prevented the Jewish Holocaust."[189] Recognizing the genuine concern expressed in the Armenian inquiries, Saul Rittenberg, speaking for MGM in August 1969, informed the Diocese through Colonel Juskalian that plans in August 1969 were only in a preliminary stage. He did not know if the movie would ever go into production and expressed the studio's appreciation of the support by the Armenian organizations, but he felt that any action would be ill advised.[190] In October 1969, MGM spent $15,000 for Howard Clewes' screenplay.[191]

On December 11, 1969, Jerry Gershwin informed the studio that Clewes' screenplay had been completed and delivered in London.[192] Eighteen days later, the decision was made to cancel the Gina Productions' *Musa Dagh*.[193] Before the New Year was three days old, Gershwin and Kastner were officially advised that MGM had elected not to proceed with financing and producing *The Forty Days of Musa Dagh*.[194] Considering the on-again off-again experiences *Musa Dagh* had been subjected to over the years, many *Musa Dagh* advocates wonder if the powers at Loew's/MGM were periodically bought off to terminate the production of Franz Werfel's *The Forty Days of Musa Dagh*. It is a question still posed by *Musa Dagh* proponents that has never been thoroughly investigated.

Ironically, *Musa Dagh*'s ordeal coincided with the gradual demise of the Hollywood studio system and the Hays Office. Today movie productions are constantly plagued by corporations and banks delving into areas in which they are unfamiliar; screenplays are written and rewritten; directors and actors find themselves playing musical chairs; studio machinations and gamesmanship are the order of the day; and lawsuits multiply. Nothing changes.

By the end of the 1960s, the film production of *The Forty Days of Musa Dagh* remained an impossible dream, but with the advent of the 1970s came a new hope, a new *Musa Dagh* champion. Enter the Armenian.

NOTES – BOOK V

BABYLON REDUX

Chapter 19

MUSA DAGH INCOGNITO

1. *MGM Archives, Musa Dagh File*, Memo: Al Block to Louis B. Mayer, 12/19/45.

2. Due to Turkey's reluctance to help the Allied war effort, the Allies cut off all aid to Turkey. One week before the war was over in Europe, the Turkish government joined the Allies.

3. *MGM Archives, Musa Dagh File*, Memo: Al Block to Louis B. Mayer, 12/19/45.

4. Ibid., Memo to Saul Rittenberg: Chronology of Musa Dagh Writers, Exhibit "A," 9/3/70.

5. Ibid., Letter: Robert Vogel to Eddie Mannix, Ladiman, and Cohn based on advice in a telegram from David Blum, 3/2/46.

6. Ibid., Letter: Charles A. Vertanes, Secretary, American Committee for Armenia, to Eddie Mannix, 9/10/47.

7. During World War I, President Woodrow Wilson had called for an American mandate of Armenia that included the provinces of Kars, Ardahan, and Erzerum.

8. Charles A. Vertanes, *Armenia Reborn*, New York: Armenian National Council of America, 1947, pp. 143-153.

9. *Los Angeles Times*, "The Forty Days of Musa Dagh," 12/11/50.

10. *MGM Archives, Musa Dagh File*, Letter: Kathryn Barnes to Hendrickson, 12/11/50.

11. *The Hollywood Reporter*, 11/29/51, p. 2.

12. *MGM Archives, Musa Dagh File*, Communiqué: Comedia Films of Rome to MGM, 12/3/52.

13. Ibid., Letter: Kenneth MacKenna to Charles Moscovitz (Loew's), 1/19/53.

14. Ibid., Letter: J. Robert Rubin to Orville Crouch, Loew's Capitol Theatre, 8/17/53.

15. Ibid.

16. Ibid.

17. Ibid.

18. Ibid., Telegram: Alma Werfel to MGM Legal Dept., 1/26/47.

19. Ibid., Letter: Thomas J. Robinson to Rudi Monta, 12/8/53.

20. Ibid., Memo: Dore Schary to Rudi Monta, 12/15/53.

21. Ibid.

22. Ibid., Letter: Felix Guggenheim, Esq., representing Alma Mahler Werfel, to MGM Legal Department, 5/29/55. Paul Zsolnay, through whom MGM had bought the rights in 1934, and a possible claimant, was Franz Werfel's former Viennese publisher and the Werfels' ex-son-in-law, who had married and divorced Alma's daughter, Anna Mahler.

23. Ibid., Telegram: Elia Kazan to Kenneth MacKenna, 12/7/56.

24. Ibid., Memo: Kenneth MacKenna to William Fiddleson, 12/19/56.

25. Ibid., Memo to Saul Rittenberg, 12/24/56.

26. Ibid., Memo: Kenneth MacKenna to Stuart Miller, 4/21/58.

27. Ibid., Memo: Sol Siegel to Kenneth MacKenna, 4/8/57.

28. Ibid., Memo: Sol Siegel to Kenneth MacKenna, 5/8/57.

29. Ibid., Memo: Kenneth MacKenna to Stuart Miller, 4/21/58.

30. Ibid., Memo: Kenneth MacKenna to Rudi Monta, 4/22/58.

31. Stanley Kubrick's star was on the rise at the time, based on such films as *The Killing* ('56), and *Paths of Glory* ('58).

32. *MGM Archives, Musa Dagh File*, Memo: Marjory Thorsen to Sol Siegel, 6/16/58.

33. Ibid., Memo to Saul Rittenberg: Chronology of Musa Dagh Writers (since 1934), Exhibit "A," 9/3/70.

34. Ibid., Memo: Milton Beecher to Sol Siegel, 12/21/58.

35. Carey Wilson, Frances Marion, Talbot Jennings, Henry Bellous, Jan Lustig, Elick Moll, Cortland Fitzsimmons, Ben Maddow, Kathryn Berman, Neil Paterson, Guy Green, Ronald Harwood, Howard Clewes, and Larry Hilbrand were among some of the screenwriters who scripted *Musa Dagh* over the long haul.

36. *MGM Archives, Musa Dagh File*, Memo: Leonard Fields to Sol Siegel, 8/14/58.

37. Ibid.

38. Ibid.

39. Among Julian Blaustein's credits as a producer: *Broken Arrow* ('50), *Mister 880* ('50), *Desireé,* ('54) and *Bell, Book and Candle* ('58).

40. *MGM Archives, Musa Dagh File*, Letter: Sol Siegel to Julian Blaustein, 3/30/59.

41. Ibid., Memo: Robert Vogel to Helen Shanks, 7/20/61.

42. Ibid., Letter: Julian Blaustein to Sol Siegel, 5/26/59.

43. In the preparation of the screenplay, MGM changed the title, locale, theme, and some of the names of the characters to make them more euphonious and to throw off its detractors.

44. *MGM Archives, Musa Dagh File*, Memo: Sol Seigel to Julian Blaustein, 6/21/59.

45. Ibid., Letter: Luther Davis to MGM, 7/22/59.

46. Ibid., Letter: Rudi Monta to Luther Davis, 8/6/59.

47. Ibid.

48. Ibid., Memo: Rudi Monta to Daniel Melnick, 6/12/59.

49. Ibid., Letter: Rudi Monta to Kenneth MacKenna, 1/28/59.

50. Ibid., Memo: Kenneth MacKenna to Rudi Monta, 7/9/59.

51. Ibid., Exhibit "A," Chronology of *Musa Dagh* history since 1934, Agreement: MGM and Anna Mahler and Alma Mahler Werfel, 9/28/60.

52. Ibid., Memo: Kenneth MacKenna to Rudi Monta, 7/9/59.

53. Ibid., Letter: Edith Tolkin to Saul Rittenberg, 8/20/64.

54. Ibid., Update: History of the Werfels, 1965.

55. Ibid., Exhibit A, 9/28/60.

56. Alma Mahler Werfel, *And the Bridge is Love, Memories of a Lifetime*, in collaboration with E. B. Ashton, New York: Harcourt, Brace, 1958, title page. The title is taken from a poem in *The Bridge of San Luis Rey* by Thornton Wilder. Copyright, 1928. The Wilder Family LLC. Reprinted by arrangement with The Wilder Family LLC and the Barbara Hogenson Agency, Inc. All rights reserved.

57. Mahler Werfel, *Bridge*, p. 286.

58. Monson, *Muse to Genius*, p. 319. (*New York Times*, 12/16/64.)

59. *MGM Archives, Musa Dagh File*, Letter: Rudi Monta to Robert Weitman, 8/13/62.

60. Ibid., Letter: John Barry Knorp to Rudi Monta, 10/20/59.

61. Ibid., Letter: Sol Siegel to Robert White, 11/6/59.

62. Elia Kazan won Academy Awards for Best Picture and Best Director for *Gentleman's Agreement* ('47) and On *the Waterfront* ('54). In 1963, Kazan made *America, America* ('63), tracing the odyssey of his uncle's emigration from Ottoman Turkey. There were several scenes and references in the film to the persecution of the Armenians during the reign of Sultan Abdul Hamid.

63. Ibid., Letter: Rudi Monta to Dan Melnick, 9/1/60.

64. Ibid., Letter: Rudi Monta to George (surname missing), 10/20/60.

65. Ibid., Letter: Saul Rittenberg to Myron L. Slobodian, 12/28/60.

66. *Variety*, 2/3/61.

67. *Hollywood Reporter*, 1/23/61.

68. Carl Foreman had been blacklisted during the McCarthy era. Among his screenwriting credits were *Champion* ('49), *The Men* ('50), *High Noon* ('52) and *The Bridge on the River Kwai* ('57).

69. *Hollywood Reporter*, 6/29/61.

70. *MGM Archives, Musa Dagh File*, Musa Dagh Chronology, 4/5/61.

71. Ibid., Musa Dagh Chronology, 4/20/62.

Chapter 20

"OPERATION ROXBURY"

72. *The Illustrated Who's Who of the Cinema*, Ann Lloyd and Graham Fuller, eds., New York: Portland House, 1987, p. 41.

73. Leslie Halliwell, *The Filmgoer's Companion*, Sixth Edition, New York: Hill and Wang, 1977, p. 70. At RKO Berman produced sixty-eight movies among which were *Morning Glory* ('33), *Top Hat* ('33), *Stage Door* ('37), *Gunga Din* ('39), and *The Hunchback of Notre Dame* ('39). Among his forty-five movies at MGM were *National Velvet* ('44), *The Picture of Dorian Gray* ('45), *Father of the Bride* ('50), *Ivanhoe* ('53), and *The Blackboard Jungle* ('55).

74. Oral Interview of Pandro S. Berman, prepared and conducted by Mike Steen, American Film Institute, Louis B. Mayer Foundation, Los Angeles, Calif., 8/4/72.

75. *MGM Archives, Musa Dagh File*, Memo: Rudi Monta to Margery Thorsen, 10/2/62.

76. Ibid., "Musa Dagh Chronology," 5/23/62.

77. Ibid., 8/9/62.

78. Ibid., 5/18/62.

79. Ibid., 7/15/62.

80. Ibid., Berman Productions, 10/17/62.

81. Interview of Hank Moonjean by the author, Los Angeles, Calif., 6/16/92. Berman's *Musa Dagh* was eventually recoded "Operation Roxbury" during the planning stage to conceal the subject of the production, particularly from the Turks.

82. *MGM Archives, Musa Dagh File,* Berman Productions, 8/62.

83. Ibid., Memo: Robert Weitman to Peter Shaw, 8/15/62.

84. Ibid., Memo: Pandro Berman to Robert Weitman, 8/23/62.

85. Ibid.

86. Ibid.

87. Louis B. Mayer had been replaced by Dore Schary in 1951. He was followed by Sol C. Siegel in 1958, who in turn was replaced by Robert M. Weitman in 1962.

88. *MGM Archives, Musa Dagh File,* Letter: Joseph R. Vogel to Robert Weitman, 8/22/62.

89. Ibid., Outside Production No. 16 File, Berman Productions, Letters to MGM from concerned Armenian Americans: Robert Hewson (Washington, D. C.), Harry Baronian (San Mateo, Calif.), Gary Miller (Ill.), Everett Beshair (White Plains, N.Y.), Jack Tutelian (Cincinnati, Ohio), Ara Der Mardirosian (Kingston, R.I.), Suren Tashijian (Watertown, Mass.) and Diran Kirk (Bloomfield, N.J.), 1962.

90. Ibid., Outside Production No. 16 File, Berman Productions, Letter: Yervant Hadidian to MGM, 8/62.

91. Ibid., Letter: Leon Surmelian to Pandro Berman, 8/26/62.

92. Ibid., Letter: Margery Thorsen to Leon Surmelian, 9/5/62.

93. Ibid., Letter: Robert Weitman to Pandro Berman, 4/22/63.

94. Ibid., Research Department, Test-Survey, Screen Directors Guild Theater, Hollywood, Calif., 2/19/63.

95. Franz Werfel, *The Forty Days of Musa Dagh,* New York: Pocket Books, Inc., Cardinal Edition, 680 pages, First Printing, 1961, Giant Cardinal Edition, 1962.

96. *Publishers Weekly,* 11/5/62.

97. *MGM Archives, Musa Dagh File,* "Musa Dagh Chronology," 10/24/62.

98. Ibid., Berman Productions, Letter: Raymond A. Klune to Robert Weitman, 1/10/64.

99. Ibid., Transcript of Conference: Pandro Berman and Robert Weitman, 1/10/64.

100. Ibid., *Musa Dagh* Chronology, 9/20/62.

101. Ibid., 3/11/64.

102. Ibid., Berman Productions, Transcript of Conference: Pandro Berman and Robert Weitman, 1/10/64.

103. Ibid.

104. Ibid.

105. Ibid., Berman Productions, Letter: Raymond A. Klune to Robert H. O'Brien, 2/6/64.

106. Ibid.

107. Moonjean Interview, Los Angeles, Calif., 6/16/92. Hank Moonjean (Henry Moomjian), a Turkish-speaking Armenian American, graduated from the University of Southern California School of Cinema in 1952. He joined MGM, where his first screen credit was *Butterfield 8* ('60) as assistant director. He remained at the studio until 1972. His Armenian credentials made him Berman's natural ally and asset on the *Musa Dagh* production team.

108. *MGM Archives, Musa Dagh File,* Letter: Bob Weitman to Robert O'Brien, 3/13/64.

109. Ibid., Letter: Raymond A. Klune to Arvid Griffen, 3/30/64.

110. Ibid., Letter: Elliott Morgan to Ray Klune, 4/20/64.

111. Ibid., Outside Productions No. 16, Letter: Ray Klune to Arvid Griffen, 4/16/64.

112. Ibid., Memo to Robert H. O'Brien, 4/21/64.

113. Ibid., Memo to Robert H. O'Brien, 4/20/64.

114. Ibid., Outside Productions No. 16, Memo: Berman Productions to Rittenberg, 7/64.

115. Moonjean Interview, 6/16/92.

116. *MGM Archives, Musa Dagh File,* Outside Productions No. 16, Letter: Arvid Griffen to Raymond Klune, 6/10/64.

117. Moonjean Interview, 6/16/92.

118. *MGM Archives, Musa Dagh File,* Outside Productions No. 16, Letter: Arvid Griffen to Raymond Klune, 6/10/64.

119. Ibid., Memo: Hank Moonjean to Pandro Berman, 6/22/64.

120. Ibid., Memo: Billy Kaplan to Pandro Berman, 7/3/64.

121. *MGM Archives, Musa Dagh File,* Outside Productions No. 16, Memo: Billy Kaplan to Pandro Berman, 8/3/64.

122. Ibid., Inter-Office Memo: Raymond Klune to Robert O'Brien, 8/16/64.

123. Good Friday, Easter Sunday and Monday, Ascension Day, Labor Day (May 1), and four national holidays, including one in honor of King Paul I.

124. Ibid.

125. Ibid., Berman Productions, Outside Production No. 16, "Operation Roxbury," *Musa Dagh* Production Boards I and II.

126. Franz Werfel's handwritten research notes, the screenplays of Carey Wilson, Neil Paterson, and Ronald Harwood, and Hank Moonjean's production boards provided some of the most exciting and rewarding moments in the author's research.

127. *MGM Archives, Musa Dagh File,* Outside Production No. 16, Memo: Billy Kaplan to Pandro Berman, 9/9/64.

128. Ibid., Memo: Guy Green to Pandro Berman, 9/21/64.

129. Ibid., Memo: Guy Green to Pandro Berman, 9/20/64.

130. Moonjean Interview, 6/16/92.

131. *MGM Archives, Musa Dagh File*, Berman Productions, Outside Production No. 16, "Operation Roxbury," Memo: Guy Green to Pandro Berman, 9/9/64.

132. Ibid., 9/11/64.

133. Moonjean interview, 6/16/92.

134. Ibid.

135. *MGM Archives, Musa Dagh File*, Memo: Arvid Griffen to Ray Klune, 12/14/64.

136. Moonjean interview, 6/16/92.

137. *MGM Archives, Musa Dagh File*, Outside Production No. 16, Memo: Hank Moonjean to Ray Klune, 3/26/65.

138. Ibid.

139. Ibid., Memo: Hank Moonjean to Ray Klune, 4/19/65.

140. Ibid., Outside Production No. 16, Memo: Pandro Berman to Robert Weitman, 7/14/65.

141. Ibid., 7/9/65.

142. Ibid.

143. Moonjean interview, 6/19/62.

144. *MGM Archives, Musa Dagh File*, Outside Production No. 16, Memo, 7/31/65.

145. Ibid., Outside Production No. 16, Memo from Pandro Berman, 8/13/65.

146. Ibid., Memo: Russell Thatcher to Robert H. O'Brien, 8/16/65.

147. Ibid., Letter to Tom DeVine, New York City, 10/5/65.

148. Moonjean interview, 6/16/92.

149. *MGM Archives, Musa Dagh File*, Letter: Stanley Goldsmith to Ray Klune, 10/20/65.

150. Ibid., Letter: Saul Wittenberg to Edith Tolkin, 1/27/67.

151. Ibid., Berman Productions, Outside Production No. 16, 1966.

152. Moonjean interview, 6/16/92.

153. *MGM Archives, Musa Dagh File*, Berman Productions, Memo, 4/22/66.

154. Ibid., Berman Productions, Memo, 4/25/66.

155. Interview of Pandro S. Berman, a tape recording by Mike Steen, American Film Institute, Louis B. Mayer Foundation, Los Angeles, Calif., 8/4/72. After his retirement, Berman was asked to rate the MGM executives. He called studio manager Eddie Mannix a tower of strength, praised J. Robert Rubin and Kenneth MacKenna, and slammed Robert H. O'Brien as "miserable."

156. Ibid., Inter-office Memo: Raymond Klune to Robert H. O'Brien, 7/16/64.

157. Moonjean interview, 6/16/92.

158. *MGM Archives, Musa Dagh File,* Berman Productions, Memo, 4/25/66.

159. Moonjean interview 6/16/92.

160. *MGM Archives, Musa Dagh File*, Berman Productions, Memo, 4/25/66.

161. Ibid., Berman Productions, Memo, 8/4/66.

162. Ibid., Outside Berman Productions, Memo, 8/29/66.

163. Ibid., Memo, 8/22/66.

164. Ibid., Memo, 9/1/66.

165. Ibid., Letter to Pandro Berman, 10/23/66.

166. Moonjean interview, 6/16/92.

167. *MGM Archives, Musa Dagh File*, Berman Productions, Inter-office Communication: Barry Brunet to Saul Rittenberg, 9/29/66.

168. Moonjean interview, 6/16/92.

169. *MGM Archives, Musa Dagh File*, Berman Productions, Memo, 10/17/66.

170. *Moonjean Interview*, 6/16/92.

171. *The Hollywood Reporter*, 11/4/66.

172. Whatever responsibility Omar Sharif may have had, if any, in scuttling Berman's *Musa Dagh*, he made up for it in Henri Verneuil's (Ashod Malakian) excellent productions of *Mayrig* ('91) and *588 rue Paradis* ('92). These French films trace the odyssey of an Armenian family from the Genocide to their resettlement in Marseille, France. In reality they told the story of Verneuil's parents and his prominence in theater and motion pictures. Sharif played the part of Verneuil's father.

173. *MGM Archives, Musa Dagh File*, Outside Production No. 16, Letter: Henri Troyat to MGM, 2/27/67.

174. Ibid., Letter: Saul Rittenberg to Edith Tolkin, 1/27/67.

175. Ibid., Memo from Ray Klune, 2/27/67.

176. Ibid., Letter: Elliott Kastner to MGM, 4/7/67.

177. Ibid., Letter: Mark Robson to MGM, 8/14/67.

178. *The Hollywood Reporter*, 9/1/67, p. 2.

179. *MGM Archives, Musa Dagh File,* Outside Production No. 16, Memo: Re: John Sturges, 9/13/67.

180. *Variety*, 6/12/68.

181. *MGM Archives, Musa Dagh File*, File 7940-D, Gina Productions, 11/21/68.

182. Ibid., Letter: George Juskalian, Col., U.S. Army, Ret., to MGM, Culver City, Calif., 3/22/69.

183. Ibid., Letter: Lindsay Parsons, Jr., to George Juskalian, 4/8/69.

184. *The Hollywood Reporter*, 4/10/69, p. 2.

185. *Variety*, 4/16/69, p. 3.

186. *The Hollywood Reporter*, 4/10/69, p. 2.

187. *Variety*, 4/10/69.

188. *MGM Archives, Musa Dagh File*, Unsigned Letter to Lindsay Parsons, Jr., 6/13/69.

189. Ibid., Telegram: Archbishop Torkom Manoogian to Lindsay Parsons, Jr. 6/27/69.

190. Ibid., Letter: Saul Rittenberg to George Juskalian, 8/20/69.

191. Ibid., Outdoor Production No. 16, Letter: Frank Rinaldi to Mark Windbourne, 10/1/69.

192. Ibid., Gina Productions, File 7940-D, Letter: Jerry Gershwin to Frank Rinaldi, 12/12/69.

193. Ibid., Communication: Herbert Solow to Russell Thatcher, 12/29/69.

194. Ibid., File 7940-D, Letter: Saul N. Rittenberg to Gina Productions, 1/2/70.

39 Elia Kazan, tenacious as ever, wanted to make a play and movie of *Musa Dagh*.

40 Dore Schary, believed *Musa Dagh* was one of the few great books written since *War and Peace* and dreamed of making the movie.

41 Sol C. Siegel, as much as he questioned the filming of *Musa Dagh*, extended the contract to lock in MGM's rights.

42 Pandro S. Berman, "*Musa Dagh* was announced by Metro forty times in forty years and each and every time aroused Turkish indignation to the point it had become routine."

43 MGM studio boss, Robert M. Weitman, "*The Forty Days of Musa Dagh* would be the first picture produced under terms of Berman's new contract."

44 Joseph R. Vogel, President, Loew's, Inc. "Every time the project was reintroduced MGM was subjected to pressure from our own State Department. The present Turkish government would not admit to a black page of its history, because it had a blind spot about it." August 22, 1962.

45 Robert H. O'Brien was responsible for terminating Berman's *Musa Dagh* production.

BOOK VI

The Seduction
Of The Silver Screen

... for the time is at hand.
—The Revelation of St. John the Divine 1:3

Chapter 21

THE FORTY "YEARS" OF *MUSA DAGH*

It would still make a great movie

The termination of the Gershwin-Kastner *Musa Dagh* production did not diminish the concerns of *Musa Dagh* zealots or the vigil maintained by Werfel's stepdaughter, Anna Mahler, the administrator of the Werfel estate.[1] Due to an advisement from MGM to Mahler[2] to review the copyright documents of Werfel's novel,[3] an inquiry was initiated by her attorney, Felix Guggenheim. In February 1970, Guggenheim wrote to MGM expressing Anna's concern as to the status of the *Musa Dagh* movie. He informed the studio that a London group was interested in acquiring the rights to *Musa Dagh* for $50,000. In essence, he was reminding the studio that the Werfel estate was legally entitled to purchase the rights if the picture was not produced by 1971.[4] Guggenheim's letter compelled MGM to pay $25,000 to Mahler to retain its rights until 1975, even though it had no immediate plans to make the picture.[5]

Concurrently, the Hollywood press announced Kirk Kerkorian's majority acquisition of MGM. With Kerkorian, an Armenian American, controlling MGM, many Armenians came to believe that *Musa Dagh* would finally make it to the screen. George Mason, publisher of the English language Armenian weekly *The California Courier* and an employee of Kerkorian's Tracy Investment Company, became a member of MGM's Board of Directors. To a letter of inquiry by the author, Mason suggested that if the Armenian community raised the money to make a movie of *Musa Dagh*, he could make certain that MGM would treat the matter fairly and equitably.[6]

The following August, Claude Heilman offered to buy MGM's rights to *Musa Dagh*. He proposed a $5 million budget with John Frankenheimer[7] as the director and that Omar Sharif or Rod Steiger would star, along with Audrey Hepburn and Jean Paul Belmondo.[8] Like so many of his predecessors, Heilman's efforts proved futile because there was another deal in the offing.

Metro-Goldwyn-Mayer, the studio that had so tenaciously guarded its claim to *Musa Dagh* for thirty-six years, for the first time seriously considered giving up its rights and relieving itself of what many at the studio thought was its most burdensome and controversial property. After turning a deaf ear to a score of offers over the years, the news that MGM was on the verge of concluding a deal with a businessman outside the movie industry was startling. For a potential motion picture that had probably set a Hollywood record in postponements and conflict, could a movie novice, albeit a successful entrepreneur, make a movie of *Musa Dagh* when MGM, one of the most powerful and successful motion picture companies in the world, had failed. The businessman was John Kurkjian, an Armenian American.

John Kurkjian, a native of Kharpert (Harpoot), Turkey, was a survivor of the Armenian Genocide. Like many of his compatriots, he found refuge and opportunity in America. After World War I, he got his start in the dry-cleaning business in Lynn, Massachusetts. The depression of the 1930s and the opportunities in California convinced him to leave the Bay State. He and his wife Mary, nee Sarness, eventually settled in Los Angeles in July 1946. Fortune smiled on him. Having briefly studied architectural engineering and acquiring a cursory knowledge of the discipline, he saw his chance in real estate development, initially in home construction, and gradually upgraded himself by building shopping centers. In partnership with five non-Armenians, his primary job was to scout locations and then build and lease or sell the properties. He retired in 1970 from the business and managed to live comfortably on the income realized from his real estate investments.[9]

In time, his success allowed him to take an active role in Armenian community affairs, particularly at St. James Armenian Apostolic Church in Los Angeles. His contributions and leadership were recognized by the Supreme Catholicos of All Armenians, Vasken I, at the Holy See in Etchmiadzin, Soviet Armenia, with the highest honor the Mother Church could bestow, The Order of St. Gregory the Illuminator. Kurkjian also spearheaded the Armenian fund-raising drive in California in the worldwide campaign for the restoration of the Holy Sepulchre in Jerusalem. For his efforts, he was awarded the Holy Sepulchre Gold Medal, the highest honor of the Jerusalem Armenian Patriarchate. Kurkjian eventually had a falling out with the church hierarchs in the Diocese. As a result he became a topic of gossip in the Armenian community and withdrew from church activities. Despite this setback, he did not abandon his sense of national pride and commitment. Determined to restore his standing in the community, he began to sponsor cultural programs, particularly as impresario of the *Folk Dance Ensemble of Soviet Armenia* tour of the United States.[10] In time he found his greatest satisfaction in another new venture, making Armenian-themed movies.

His first film was a short documentary about the Armenian Genocide, *Where Are My People?* ('65). It was shown on Los Angeles television and made available free to churches, schools, and cultural organizations. He followed with other Armenian films.

Like many Armenians, Kurkjian had read *The Forty Days of Musa Dagh* when it was first published in this country in 1934. It had instilled in him a born-again faith that someone, at last, had remembered the Armenian Genocide of World War I. The icing on the cake in 1934 was the news that it was to become an American-made movie bearing the logo of the most prestigious movie company in the world, Metro-Goldwyn-Mayer. To John Kurkjian, *Musa Dagh* became the dream that would dispel the stereotyped epithet of the "starving Armenians" in its epic portrayal of heroism and the more positive traits of the Armenian character.[11]

In 1970, during a luncheon Kurkjian had with an attorney friend with MGM connections, the conversation turned to MGM's financial crisis. The studio that had once boasted having "more stars than in heaven" was liquidating some of its assets by auctioning props, costumes, and memorabilia to collectors. Kurkjian inquired if MGM was willing to part with its rights to Werfel's *The Forty Days of Musa Dagh*, which it had recently renewed for five years. The attorney immediately checked it out and the response, surprisingly, was affirmative. Kurkjian's lawyer friend, Gary Cooper (no relation to the movie star), believed it was just a matter of wading through the technicalities and banalities of the legal process.

MGM's recent contract had stipulated that the Werfel estate had the option to reassert its rights if the studio's production was not under way by August 1975.[12] Before the Werfel estate was able to exercise its rights and assume ownership of *Musa Dagh*, an agreement was executed on September 2, 1970, between Frank Davis, MGM's chief legal counsel, and attorneys representing John Kurkjian's High Investments, Inc., to buy MGM's rights to *The Forty Days of Musa Dagh*.[13] MGM wanted $250,000 cash for the property. Kurkjian's counter-offer of $125,000 was accepted. MGM was to receive an additional $50,000 if the film was produced and have ten percent of the net profit from distribution in perpetuity, but only after Kurkjian recouped distribution fees, expenses, and costs of the film's negative. As part of the deal, Kurkjian fell heir to nine large boxes from the studio, which contained *Musa Dagh*'s sixteen complete screenplays, adaptations, and treatments, and under separate cover, five copies of the "historic" agreement between him and MGM.[14] He made the front pages of the Armenian press and the Hollywood trade journals. He had scored a real coup by purchasing MGM's rights to *The Forty Days of Musa Dagh*.

The news electrified the Armenian community throughout the country and overseas. Renewed hope and interest were born in the hearts of many *Musa Dagh* devotees. Werfel's novel was coming off the shelf again. Surely, in the hands of an Armenian producer and with an Armenian owning MGM, the time was opportune for an unqualified success. Astonishingly, an Armenian American, John Kurkjian, had become the sole owner of the film rights to Franz Werfel's *The Forty Days of Musa Dagh*. If the response could have been measured in decibel levels when the news reached the Armenian media throughout the world, it would have been deafening. The motion picture production of *The Forty Days of Musa Dagh* became Kurkjian's most passionate endeavor.

When MGM story editor Samuel Marx was informed of Kurkjian's purchase of *Musa Dagh*, he told the author "some of the *Musa Dagh* screenwriters were absolutely ridiculous." Even though thirty-six years had passed since MGM bought Werfel's novel, it was Marx's conviction that it would still make a great movie. But he was pessimistic, knowing *Musa Dagh*'s history. Marx opined that MGM presently was looking for upbeat stories unlike *Musa Dagh* that could be made with a $10 to $15 million budget ceiling.[15]

During the negotiations, Kurkjian was repeatedly told that the movie had to be made by 1975, or he would forfeit his film rights to the Werfel estate.[16] Whenever the deadline for the rights renewal was pending, MGM had paid the Werfel estate to retain its ownership, as it did again in early 1970. Kurkjian felt confident that it was worth a gamble that the picture could be made within the four years remaining in the current MGM-Werfel agreement.[17]

Kurkjian knew that Turkish pressure on the State Department had been the major factor aborting the *Musa Dagh* film productions in the past.[18] Bolstering possible State Department pressures on MGM could be new issues concerning national defense. The Cold War had compelled the United States to establish military bases in Turkey on Soviet Russia's border during the Truman administration. There was always the possibility that *Musa Dagh* would incite Turkey to cancel the bases agreement.[19]

Through attorney Cooper, Kurkjian hired a Hollywood hand of thirty years, Samuel White,[20] who happened to be Cooper's father-in-law, to oversee the mechanics of the *Musa Dagh* project. After reading all the screenplays, treatments, adaptations, and Werfel's novel again, Kurjkian and White decided on a new script within a year. Their intention was to rewrite the story because, in their collective opinion, "what you had two years ago wouldn't work today."[21]

Despite *Musa Dagh*'s protracted history, the news of Kurkjian's deal produced a positive reaction in the film world. Dino De Laurentiis, the Italian film producer,[22] proposed a joint venture with Kurkjian to make *Musa Dagh* with Sylvana Mangano as Iskouhi. Everything seemed to be going well until it came to the issue of distribution of the film. The Roman "angel" knew that MGM had first right of refusal in the matter, but he was not deterred. With Kurkjian's blessing, De Laurentiis sought out his counterparts at MGM. Since he had his own distribution network, he wanted to take over *Musa Dagh*'s theater engagements. The meeting degenerated into high-volume obscenities when the studio turned him down. Frustrated, De Laurentiis stormed out of the meeting. He felt he had been intentionally insulted because MGM's bosses did not like him as a competitor. He was convinced that the studio had deliberately set him up just to aggravate him. When Kurkjian was told by MGM that he could not eliminate the studio's connection, De Laurentiis was no longer interested in any co-venture. He was absolutely uncompromising about the distribution rights. Kurkjian offered to mediate the controversy but to no avail. The Italian film producer's parting advice to his much-chagrined potential partner was to put as much distance between himself and MGM as soon as possible. If the studio's intention was to infuriate De Laurentiis so that he would lose interest in *Musa Dagh,* the strategy worked.[23] For John Kurkjian, the stress and strain of making a major movie was just beginning.

Soon after the De Laurentiis incident, MGM turned its plummeting financial situation around by paying off its obligations and filling its coffers under Kerkorian's management. Kurkjian was contacted by MGM's studio executives and politely scolded for thinking of striking a deal with "that Italian."[24] To Kurkjian's immense delight, MGM proposed a co-venture with High Investments, Inc.[25] Kurkjian accepted the co-venture offer with unabashed celerity.

MGM had had second thoughts after it sold *Musa Dagh* to Kurkjian due to an inquiry by one of Hollywood's eminent attorneys. In January 1974, Greg Bautzer, a prominent filmland legal counsel and man-about-town, informed MGM President Frank Rosenfelt that he was representing a client who was willing to spend $8 million to make *Musa Dagh*.[26] Bautzer's letter may have been the factor that compelled MGM to initiate negotiations for a *Musa Dagh* co-venture with the Kurkjians' High Investments, Inc. What was most enticing to Kurkjian was the partnership guaranteed MGM's distribution facilities and an office on the studio lot.

From the very start of co-venture negotiations in May 1974, Kurkjian said MGM was in charge. Dissatisfied with the sixteen screenplays on record and the Kurkjian-White script, the studio insisted on a new script. Satisfying this stipulation alone resulted in a five-month delay. The following August, four years after acquiring *Musa Dagh*'s rights, Kurkjian was notified by MGM that he had to extend his rights to *Musa Dagh* with the Werfel estate before August 1975. Acceding to Anna Mahler's demand, Kurkjian paid her $25,000. Now he had until September 1978 to complete the movie; otherwise the Werfel estate could claim *Musa Dagh*.[27]

If the historic struggle to film *Musa Dagh* were an indication, an indomitable will would be required to overcome the adversities posed by the studio bosses and the film's obstructionists. Kurkjian could not believe that the script prepared by White and himself was rejected because it was "too much like the book."[28] To him the argument was specious and unworthy of a great motion picture studio. According to Kurkjian, there never was a moment during the exacerbating negotiations when MGM was not represented by a battery of intimidating lawyers. "You agreed to certain things and the next day there were changes."[29] It was the studio's modus operandi. Kurkjian toughed it out because he depended on MGM's facilities and prestige. Besides, having an office on the lot enabled him to keep an eye on his project. Initially he had been elated with MGM's renewed interest in *Musa Dagh* and was convinced of its sincere intent to make the movie. He had been attracted to work with the studio because of its track record and its standing in the film world. But when weeks and months passed and there still was no co-venture contract, Kurkjian, frustrated and angry, confronted MGM chief counsel Frank Davis, insisting that "... the contract should have been ready and signed in four days, not seven months."[30] Kurkjian soon learned from this experience that delays and postponements were normal in Hollywood.

Finally, on January 14, 1975, Davis instructed associate general counsel Karla Davidson to prepare a contract between MGM and Kurkjian. The agreement was to stipulate that MGM receive, up front, $125,000 and 5 percent of 100 percent of the net profit from film distribution. A new screenplay was to be part of the deal, as well as the selection of a producer in consultation with Kurkjian. The executive producers would be John Kurkjian and Samuel White, who would receive $150,000 each. The picture's cost was not to exceed $7 million, exclusive of overhead.[31] Of particular reassurance to Kurkjian was the knowledge that two Armenian American appointees of Kirk Kerkorian—James Aljian and George Mason—were on MGM's Board of Directors.[32]

Kurkjian, concerned about the deadline with the Werfel estate and intent on completing shooting by September 1978, continued to apply pressure on MGM President Frank Rosenfelt. In July 1975, five years after he bought the rights to *Musa Dagh* and fourteen months after negotiations had begun, Kurkjian was immensely relieved when all agreements with MGM were finally approved and signed.[33] Adding to his elation was Rosenfelt's assurance that he was in full accord with Kurkjian and that MGM was ready to proceed immediately as it, too, wanted the picture completed as quickly as possible. He instructed Kurkjian to get together with the new production chief, Daniel Melnick, to select a writer.[34]

Selecting from a list of screenwriters proposed by Melnick, Kurkjian and White favored Edward Anhalt.[35] Vice-President Ray Wagner of the production staff disagreed, thus prolonging the process. Concerned about the unexpected delays he had already endured, Kurkjian stressed the need for a schedule and game plan to expedite the production. Sam White drew up a guideline, and copies were sent to Wagner and Melnick on September 18, 1975 (Appendix XII). Kurkjian was convinced that they never considered the game plan.

Ignoring Kurkjian and White, Melnick sent Werfel's novel to screenwriter James Goldman[36] and to the English playwright John Osborne.[37] Osborne turned it down. A month later, Melnick called White to tell him that James Goldman loved the book and wanted to do the screenplay. His agent demanded $250,000 plus a percentage of the net profits with no deferment of payment. Melnick urged High Investments to come up with an immediate $50,000 as a demonstration of good faith. White suggested that MGM and United Artists (another Kerkorian acquisition) put up the difference. What disturbed Kurkjian and White was the stipulation that if a script did not materialize, resulting in an aborted production, Kurkjian and White would be responsible for the entire $250,000 demanded by Goldman's agent. Kurkjian was incensed because Melnick knew that $150,000 had been budgeted for a screenwriter.[38] The Goldman deal was vetoed.[39]

Melnick then gave Werfel's novel to Carl Foreman, hoping that Foreman would write the screenplay and produce the picture. In November 1975, MGM/United Artists refused to come up with any more money because Melnick had failed to wrap up a deal with Foreman or Goldman or someone else of equal stature. Honoring his *Musa Dagh* commitment, Melnick assigned Wagner to find a less expensive but qualified writer to do a treatment.[40]

Realizing they could not rely on MGM for a screenwriter, and since time was of the essence, White called Ben Kamsler of the H. N. Swanson Agency, who suggested British writer Ronald Harwood. White, Kurkjian, and Wagner were impressed with Harwood's credits.[41] A deal was developed subject to Harwood's meeting with Melnick in London.[42]

Commensurate with its MGM dealings, Kurkjian's High Investments produced an eight-page brochure for potential "angels" touting its "coming attraction," *The Forty Days of Musa Dagh*. A full-page photo was captioned "John Kurkjian and Frank Rosenfelt, MGM President,[43] concluding an $8,000,000 contract to film *Musa Dagh*."[44]

The pamphlet was designed to create a positive first impression in the minds of investors. In large type, it extolled the history of Franz Werfel's novel, recounting its initial public acclaim in 1934 and 1935 and MGM's purchase of the film rights as an Irving Thalberg production. A brief review of the Armenian Genocide was incorporated in the advertisement, noting that the victory of the Musa Dagh defenders was historical fact. It emphasized the Turkish government's successful protests through the State Department, that MGM had already spent $1,500,000, excluding large sums paid to the Werfel estate, and that Armenians had waited many years to see Werfel's novel on the screen. To hold the reader's interest, reference was made to the gross receipts in millions of dollars of blockbuster movies such as *The Godfather* ('72) $85m+, *The Towering Inferno* ('74) $48m+. The presumption was that *The Forty Days of Musa Dagh* should conservatively return $50 million worldwide. The advertisement's cachet was in dropping the names of movie luminaries as possible participants in the film: Actors: Al Pacino, Omar Sharif, Dustin Hoffman, Robert Redford, Warren Beatty, Faye Dunaway, Sophia Loren, Liv Ullman, and Catherine Denueve; directors Sidney Pollack, *The Way We Were* ('73) and Francis Ford Coppola, *The*

Godfather ('72); and screenwriters Robert Bolt, *Doctor Zhivago* ('65), Dalton Trumbo and Lorenzo Semple, Jr., *Papillon* ('73). The brochure's salient point was to extend an invitation to investors to join Kurkjian in financing "this motion picture memorial." In reality he was hoping to attract his fellow Armenians. Noting that Kurkjian himself was a survivor of the 1915 genocide, the brochure described his contract with MGM wherein he acquired all world rights, title, and interest in and to the property of Werfel's novel. The pamphlet credited Kirk Kerkorian with acquiring control of MGM and restoring its rightful place as one of the major entertainment forces. MGM's net income for the first quarter of fiscal 1975 was stated to be the best in twenty years. The brochure also emphasized the rebirth of movies replacing the "new wave." Potential backers were told that Kurkjian had refused offers to sell *Musa Dagh* to a mysterious buyer for a profit of $500,000. (Kurkjian was convinced that the anonymous buyer was Turkish.) "This is not a standard business venture. It is a crusade of the Armenian people to show the world once and for all that they are united."[45] He projected an $8 million budget, half financed by MGM with the balance privately financed through High Investments. Four million dollars would be placed in escrow, earning 8 percent until completion of the movie. The offer to investors was a 50/50 first position to recoup the initial investment with MGM. Thereafter, investors would receive 60 percent of the net profit from High Investments' share after all distribution costs were redeemed in addition to the many tax shelter advantages the investment offered.[46]

On the back of the pamphlet was a sketch of a "Memorial to the fallen Armenians as it stands today on Mount Musa Dagh." (Following the evacuation in 1939 of the Musa Dagh Armenians from the region, the memorial that was dedicated in 1932 was destroyed by the Turkish government.) In September 1993, a group of Armenian American tourists visiting the Musa Dagh area found no evidence that a heroic stand had ever taken place there in 1915. What they witnessed was the rubble of what once was a memorial.[47]

To arouse the general public's interest, an Associated Press release was made available to the media recounting the events in Werfel's novel and alerting the readers to the impending production of *The Forty Days of Musa Dagh*.[48] In spite of Kurkjian's prodigious efforts, the media publicity and the brochure did not generate the expected monetary response; not enough prosperous Armenians responded.[49] The project required big money from such Armenian American multimillionaires as the Manoogians, Kerkorians, Mardigians, Hovnanians, and Mugars.

While Kurkjian was making his appeal for financial support, MGM production chief Daniel Melnick met with Ronald Harwood in London in January 1976 and was favorably impressed. An agreement to write the screenplay stipulated that the contract was for thirty-four weeks at a fee of $50,000. Harwood was furnished a first-class round-trip airfare ticket from London to Los Angeles, an expense account of $600 a week, and a Beverly Hills apartment.[50] If the *Musa Dagh* script count were correct, that would make Harwood's screenplay number eighteen. Kurkjian was distressed at MGM's lack of professional courtesy to a partner when Harwood's contract was relayed to him one week after Melnick returned to Culver City on January 24, 1976. Two weeks later, Harwood arrived in Los Angeles and met with Melnick and Wagner to discuss the screen treatment. Once again, Kurkjian was snubbed. Before arrangements were made by MGM for Sam White to meet with Harwood, White was told not to discuss High Investments' thoughts about the screenplay. Melnick and Wagner wanted Harwood to write the screenplay based solely on Harwood's initial inspiration. Almost two months passed before Harwood turned in a treatment.[51]

Nine months had elapsed from the time Kurkjian had signed agreements with MGM until he received Harwood's treatment. To compound Kurkjian's frustration with the process, he had called Wagner to set up a meeting so that they could discuss Harwood's work. A week later, April 20, 1976, Kurkjian and White were visibly upset to learn that Wagner, with Melnick's blessing, planned to hire James Harris to produce the picture. Without their knowledge, Wagner had not only given Harris the Harwood treatment to read but had met with him and decided that his ideas and theirs were compatible. Harris had not made a film since 1965.[52]

Wagner and Melnick were adamant about hiring Harris, even though it was contrary to a technicality in the contract that a producer would not be hired until both parties had approved a screenplay. MGM wanted Harris to go over the script with Harwood and come up with something "Up beat! Current!"[53] They pressed their position and requested that a technicality not stand in the way of the script. Kurkjian reluctantly consented. To compound his anxiety he was expected to assume all expenses. A contract was signed May 4, 1976, which offered Harris $12,500 during the development stage, against a production fee of $125,000 plus 3 percent of the net profit.[54]

The situation continued to deteriorate when White was turned down for asking to see the treatment from Harwood and Harris and again when he suggested that he sit in on the meetings and work with them. Harris told him they could not write a script by committee. White protested to Wagner but to no avail. When White asked to see the first fifty pages of script, Harris refused again, but he agreed to let White and Kurkjian read the completed script before anyone else, as set forth in the contract. Kurkjian said it never happened. It had taken Harris and Harwood so long to finish the script that it had to be distributed to everyone immediately. During the entire writing period, neither Wagner nor Melnick contacted Kurkjian or White. Nor did Harris or Harwood ever consult or collaborate with them on the script.

These Byzantine machinations were hardening John Kurkjian, more so when he learned that Melnick was stepping down in July 1976 and was to be replaced by Dick Shepherd. Highly perturbed, White met with studio boss Frank Rosenfelt demanding to know *Musa Dagh*'s status. Rosenfelt promised him that MGM intended to proceed with the project without interruption and had communicated that to Harris and Wagner. He reassured White by telling him that his good friend Stanley Kubrick had recommended Harris and had praised him to the sky.[55] Finally, on August 23, 1976, MGM made it official with a press release:

> Raymond J. Wagner, Vice-President of MGM Production, announced that James B. Harris had been signed to produce The Forty Days of Musa Dagh *for MGM, and that Ronald Harwood was to write the screenplay, with John Kurkjian and Samuel White serving as Executive Producers.*[56]

The blurb cited Harwood's screen credits and mentioned that Harris was an associate of Stanley Kubrick in *The Killing* ('56), *Paths of Glory* ('58), and *Lolita* ('62), and had produced and directed *The Bedford Incident* ('65) for Columbia. It went on to say that Werfel's novel had been translated into thirty-one languages and read by millions and had never been out of print and that *Musa Dagh* was to be one of MGM's most ambitious productions.[57]

Another seventeen weeks passed before Kurkjian and White finally saw Harwood's screenplay. They were dissatisfied with it but felt that a rewrite incorporating much of the material that was left out might make it acceptable. The studio was more decisive. Sherry Lansing of the production staff gave orders that Harwood's services were completed as of September 24, 1976.[58] In addition to Harwood's salary of $50,000, Kurkjian had also paid his expenses during his entire stay in Los Angeles, which had cost him over $11,000 (Appendix XI). Owning the rights to *The Forty Days of Musa Dagh* had made Kurkjian responsible for financing the entire project.

Kurkjian and White were extremely agitated when they met with Wagner and Harris in production chief Dick Shepherd's office to evaluate Harwood's script. With the exception of Harris, none of them liked it. Shepherd said that Harwood's screenplay would cost $12 million whereas the budget was set at $7 million,[59] and none of the things he remembered from the book were in the Harwood script. To his credit, Shepherd was specific about all the book's situations, characterizations, and scenes missing from the script. White and Kurkjian protested that their script, which had been submitted to MGM when negotiations had begun in May 1974, contained everything that Shepherd had mentioned. They were convinced that Wagner had never read the Harwood script. Wagner was supposedly "riding point" on this project and constantly telling Kurkjian and White that a fresh approach was needed and that the thing was outdated. To mollify Kurkjian, Shepherd agreed to read the High Investments script. [60]

Another month passed before Shepherd called Kurkjian in to tell him that their script would have to be re-evaluated before it could be made into a viable screenplay. Kurkjian was completely taken off-guard when, out of the blue, Shepherd said the project was too chancy and that the movie based on their script could never be made for less than $10 million to $12 million. It was his judgment that MGM should not gamble that much money on such a questionable production. He had discussed it with Rosenfelt and others. They had concurred and decided not to proceed.[61] In the contract signed by Kurkjian and Rosenfelt, there was a provision that the studio could terminate the agreement after first delivery of the screenplay.[62]

Kurkjian was perplexed. Six years had gone by since he had bought the rights. It was twenty-eight months from the start of co-venture negotiations to his last meeting with Shepherd. Kurkjian said in all his years of business dealings he had never experienced anything like it. It was incredible that the same things that had happened so many times before to Musa Dagh were happening again. *The Forty Days of Musa Dagh* had gestated into the forty "years" of *Musa Dagh*. He had "entered into a deal with MGM with high hopes, confidence, and complete trust in their ability to do everything they said they would. It was incomprehensible."[63] For Kurkjian, it was an introduction to the real Hollywood.

In a statement prepared by White to attorney Greg Bautzer tracing the chronology of the Kurkjian-MGM co-venture, Kurkjian was vehement in his denunciation of MGM. He was in a quandary. The money he had spent was lost without a single compensatory result. As of September 1976, $2.5 million had been committed, all predicated on the MGM deal. He had less than two years to make the picture before the rights reverted to the Werfel estate. If that happened, he stood to lose over $500,000.[64] Despite the enormity of the setback, Kurkjian was still determined to bring *Musa Dagh* to the screen.

MGM associate general counsel Karla Davidson rebutted (White) Kurkjian's letter to Bautzer. While she agreed with Kurkjian's chronology, Davidson said that Kurkjian had misunderstood the contract or did not want to understand it and insisted that MGM had complied with the spirit and the letter of the agreement that Metro was merely entering into a development deal. As for the overall time factor, this was "quite prompt as things go." [65] She admitted that the Harwood deal had exceeded the contract by two months and excused it as being not unusual with writers in Hollywood. While she agreed that Kurkjian was accurate regarding the contract's stipulation that "We shall supervise all writing and in connection with such supervision, there shall be consultation and collaboration between you and us,"[66] she defended MGM's right to delegate supervision to producer James Harris because he was hired with Kurkjian's approval. She charged the novice Armenian producer with ignorance, claiming that Shepherd had informed Kurkjian that the screenplay he originally brought in would have required at least $10 million to $12 million budget. It was unfortunate, said Davidson; the co-venture had not worked out. After all, Kurkjian still had almost another two years to put his package together elsewhere.[67] If it was any consolation to Kurkjian, his recounting of the co-venture events with MGM in his correspondence to Greg Bautzer of October 29, 1976, was verified in Davidson's rebuttal.

Kurkjian said his relationship with MGM executives Rosenfelt and Davis had always been on a first-name basis. It had included social visits and dinners due to Kurkjian having an office on the Culver City lot for a year and a half. To assuage his hurt pride, they offered to help. Kurkjian's response was to insist that Dick Shepherd be dealt out so that he could continue to do business directly with the studio through Rosenfelt. Rosenfelt suggested he call Kirk Kerkorian, who really owned the studio.

Kurkjian in a one-on-one meeting with Kerkorian unburdened his woes. He accused Shepherd of attempting to take him down a financial drain. He charged that MGM's screwball antics to sex up *Musa Dagh* (a nude scene had been incorporated in the new screenplay) would have resulted in a cheap film and a discredit to the Armenian people.

He pleaded with Kerkorian to convince Rosenfelt and Shepherd that the film must be made properly. According to Kurkjian, Kerkorian told him that he preferred to leave the studio's concerns in the hands of his more experienced MGM staff. Kurkjian was bitterly disappointed. Despite his knowledge of *Musa Dagh*'s stormy history, he had come to believe that this time, with an Armenian in control of MGM, it would be different. "Despite changes, nothing changes in Hollywood."[68] He had become one more victim in the MGM *Musa Dagh File*. Kurkjian's failure to convince Armenian millionaires to join him in the project gave the studio heads a loophole to pull out after delivery of the screenplay. The upshot of all this was Kurkjian's realization that, if *The Forty Days of Musa Dagh* was ever to reach the silver screen, he would have to do it the hard way—alone!

Chapter 22

SEARCHING FOR ANGELS

Achilles heel

John Kurkjian was now on his own. With the MGM fiasco behind him, and still confronted with the expiration date of September 1978 to his *Musa Dagh* rights, he regrouped. A second promotional brochure had already been sent to prospective angels in 1977. The objective this time was to raise $2.5 million in a limited partnership called Musa Dagh, Ltd., offering twenty-five units at $100,000 each. To persuade the prospective client that this was a new undertaking, the booklet included a picture of the new High Investments team responsible for the film production.[69]

As with the first public relations promotion, the new brochure reviewed the history of Werfel's inspiration to write the novel and stressed the potential of *The Forty Days of Musa Dagh* film to become another monumental movie like *Gone With The Wind*, *Lawrence Of Arabia*, and *Doctor Zhivago*. The prospectus informed the potential investor (angel) that High Investments intended to present the project to European investors and distributors as well.

Kurkjian's offer required that each investor have a net worth of $250,000 exclusive of residence, furniture, furnishings and autos. At least some portion of the annual gross income of each angel had to be subject to a federal income tax at a rate of at least 50 percent. In exchange for their investments, the limited partners would recoup their total contributions and 60 percent of the income while the general partners, Kurkjian/High Investments, would realize 40 percent. To impress investors, Paul Schreibman, High Investments legal counsel, was mentioned as having represented Toho Films of Japan, one of the largest film producers and exhibitors in the world.[70]

As the deadline to Kurkjian's *Musa Dagh* film rights approached, Kurkjian lowered his expectations by suggesting to MGM the possibility of a TV movie.[71] There was no response. Previous to this, in May 1977, Karla Davidson had been contacted by the Harcourt Management Corp. of Scarsdale, New York and told that there were clients interested in obtaining the rights to *Musa Dagh*. They asked if MGM was the right organization to deal with.[72] This information was not passed on immediately to High Investments. Kurkjian believed the offer came from Turks whose intention was to bury *Musa* Dagh forever as a motion picture.[73]

In the process of launching his project, Kurkjian was upset when *Variety* announced that Golan-Globus Productions claimed to have acquired the rights from Kurkjian and planned a $10 million production of *Musa Dagh*.[74] No such deal had been made with the two Israeli movie producers. He was livid when he denounced them in a phone call.[75] At least interest in *Musa Dagh* had not waned.

The poor reception to his second promotional brochure and to his advertisements in the Armenian newspapers were very distressing. He had been confident that the Musa Dagh, Ltd., offer would have no trouble finding 25 investors. Even his personal solicitation of wealthy Armenian American investors was only partially successful. The necessary seed money just was not there. In particular, he was counting on his friend Alex Manoogian. There was no question of Manoogian's financial capabilities. He had built his Michigan-based Masco Corporation into a Fortune 500 company. Manoogian, a naturalized American citizen, was already recognized as one of this country's eminent industrialists and philanthropists. He was not only the president of the Armenian General Benevolent Union (AGBU), the largest, most solvent, and influential non-religious Armenian charitable organization in the world, but also the major benefactor of the Armenian Apostolic Church and its Etchmiadzin Catholicate.

Kurkjian personally asked Manoogian to finance the film. Manoogian discussed the film project with board members of the AGBU Alex Manoogian Cultural Fund. Dr. Dennis Papazian (director of the Armenian Center, University of Michigan, Dearborn), board chairman of the Cultural Fund at the time, says Kurkjian's proposal was examined. Board members wondered if Kurkjian, who had never produced a major film, was up to the challenge. Any grant or loan would have meant cutting back on other projects, which were vital to the welfare of the Armenian community in the United States and abroad (educational institutions, publications, cultural activities, the arts). Besides, the Cultural Fund was not wealthy then. The board could see the potential and the advantages of having a first-class film of *Musa Dagh* and was sympathetic but did not think the Armenian community, particularly AGBU members, would have understood such an expenditure on this project. Papazian contends that the AGBU Board of Directors could have been sued if it had invested in a Hollywood film and lost money. To oversee such an investment would have required lawyers and accountants, which would have added to the costs. Papazian defended Manoogian as a prudent man who became rich because he understood his limits as well as his virtues. "Why should he take money out of something he knew and put it into something he really did not understand?" [76] The Cultural Fund members felt that filmmaking was speculative and that there would be no end to trouble and liability if the film failed. Papazian said that Kurkjian was not seeking an investment or a loan from the AGBU but a grant.[77] Kurkjian contended that "All Manoogian had to do was to give the go ahead for the AGBU to invest in *Musa Dagh* and we've got a movie."[78]

Extremely disappointed in his friend, Kurkjian felt that if Manoogian was averse to backing the movie, he could have at least publicly encouraged the making of *Musa Dagh*. Among Kurkjian's other major disappointments was the lack of support from other wealthy Armenian Americans, the most distressing of which was the absence of Kirk Kerkorian. Even though there was sincere encouragement from Armenians generally, individually they just would not venture into untried waters with a novice.[79]

Kurkjian's next ordeal on the *Musa Dagh* roller coaster involved Franz Werfel's stepdaughter, Anna Mahler.[80] At the time Kurkjian purchased the rights to *Musa Dagh* from MGM in 1970, he had four years to complete the film.[81] He believed that forty-eight months would have been more than adequate to make *Musa Dagh*. If not, he did have the option to renew his rights. As it happened, he was compelled to renew his claim twice.

On the first occasion Kurkjian had paid $25,000.[82] From the moment Kurkjian owned the rights, he became the involuntary benefactor of the Werfel estate. Felix Guggenheim, the attorney who had represented the Werfel estate, had died and was succeeded by his son, Alfred Kim Guggenheim. Mahler and young Guggenheim saw in Kurkjian a tenacious adversary whose Achilles heel was his commitment to *Musa Dagh*. Kurkjian felt that they had taken advantage of him.

As the expiration date approached in 1978, Guggenheim informed

Kurkjian that another party was making a better offer. Since he was duty-bound to do his professional best for his client, Guggenheim would recommend that Anna Mahler sell the rights to the highest bidder. Aware that he could not produce the film by 1978, Kurkjian offered $30,000. Guggenheim wanted $60,000 because "someone else" had already made a six-figure bid, or so Kurkjian was led to believe. Kurkjian told Guggenheim that if the "someone else" were the Turks, which seemed to him to be the implication, Guggenheim should be aware of retaliation. He reminded his legal adversary of his reasonableness and of the money and energy already poured into the venture.[83] Two days later, Anna Mahler agreed to settle for $30,000 to renew Kurkjian's rights for three years and another $30,000 if the movie were sold to television.[84]

Kurkjian now had an extension through August 15, 1981, with no plans for renewal. Over the span of ten years, the Kurkjians had personally spent over $500,000 on their *Musa Dagh* movie project.[85] Kurkjian was convinced that the Werfel estate, having an understandable vested interest in its own welfare, was acutely aware of its advantage, and, rather than sell the rights permanently, perceived it as a source of reliable income by selling the renewal rights for a limited period of time. For now, he had bought himself a reprieve.[86]

Realizing the difficulty of making the film in the United States, Kurkjian decided to investigate the European film industry. In December 1976, he hired Ika Panajotovic of Nobla Film to be a member of his new production team. An American of Yugoslav ancestry, Panajotovic's assignment was to secure investments and distribution rights in Europe. Contacts had already been made in Yugoslavia, West Germany, Italy, and with Rank Films in London. Panajotovic, applying his ethnic credentials, conferred with Inex Film and Kosutnajk Studios in Yugoslavia to secure supply services, facilities, studio stages, equipment, wardrobe, and other necessities valued at $1.2 million. Most encouraging was the Tito regime's promise to fill all the movie's needs.[87] Then, before contracts could be finalized, President Carter's Human Rights Program was launched, much to the consternation of the Yugoslavs. Kurkjian was told that, under the circumstances, Tito had no desire to do business with Americans until the human rights issue was eliminated.[88]

Offsetting this setback was the possibility that Cinema 77 in West Germany would consider an investment of $1.5 million. Massino Ferrara, representing major film companies in Italy, expressed the possibility of providing between $400,000 and $750,000. Rank Film Laboratories expressed willingness to grant a credit of $100,000 for one year of lab costs. Another $500,000 was possible from distribution contracts in the United Kingdom, South Africa, and Australia. Japan and Southeast Asia were also possibilities. The support of these potential angels was contingent on a final screenplay, selection of an esteemed director, casting of the major acting roles, and a production budget. It was estimated that the cost of this joint-venture production would be at least $6.5 million.[89]

To keep these possibilities alive, the *Musa Dagh* project next crossed the Danube to deal with the Communist regime in Bucharest. The Romanians were aware of *Musa Dagh's* trials through their foreign distributors. Initially, the Ceaucescu government's overtures convinced Kurkjian of their sincerity.[90] An additional advantage was the sizeable Armenian population there to draw from as actors and extras. Many of them were the survivors of the Genocide or the descendants of those who had escaped from Turkish persecution.[91]

Again, Kurkjian's elation was short-lived. When the media publicized the news about *Musa Dagh*, the Turkish government threatened the

Romanians with an embargo on their ships seeking passage through the Bosporus and the Dardanelles. Bucharest had to weigh a movie production's worth against a blockade that would adversely affect the country's economy. Romania reneged. Undaunted, Kurkjian sent feelers to Greece and was told the picture would be sabotaged and that he should stay out of Greece.[92]

Depressed by the turn of events, but persistent, Kurkjian explored yet another avenue. After seeing a Soviet Armenian movie, *Mekhitar Nahabed,* he was so impressed with its quality that he decided to contact the Yerevan (capital of Soviet Armenia) authorities. To Kurkjian, an encouraging factor was the extant agreement between the United States and the Soviet Union permitting their peoples to engage in co-venture movie projects. Seizing the initiative in 1978, Kurkjian wrote to the Armenian government informing it of his rights to *Musa Dagh* and indicating his interest in exploring the possibilities of making the movie in Soviet Armenia. Kurkjian was delighted to hear that the Armenian authorities would be honored to participate in the production of such a picture. On that note, Kurkjian packed his bags and made ready for a journey to the Armenian homeland, the land of his ancestry.

With several scripts in hand, he alighted at the Yerevan airport. Kurkjian's main contact in Yerevan was the top echelon of Armenia's film industry. The meeting was cordial and encouraging. Kurkjian was overwhelmed when they offered to secure everything he needed. How ironic that after all the ups and downs, *Musa Dagh* was finally and most appropriately to be brought to the screen by Armenians and in Armenia. It was still Kurkjian's intention to use American actors in the leading roles and Armenians as extras. Shooting the film in Armenia presented an inspirational opportunity, especially after Kurkjian's meeting with Musa Daghians from Anjar, Lebanon, now living in Musa Ler (a village that was created for them near Etchmiadzin, the ecclesiastical seat of the Catholicos of All Armenians). To Kurkjian, the omens seemed positive. But, there was the matter of a formality, a simple technicality, a matter of courtesy—a trip to Moscow! Official approval by the Soviet government there was mandatory, and his chances were 50/50 because the political climate changed on a daily basis.[93]

After spending two weeks in Armenia, where he was accorded all the amenities of a VIP, including a thorough inspection of the Armenian film industry's studios and facilities, he made arrangements through the Armenian Consul in Moscow for his meeting with the Soviet film authorities. The power vested in the Soviet movie bosses was much different from that of their Hollywood counterparts. In the Soviet Union, the film industry was one adjunct of the Soviet government, whereas in Hollywood, it was part of the free enterprise capitalist system, having no official connection to the government in Washington. However, Kurkjian was well aware that, like MGM's encounter with the State Department, his venture in Armenia would also be determined by a political decision, this time by the Kremlin.

In Moscow, Kurkjian was ready to offer the Soviets distribution rights to *Musa Dagh* in the Soviet Union in exchange for retaining the American, Canadian, and world rights. Knowing the Soviets had an undisguised passion for United States currency, he would promise the Soviets 25 percent of the net in American dollars. He was furnished a car and a chauffeur and an appointment in the Kremlin. Contrary to the scenario in his mind, he was pleasantly surprised when he was introduced to his host. Expecting to meet a tough looking, hardline Soviet Communist, he was taken aback to shake hands with a Russian "Robert Redford." Alexander Sirakov, about forty-eight years old, blond, blue-eyed, handsome, smiling, and oozing with old world charm and warmth, offered a hospitable greeting. Vice-president of the Soviet film industry and influential decision maker, Sirakov was appointed by his father, the president of the Soviet Union's motion picture industry. Kurkjian was immensely pleased with Sirakov, who proved to be an attentive listener as Kurkjian reviewed the history of the *Musa Dagh* film project and detailed his plans for the production of the movie in Armenia. Kurkjian updated Sirakov about his experience as a moviemaker, maintaining that he was capable of producing a quality movie if he had the cooperation of the Soviet government.[94]

He shared with Sirakov vignettes of his brief stay in Armenia. There was the government official in charge of all roads and bridges in Armenia, who had chauffeured him to the prominent sites. He was absolutely sure that the people in Armenia would support the making of *Musa Dagh* there. There was another story of an eighty-nine-year-old Musa Dagh survivor in Musa Ler, who told him that he was going to be a king in the eyes of the Armenian people and that all the villagers in that remote "atheistic" corner of the globe were going to pray for him. Sirakov responded with an oration, singing the praises of the Armenians, from whose ranks came 64 generals, including Ivan Bagramian, who had participated in the capture of Berlin in 1945. Sirakov was so enthusiastic about Kurkjian's project that he envisioned four or five pictures. Kurkjian was captivated by his host, who then told his guest that the scripts would have to be examined for their capitalistic ramifications. Kurkjian reminded Sirakov that the incident at Musa Dagh had occurred before the Russian Revolution and the founding of the Soviet Union. Nevertheless, Sirakov was optimistic that a positive decision would be made within a month. Kurkjian expressed his gratitude to his Russian host by presenting him with a gold pen and pencil set. Sirakov reciprocated with an elaborate buffet. As the Russian accompanied his Armenian American guest to his car, he promoted his seventeen-year-old daughter for a part in the film and promised Kurkjian a gift on his return. All Kurkjian had wanted was an unequivocal and emphatic "Da!" to go ahead with his cherished project.[95]

On his return to Los Angeles, Kurkjian grew impatient awaiting Sirakov's answer. After more than a month passed, Kurkjian sent a cablegram to Sirakov, who immediately responded. Due to the deterioration of the political climate between the United States and the Soviet Union (a result of the Soviet invasion of Afghanistan in 1979), Sirakov believed the atmosphere had become so clouded that it would be better to wait until the diplomatic air cleared for a better chance of a favorable decision. Kurkjian was extremely disappointed. He asked Set Momjian, a supporter and a friend of President Carter, to intervene with the State Department. Kurkjian was informed that the United States government frowned upon American citizens conducting private business with the Soviet Union in light of the present situation, at least, until relations improved.

First MGM, then Yugoslavia and Romania, followed by Greece, and now the Soviet Union. It was a most discouraging pattern. More than seven years had passed since he bought the film rights, and he was no nearer to production than on the day he took over *Musa Dagh*. The money and the energy expended were considerable, but more significantly, there was no recovery for the time lost. And Kurkjian was not a young man. He had reached the point of no return. His overseas feelers had cost him dearly. He realized that shooting *Musa Dagh* abroad was too problematic. He had no other choice but to make the film in California, and if necessary on a low budget.[96]

The silver screen and *Musa Dagh* had so seduced John Kurkjian that there was no turning back. He had no other recourse but to produce the film independently, despite the criticisms of his earlier low-budget films designed for the Armenian trade. Nevertheless, he thought he had gained enough experience to pursue his objective.[97] John Kurkjian was about to enter to the real world of moviemaking.

Chapter 23

THE FINAL CUT

Gone too far to back out now

Even though there was sincere encouragement from Armenians universally, they just would not venture into untried waters with a novitiate. It is possible that Kurkjian's dispute with the Church had given him a dose of bad publicity in the Armenian community. Regardless of his sincerity where the production of *Musa Dagh* was concerned, the necessary monetary support would not be forthcoming.

If *The Forty Days of Musa Dagh* was ever to reach the screen, John Kurkjian knew he had to do it on his own and before his rights to Werfel's novel expired. He felt that MGM's bosses had deceived him by their fawning interest and gamesmanship. Time after time they had failed to make good on their promises. He had been worn down by attorneys with their exploitive fees, by MGM, and by Werfel's heirs, who had whittled down his savings. It had been a debilitating lesson affecting his health. To maintain his rights to the book, he had to get his film "in the can" by August 15, 1981. He decided to personally produce his dream movie in Los Angeles. With limited resources, he launched his life's most challenging project.[98]

Extremely disappointed that wealthy Armenians would not back him, Kurkjian remained confident that the Armenian community in

Los Angeles would support him. After a forty-year wait, he believed they would appreciate a fellow Armenian who was going to bring their Armenian treasure to the screen, regardless of Turkish and State Department pressures. John and Mary Kurkjian felt that they had gone too far to back out now. After securing loans from various banks, friends, and business firms, they also raised additional funds by mortgaging their home, cashing insurance policies, and selling their jewelry.[99]

The first order of business was to disband the production team, with the exception of Paul Schreibman, who stayed on as legal counsel. Kurkjian refused to entrust the operation to anyone, regardless of their résumé or capacity to perform. He became the sole hands-on chief of the entire production and was determined to oversee every minuscule detail if necessary. On that basis he began to assemble his new production team, cast, and crew.[100]

Considerably downgraded from its MGM facility, High Investments, Inc., moved its operations to an office in a Van Nuys radio and television studio where the weekly *Armenian Teletime Hour* was taped. To control expenditures for his first major movie production, a plan was devised for an April to May 1981 shooting schedule, a June to July editing session, and a post-August distribution. There was the absolute need for celerity to complete the film before the rights deadline. Once the movie was shown to an audience, the rights to *Musa Dagh* would be forever sealed in his name. Recognizing his monetary fix, Kurkjian intended to shoot the exterior scenes in the Santa Monica Mountains just a few miles from his home and to use unemployed actors. Rather than go through a Hollywood-casting agency, he hoped to draw on the Armenian population of Los Angeles,[101] believing that the expense of extras could be minimized since Armenians would be willing to work for minimum wage on their Armenian treasure. He had already investigated the possibility of a television mini-series similar to *Roots* and *Shogun,* but he was told the time for *Musa Dagh* had passed and something more current was needed.

Nevertheless, Kurkjian was convinced that even a low-budget *Musa Dagh* could be profitable. He based his projection on a demographic analysis of potential ticket buyers: 35 million—Greeks, Yugoslavs, Rumanians, Bulgarians, Syrians, Lebanese, Arabs, Jews, and Armenians in the Americas alone. All of them had a history of suffering at the hands of the Turks. He was also determined to erase the old stereotype about starving Armenians and the more recent conception of Armenians targeting Turkish diplomats. He envisioned his production as an opportunity to give the younger generation of aspiring Armenian Americans jobs in his films and possible stardom. Initially, he planned on a two-to three-hour movie that would keep to the essential theme Werfel had established in his masterpiece, but within the confines of a limited budget.[102]

Kurkjian was pleased that a low-budget "sleeper" like *Midnight Express* ('78), about the incarceration of an American hashish smuggler in a Turkish prison, had proved to be a box office bonanza for Columbia Pictures. Turkish protests against the movie were to no avail. He suspected that pro-Turkish organizations in the United States and the Turkish Embassy in Washington had access to the Armenian print media and Hollywood journals and were aware of his *Musa Dagh* plans.

At first, Kurkjian did not expect any trouble from the Turks. After all, the 1930s were history. But Kurkjian's suspicions had been aroused soon after purchasing the rights to *Musa Dagh* from MGM in 1970. Two agents from New York City who refused to identify themselves had paid him a visit. Kurkjian called them Mr. X and Mr. Y. They were representing a client who also wished to remain anonymous and offered to buy him out at a handsome profit. The mysterious identity of the client caused Kurkjian to think that the source was Turkish. He rejected the offer. A month later, the same agents proposed to pay all of Kurkjian's *Musa Dagh* expenditures plus a bonus of $500,000 in the form of a certified check. Kurkjian demanded to know the name of their client. Messrs. X and Y told Kurkjian they were not at liberty to divulge the identity of their patron. Kurkjian concluded that the mysterious benefactor had to be a Turk, probably a New Yorker, who was determined to prevent Franz Werfel's *The Forty Days of Musa Dagh* from ever reaching the silver screen. Even when the agents emphasized the sincerity of the offer and the authenticity of the check, Kurkjian remained steadfast.[103]

THE PRELIMINARIES

Proceeding to assemble his team, Kurkjian hired a production manager at $1200 a week for fourteen weeks, with the understanding that Kurkjian was to be kept informed as to the daily proceedings and that all decisions would rest with him.[104] The production crew they put together was an ethnic mix of Armenians, Hispanics, Jews, and Anglo-Americans, hired because of their availability and willingness to accept minimal salaries.

For a film once linked to the names of such outstanding producers as Thalberg and Berman and such renowned directors as Kazan, Lean, and Mamoulian, the selection of *Musa Dagh*'s director was vital to establish credibility in the film community and with a potential audience. Kurkjian said that David Lean would have been his first choice,[105] but the stark reality of an inadequate treasury and the approaching expiration date of the rights made contacting Lean prohibitive.[106] There is no question that Lean could have shaped Werfel's novel into a monumental screen achievement, but only with an unrestricted budget worthy of his talents.

The media publicity about *Musa Dagh* soon caught the attention of director Richard Sarafian's wife. On her initiative, a meeting was arranged between her husband and Kurkjian. Sarafian had established himself in television and movies as one of the "new wave" in the 1960s and 1970s. Between 1969 and 1973, Sarafian had directed six films that demonstrated that he was capable of good work in many genres, but more impressive was the caliber of the actors he directed.[107] His films were generally well received and adequate for many television screenings. In addition to his directorial duties, Sarafian offered to drum up financial support for *Musa Dagh*. A disagreement over compensation terminated the matter.[108] After Kurkjian's *Musa Dagh* was premiered in April 1982, Sarafian told Krikor Satamian, a talk show panel moderator, that he would have gladly directed the movie for nothing.[109]

The selection of Sarky Mouradian, a long-time acquaintance of Kurkjian, as the director of *The Forty Days of Musa Dagh,* predicted that it was not to be a major production. Mouradian, a native of Beirut, Lebanon, and a graduate of the National School of Music there, had made his theatrical debut as a song composer. After immigrating to the United States in 1958, he attended the New England Arts Theater in Boston. He moved to California in 1961 to attend the Academy of Arts, Television and Motion Pictures in Beverly Hills, where he studied scriptwriting, motion picture sound and editing, set construction, cinematography, and directing. While in school, with the support of Armenian individuals who provided $50,000, he made his first film, *Debt of Blood*, with Vic Tayback. The screenplay was based on a nationalistic theme by the noted Armenian writer, Avedis Aharonian. Unable to find a distributor, he dubbed it in Armenian and made money by renting theaters and advertising to Armenian audiences. The movie eventually played in the Middle East, which proved to be its biggest market.[110]

In the meantime, Mouradian had made contacts in the film colony and widened his experience as a boom and sound man, sound and music editor, camera operator, and gaffer (setting up electrical equipment). His early movie experience was primarily in the production of "skin flicks." When the films evolved into pornography, he got out. But he learned much from the experience: how to work on a tight budget and how to work with amateurs and untalented people. His first movie credit as a director of an American film was *The Agency* ('65) which had a run in Europe. He also made a movie with Jack Palance and worked on Peter Bogdanovich's American Film Institute documentary about John Ford. Active in the St. James Armenian Apostolic Church in Los Angeles, he organized a theatrical group while serving as an Armenian language instructor and became acquainted with John Kurkjian, chairman of the Parish Council.[111]

In 1967 Mouradian launched the first Armenian television program in Los Angeles, which was fast becoming the largest metropolitan Armenian community outside the Soviet Union. In 1979 he founded the *Armenian Teletime Hour* in Los Angeles with outlets in Fresno and San Francisco. By 1992 Mouradian owned a small television studio and was offering four shows every weekend for Armenian audiences and one show for the Italian community.[112] It was here that Kurkjian set up his new office after the MGM debacle.

Mouradian's biggest hit was another Armenian film, *Tears of Happiness* ('74), produced by Kurkjian. It made money in the Middle East, particularly in Beirut, thanks to subtitles in English, Arabic, and French, even though they blocked out much of the picture. Other Armenian films included: *Sons of Sassoun* and *Promise of Love*, produced by Los Angeles jewelers, the Bouchakian Brothers.[113]

On the basis of his résumé, Kurkjian offered Mouradian the *Musa Dagh* director's chair. The deciding factor was that Mouradian's salary fit Kurkjian's pocketbook. Mouradian's total income as director was not to exceed $25,000.[114] The truth of the matter is that Sarky Mouradian was John Kurkjian's last and only resort. He was hired as an independent contractor and production supervisor, not as a partner or co-venturer. Mouradian warned Kurkjian that everybody who knew *The Forty Days of Musa Dagh,* especially Armenians, had already made up their minds as to what kind of movie it should be. No matter who the director and cast were, there would be criticism. As an additional incentive, Kurkjian signed Mouradian as associate editor. Mouradian gave himself an alias, "Sergio Murad," a tongue-in-cheek loose translation of his name from the Armenian to Italian and Arabic. His rationale for the pseudonym was to avoid negative criticism from those who might charge him with "braggadocio."

Sarky Mouradian and "Sergio Murad" earned about $34,000 on paper for their joint endeavors. Mouradian says he was never paid for his directorial stint, nor did he press for it or expect it. He did get paid for post-production editing. Mouradian contends he got involved in *Musa Dagh* for the opportunity and the honor to direct Werfel's Armenian treasure and not for the money. Like Kurkjian, he believed that the rights would belong forever to an Armenian once the movie was made, thus negating future hassles with the Turkish government and the State Department.[115]

Mouradian's task in developing and producing a film on Kurkjian's restrictive budget was monumental. His assignments entailed consolidating the available scripts with a screenwriter into a single full-length shooting screenplay, preparing a budget to determine cost of production, surveying and researching locations, interviewing actors, specifying all requirements for principal photography, keeping within the budget, and getting the film ready for distribution. Acceding to

Mouradian's request to lighten his load, Kurkjian hired two assistant directors.[116]

Compounding Kurkjian's mounting problems and anxiety to get the production under way was the decision about a working screenplay. Werfel's novel had been treated and mistreated by more than a dozen screenwriters over forty-five years. In his original deal with MGM, Kurkjian's rights had included ownership of all the efforts of every screenwriter who had taken on *Musa Dagh*. Screenwriters such as Carey Wilson, Neil Paterson, and Ronald Harwood had produced excellent shooting scripts. Their transpositions to the screen, although desirable, would have skyrocketed the production into millions of dollars over Kurkjian's budget. Well aware of his monetary situation, Kurkjian chose to start from scratch with another new script. In 1978, Clarke Reynolds of the High Investments production staff had produced a 220-page screenplay. That same year, due to the prohibitive cost of producing Reynolds' version, Kurkjian tried again with Larry Hilbrand.[117] After Kurkjian went over all the scripts and made his recommendations, Mouradian put together a composite adaptation in 1981.[118]

According to Mouradian, the production difficulties he encountered would have made a movie on how not to make a movie:

> *I've been in the movie business twenty-five years but this was a nightmare. I have never had problems like* Musa Dagh: *casting, mismanagement, work stoppages, money problems and on and on.*
>
> *One morning I went to work on location in the mountains. I had cast and crew ready for a shoot and before I could say "action" everything was called off due to money problems. On another occasion the union prevented me from going overtime for a one hour shot. It cost Kurkjian an extra day's pay. Then*

there was the situation where we already had rented several horses to pull a cannon when the union wranglers refused to work unless they had a contract. We had no choice but to push the cannon by hand because they took the horses away. I always had to go up to the set in the Santa Monica Mountains with a Teamsters' driver because the union rules prohibited me and others from driving to the set. I was so incensed with the union hassles that I urged Kurkjian to fire everybody including me, shut down the production, wait about a week, and then rehire who you want. He was compelled to hire more teamsters than we needed. Too much money was wasted on nonsense stuff because of the unions.[119]

Due to the pressures exerted by the unions and the rights troubles with the Werfel estate, Mouradian suggested that Kurkjian forget about Werfel's novel and base the movie on the actual incident. He suggested calling it, *The Battle of Musa Dagh* or *The Last Days of Musa Dagh*, making it an Armenian film and dubbing it in English, or making a documentary of the incident. Kurkjian rejected the idea. When Kurkjian's money problems began to mount, Mouradian told him to file for bankruptcy. To Mouradian, Kurkjian's greatest mistake was failing to hire the right people, and his greatest weakness was his meager treasury. The production was rushed, the crew was uncaring, and the lack of prominent American actors in the leading roles undermined the credibility of the film. Before any film footage was shot, Mouradian learned about inquiries to buy Kurkjian out. He was also convinced, like Kurkjian, that the interested parties were Turkish agents.[120]

On Mouradian's recommendation, Kurkjian hired many members of Mouradian's "stock company" who had worked with him on his

Armenian films: Cinematographer Gregory Sandor; music arranger/ conductor Jaime Mendoza-Nava; and actors Manuel Kichian, Maurice Sherbanee, Buck Kartalian, Victor Izay, Mark Tombazian, and Alex Hakobian. Also on Mouradian's advice, Kurkjian contracted Alex Hakobian to write a new screenplay.[121] In spite of the advantage of having access to all the outlines, treatments, adaptations, and scripts of his predecessors, Hakobian's screenplay was an inferior adaptation of Werfel's novel.[122] Mouradian was pleased to have Sandor as *Musa Dagh*'s cinematographer and spoke highly of Mendoza-Nava[123] who had to use "canned" and pre-recorded music due to budgetary restrictions. To compound his difficulties Mouradian found production management:

To be mediocre, weak, poorly organized, working with an inept budget. You need someone who is aggressive, demanding, someone who has ice water in his veins. Too many things to failed, budget breakdowns didn't work: Some days you'd expect to see 150 extras on the set and there would be forty. People were hired in the make-up and costume departments who were not needed.[124]

When money problems began to occur, many on the set suspected that the production would collapse and the movie would never be finished. As a result they lost their drive and everything became mechanical. It seemed like they did not care anymore. Involved in every movie production is an assistant director whose job is to keep the set quiet, tell extras what to do, and get everything ready for shooting. Mouradian says only assistant director Jack DeWolf was supportive.[125]

To avoid labor union problems, the effort to recruit non-union extras within the Los Angeles Armenian community was canceled. In March 1981, High Investments was compelled to strike an agreement with Kenney/Travis & Associates as the casting agency for a fee of

$10,000. The agency was to arrange interviews with performers and negotiate their compensation with the understanding that Kurkjian had final written approval.[126] To Mouradian:

> *Contracts were poorly drawn. Everyone in the movie business knows that in the preparation of a production board, it is absolutely necessary to ascertain how many days each actor is needed and, if overtime is necessary, the pay for each additional day must be specified. The casting agency and the production manager were derelict in this respect. When an actor/actress has completed his/her contractual assignment, it is the casting director's job to make sure he/she leaves the set. One of the cast members got an extra week's pay for working one day beyond the contract. It is the production manager's responsibility to coordinate all aspects of the production and always keep on top of things. Many of the people involved in Kurkjian's* Musa Dagh *realized he was a novice and milked him, not knowing where their next job would come from.*[127]

In April 1981, *Variety* alerted the movie community that John Kurkjian and the Kenney/Travis Agency were casting parts for the long-awaited movie of Franz Werfel's *The Forty Days of Musa Dagh.* The various roles to be cast were mentioned, with a brief description of each of the major characters. Particular emphasis in the article was placed on the hero of the novel, Gabriel Bagradian, calling for a "good-looking actor evincing European charm" and stressing the preference for a "star."[128]

Mouradian recalled that Kurkjian was very emotional when casting the movie. He was overly concerned about a person's character and reputation, while Mouradian was only concerned with the individual's ability to do the job. He cared less about their conduct off the set. In the final analysis Kurkjian had to settle mostly for unknowns with limited acting experience in the leading roles. As a result, no recognized actor carried the movie.[129]

For the male lead of Gabriel Bagradian, Kurkjian contacted Mike Connors (an Armenian American actor whose birth name was Krikor Ohanian) of television's successful *Tightrope* and *Mannix* series, but the deal fell through. David Hedison (Hedetsian), another Armenian American actor, also rejected the offer. Hank Moonjean recalled that Connors had called him inquiring about Kurkjian. Knowing that Kurkjian had no standing in the movie colony, Moonjean suggested that Connors stay clear of the deal.[130] Kurkjian eventually signed a British-Indian actor, Kabir Bedi, who was unfamiliar to the local movie colony and American moviegoers. His celebrity was confined to the movie-going public in Europe and India. In hiring Bedi, Kurkjian hoped for a fringe benefit. It is common knowledge that Indian audiences whose hunger for American movies are voracious would flock to see one of their own in an American film. Although Bedi looked "Armenian" and physically was right for the part of Gabriel,[131] he was an unknown, lacking box office appeal. Bedi's American film credits within the year would consist of a third-string villainous role in a James Bond movie, *Octopussy* ('83).

Mouradian remembered Bedi as a professional actor who was friendly, conscientious, always on time, knew his lines, listened, and took direction.[132] Bedi's distinction was to command the highest individual salary among cast, crew, and production team. The job lasted about six weeks for Bedi and earned him $60,000. Kurkjian had no regrets.[133]

Playing opposite Bedi as Juliette, Bagradian's French wife, was Ronnie Carol, an aspiring television actress. She counted on her participation in *Musa Dagh* for career advancement. Mouradian felt that, for the money, they should have had a more experienced actress. Ed Vasgersian, who played the sympathetic Turk, Jamal, said that Carol gave the part her best, with very little guidance from director Mouradian, who simply failed to bring out the best in the actors:

> *He never took enough time with any actor but rather was more concerned that the dialogue and framing were right on film and made no attempt to get the cast to understand what the scenes were all about. He cared less about the interpretation of the subject matter. He just wasn't the right man for the job.*[134]

The best Kurkjian could do for a minimal semblance of veteran players was to contract a handful of experienced character actors. Mouradian and Kurkjian found it a joy to work with Peter Haskell, David Opatashu, Michael Constantine, John Hoyt, Guy Stockwell, and Buck Kartalian.[135] None of them were box office draws. They and the leading man were the only ones who brought some credibility to the picture. They listened, respected their assignments and the director, came in when needed, and did not complain or put anyone down. They made it easy for the director because they were professionals. Mouradian remembered Kartalian as the best Armenian on the set; he so wanted *Musa Dagh* to succeed that, when he had additional money coming to him and got it, he returned it, knowing Kurkjian's money problems.[136]

One of the most powerful characters in Werfel's novel is the parish priest of YoghunOluk, Ter Haigasun, an epic personality. On film he should have had a scene-stealing role. Instead, the part was relegated to a virtual walk-on with a few lines of dialogue lacking any dramatic effect. Playing Ter Haigasun was Cano Graham, who had the appropriate physical presence except for his exaggerated long, thick, gray hair and flowing beard. When he spoke, the words came out like a cartoon of Gabby Hayes[137] gone spiritual. Mouradian rated him as the worst actor in the production, a nice man but totally miscast.[138]

Ever the nationalist, Kurkjian went out of his way to hire many aspiring Armenian American actors who yearned for a break in Hollywood.[139] Of all the players, Kurkjian was most incensed by one of the cast members who had a three-day stint. The part paid $5000. Upon completion of the role, Kurkjian and Mouradian noticed he was still on the set. Since his services were no longer required, they questioned his presence. His defense was that, being idle he enjoyed watching the shooting and getting a free meal. Kurkjian was sympathetic and thereafter did not take exception to his presence on the lot. About a month later, Kurkjian received a bill from the Screen Actors Guild. Kurkjian was livid. After all, the job was done and paid for. The union challenged Kurkjian on the grounds that the actor's presence on the set required payment, no matter that his part in the film had been completed or that his unnecessary presence had been questioned. Kurkjian was convinced that it was a ploy to take advantage of his ignorance and gullibility. Kurkjian reluctantly paid the actor and the guild.[140] Mouradian corroborated the episode and the union hassles.[141]

Ed Vasgersian's experience illustrates the general atmosphere surrounding *Musa Dagh*:

Familiar with the book and its controversial nature, Vasgersian was elated to learn about Kurkjian's venture in the trade papers. After a phone call to Kurkjian at his home in Thousand Oaks, he sent him a picture and a résumé. Shortly thereafter, he received a script and a $300/day offer. Though he was content that the money earned would at least pay his expenses, he was more than thrilled to have a part in Werfel's Armenian classic. He had been selected to play the part of

Jamal, a sympathetic Turk. It was a role created especially for the movie to placate potential anti-*Musa Dagh* Turkish concerns and interests. Vasgersian was perplexed that his role had been awarded solely on the basis of a picture, a résumé, and a couple of phone calls. There were no one-on-one interviews or even an audition. He began to wonder about Kurkjian's movie expertise and about the production itself. After signing a contract, he never received a copy. Vasgersian says he was paid $1500, which barely took care of his expenses.[142]

While some of the Armenians on the set knew the book and discussed it, no copies were available, nor was there an orientation or attempt to make everyone aware of the significance of Werfel's novel and the making of the movie. People just went through the motions, knew their places (marks), spoke their lines, and moved out. Vasgersian got the impression that it may have been the first film for many of them. In retrospect, Vasgersian opined that some of the people involved should have been fired because of their professional shortcomings or not hired in the first place. While he found Kurkjian congenial, he is convinced that his boss knew less about the movie business than he should have. He did not seem to appreciate the fact that the scarcity of capital was making this a mediocre operation. On the other hand, he complimented Kurkjian for his hospitality. At all times, the company was treated to first-class meals and even to wine on occasion. The food was much better than usually offered on other productions. The Kurkjians spent $65,000 for catering services. Vasgersian recalls that some members of the cast had mentioned that Kurkjian had hosted a dinner at a Hollywood restaurant for the entire company to launch the *Musa Dagh* production, but there was no wrap-up celebration after the film was "in the can." Kurkjian's presence was always felt on the set. He never intervened or interfered, but he would ask questions to appear knowledgeable and involved. When Vasgersian arrived on location in the Santa Monica Mountains, half the movie had already been shot. His stint lasted about eight working days spread over a two-week period. To this day, Vasgersian regrets his part in the movie.[143]

Before the production got under way, Kurkjian had designated himself as the movie's technical advisor based on his visits with Musa Daghians in Anjar, Lebanon, and at Musa Ler in Soviet Armenia, where he had met some of the Musa Dagh survivors and their progeny. Those brief meetings provided him with additional information about the siege and deliverance at Musa Dagh. He had taken copious notes regarding the living conditions during the siege (clothing, food, shelter, medical care, government, etc.). On the movie set, he even arranged for the presence of a Musa Dagh survivor's descendant to act as an advisor.[144]

While the production team and cast were being finalized, Kurkjian, Mouradian, and the production manager scouted the Los Angeles area for location sites and made the necessary arrangements to secure them for specific shooting dates. Not only were studio sound stages not available or affordable, to compound his problems, Kurkjian simply lacked the funds to build sets in harmony with the novel. A little more than $36,000 was expended for a month's use of eight properties. In addition, securing legal permits for police, fire marshals, rangers, lifeguards, security guards, etc. cost $8000. The rental of a family home as a set for the Bagradian residence alone was $9300. These costs had to be met before the first reel of film was shot.

THE SHOOT

Forty-seven years after MGM purchased the rights to *The Forty Days of Musa Dagh*, and almost eleven years after the Kurkjians gained the rights to film Werfel's novel, the principal photography of

Kurkjian's production finally got under way. Shooting began on April 27, 1981, the week of Armenian Martyrs Day. The first scene was shot in a Los Angeles suburb at an American Legion hall representing the Constantinople Ottoman Turkish government headquarters. Thereafter the plan was to shoot around the lead, Kabir Bedi (Gabriel Bagradian). Since he was the most expensive person on the set, it was imperative to dispense with his services as soon as possible.[145]

From the first shooting day on, there was a feeling of insecurity on the set due to the constant rumors that Kurkjian had money problems. Nevertheless, everybody stuck it out because there were no other jobs and at least they could eat well. Until the "wrap" (final shooting) of the outdoor location scenes on June 9, Kurkjian's well-being was severely tested. He recalled:

> One day I arrived on the set to find the Teamsters Union representative wouldn't allow anyone to work. I was told that we needed sixteen drivers that day when all I needed and hired were two Teamster drivers. So I had to hire fourteen more drivers than I needed at $200 each per day plus feed them. We had to do it. We were caught in a "Catch-22" situation. The unions don't play these games with the big studios because they're always doing business with them.[146]

Wanting to do right for the Armenian community, Kurkjian made sure that, on shooting days, 60 percent to 80 percent of the extras were Armenians from the Los Angeles area, even though it had no monetary advantage for him. He still had to go through the Screen Actors Guild to get a waiver to pay them the minimum of $30 to $50 a day. They were fed, insured, and provided transportation. While they were on location, bus service was available to those who preferred not to drive their own vehicles. At a designated spot, cast and crew would be picked up by a Teamster-driven rental bus and returned after each day's shooting. On remote location days, the Teamster drivers would shuttle personnel to the set after the bus had driven them in.[147]

To save time and money and to maintain discipline, Kurkjian rented house trailers and tents while shooting in the mountains. Key members of the company remained on site until shooting there was completed. Five trailers were assigned to the leading players while the crew lived in the tents. The Kurkjians had a trailer as well. They believed their presence put the necessary pressure on cast and crew to be ready to work. Being of the "old school," he was disturbed by the conduct of the company during off-hours. There was a daily unwinding involving drinking, drugs, and sex. In time he discovered that what he considered to be questionable behavior was common in Hollywood. His constant worry was that someone would get sick or have an accident and adversely affect the schedule and his budget.[148]

Mouradian said that the activity Kurkjian found offensive is normal on movie sets, particularly on location:

> It happens because many of the crew, after a job is done, is on the set on call. So, when idle, they get together and party. If there had been a strong production manager and strong assistant directors, they not only could have stopped the partying but fired them. They have the right when the rules are broken.[149]

Vasgersian disputes Kurkjian and Mouradian. He claimed he never witnessed unruly conduct on the *Musa Dagh* set or heard about anything along those lines. "Kurkjian exaggerated because he did not understand the acting profession. Because people are friendly, warm, and extroverted does not imply that they are immoral."[150] As far as the Kurkjians were concerned, the shoot in the mountains was another unpleasant experience.

There were at least fifteen unusual accidents on the set. Kurkjian suspected that the victims simply took advantage of the production's workmen's compensation insurance coverage. Accident claims were a new experience for him, and one that he abhorred. To get the project completed, he knew he had no choice but to tolerate the claims and make good on them. It was another reason why he was present on the set. On another occasion, while they were on location in the mountains, the fire marshal stopped production because of a fire hazard in the area. The cast and crew still had to be paid; otherwise they would have quit. It was one more example of an unexpected expense to a depleting budget. Frayed nerves, ceaseless worry, sleepless nights, and real and unwarranted suspicions contributed to Kurkjian's failing health.[151]

Payday was every Friday at 3:00 P.M. By mid-June it was always cash. About halfway through shooting the picture, the payroll was not ready, resulting in a strike. Kurkjian had run out of money. He was desperate. He had to finish the picture on schedule or lose everything. Reluctantly he agreed to a short-term loan of $200,000 on a usurer's terms. He had no other recourse. Cast and crew were paid the next day and work resumed. As a side effect of this unfortunate episode, Kurkjian said he was compelled by the Screen Actors Guild to deposit $100,000 as a guarantee for the protection of the actors in case he went broke again. The money was gone within six weeks. Reminding the union's representative that the $100,000 was a loan to protect the cast, he demanded to know how the money disappeared, especially since the actors had already been paid. There never was an accounting or a satisfactory answer. Kurkjian was convinced that there was collusion among the parties concerned.[152] Reviewing his movie-making experience Kurkjian contended:

> *The great majority of the cast and crew had no knowledge*
> *of Werfel's novel and cared less about my dream movie. Only a*
> *few were professional, concerned, conscientious, and decent. The*
> *trials and tribulations in making a film do not concern movie*
> *audiences. Most moviegoers are only interested in the final product.*
> *Along with Hollywood gossip and the supermarket tabloid type*
> *of titillation, the movie-going public accepts the escapades of the*
> *film colony because they focus on the movie stars. And the movie*
> *people? Their philosophy is just to get the film "in the can." Don't*
> *get hung up on the details, and don't look back, "wrap it"!*[153]

Instead of twenty weeks of shooting, Mouradian says he had six. Most days there were only the director, the cinematographer and three members of the crew on the set. Production was rushed because of budgetary restrictions. Each day's schedule produced at least three to four takes of each scene that were printed and ready for viewing the next day. After the takes were screened, one print would be selected for Kurkjian's review and approval. Once the shoot was finished, editors Tony De Zarraga and "Sergio Murad" (Mouradian) got the film "in the can" within a month at Ryder Sound Services in Burbank, which also took care of the audio re-recording.[154]

Kurkjian claimed that *Musa Dagh* cost over $3 million exclusive of the money he personally borrowed. Reflecting on the money spent, he ruefully reminisced:

> *If I had not gone into the film business and kept to my*
> *shopping center development business and bought some of the*
> *properties I had considered at the time, I would have been a*

multi-millionaire today. I could have made thirty million if I
had stayed in business in this area alone.[155]

Kurkjian was unable to distribute the film in commercial theaters, but while sound re-recording and editing were in progress he formulated a plan to premiere the movie before Armenian audiences in California. High Investments placed publicity in the Armenian media; printed brochures, programs, posters, and mailers; rented theaters; and assumed travel expenses for the Kurkjians, who made personal appearances at all the premieres. With Kurkjian increasingly applying the necessary pressure, the edited film was ready August 15, 1981. Fulfilling the contractual agreement with Anna Mahler and her attorney, A. Kim Guggenheim, an invitation was sent to Guggenheim to see the film. Accompanied by an attorney friend, they viewed a two hour and twenty minute film. Guggenheim gave his approval and wished Kurkjian good luck in its distribution.[156] One more contentious chapter in the *Musa Dagh* ordeal had finally reached closure.

WORLD PREMIERE (The author was present)

In a press release for the world premiere, particularly for the Armenian newspapers, Kurkjian announced that the $5 million movie was ready. He claimed:

> *It will blast like an atomic bomb ... it will be a thousand*
> *times stronger than the assassinations of Turkish diplomats*
> *in explaining to the world the suffering of the Armenian*
> *population at the hands of the Turks during World War I.*[157]

To their credit, the Kurkjians put on a respectable world premiere of *The 40 Days of Musa Dagh* (for greater visual impact, the numeral

"40" replaced the original "Forty" of the novel's title). Invitations were sent to state and local dignitaries, representatives of the Armenian media and cultural organizations, churches, and *Musa Dagh* devotees. The Academy of Motion Picture Arts and Sciences Theater in Beverly Hills was booked for Friday evening, April 30, 1982, to coincide with the anniversary of the 1915 Armenian Genocide.[158]

The theater lobby was adorned with large color stills of scenes from the movie, and preparations were being made for an Armenian "mezzeh" (buffet) following the screening. Black tie optional, tickets at $75 each, the lobby was thronged with "first nighters," mostly from the Los Angeles Armenian community.[159] The fashions ranged from commonplace to glitter. It was an auspicious event, carrying an air of electricity as the premiere's patrons took their seats in the auditorium. One could sense immense nervous anticipation, as the most talked-about novel and movie in the history of the Armenian Diaspora was about to be unveiled after almost a fifty-year wait. It was a nail-biter for the Kurkjians, the film's participants, the investors, the novel's patrons, and the Armenian audience.

The program preceding the screening was delayed for a half hour until 9:00 P.M. due to latecomers. The master of ceremonies, George Boyajian, introduced the principals of the movie's production team and cast along with the Republican gubernatorial nominee, Attorney General George Deukmejian and his wife, and two representatives from Soviet Armenia. The introduction of John Kurkjian prompted a standing ovation. He welcomed the audience and expressed his appreciation for the fulfillment of his dream. He said the film would carry a message the world over, intimating that the Armenians were going to have their "day in court" via the silver screen.

About 9:25 P.M., the lights dimmed and a hush fell over the audience, followed by a long, loud, receptive applause as the title *The 40 Days of*

Musa Dagh appeared on the screen. The credits were superimposed over a Technicolor scene depicting a death march as Turkish soldiers flayed away at helpless Armenians. There was the immediate perception of the scene that something was not right, with a handful of victims (extras) scattered yards apart, against a sound track stinging the ears with the incessant tattoos of cracking whips. A map of historic Armenia was introduced with an off-screen narrator highlighting Armenia as the first nation to convert to Christianity. The movie's opening scene focused on the Ottoman Turkish government headquarters in Constantinople and a discussion of the Armenians' plight in 1915.

The scene involved the historic characters Talaat (Michael Constantine), Enver (David Mauro), the German missionary and tenacious champion of the Armenians, Johannes Lepsius (Gilbert Green), and the American Ambassador Henry Morgenthau, Sr. (David Opatashu), whose official reports had provoked the United States government and the American press to protest the Turkish treatment of its Armenian subjects. The scene was inadequate, except for veteran actor Opatashu. Neither the dialogue nor the acting convincingly conveyed the subtle craftiness of the two architects of the Armenian Genocide.

Kabir Bedi (Gabriel Bagradian) looked "Armenian" and was adequate. Ronnie Carol (Juliette) tried but was unconvincing. Maurice Sherbanee's (Turkish civil governor) over-emoting exemplified "scenery chewing" at its worst. For the most part, the other speaking roles came across in a pedestrian manner, actors going through their paces and mouthing words, permissible for a rehearsal, but not the final product. Extras scattered across a set with a couple of tents on camera did not equate the stalwart community of 4000 defenders of Werfel's novel or of the actual event.

Not a single scene or line of dialogue made an impression. For those familiar with the novel's characters, scenes, and theme, too much had been omitted or distorted. If there was a suggestion of heartfelt love between Gabriel and his wife Juliette and with Karoon (Iskuhi), it was unconvincing. Overall the acting ranged from mediocre to worse. Action scenes lacked authenticity and high drama. The significance of the survivor of the Zeitoun massacre and the renegade of Musa Dagh, Sarkis Kilikian, was lost. A miniature "warship" represented the French naval squadron of six armored cruisers. A couple of lifeboats on a beach were supposedly ready to evacuate over 4000 survivors. According to Kurkjian, nearly seven hundred people were involved in the making of *Musa Dagh*. Mouradian says two hundred. The book's "cast of thousands" literally or figuratively was simply not there. To anyone keeping a running count on discrepancies between book and film, it was disturbing.

Equally disconcerting were the film's inept special effects, which critically weakened the visuals and distracted from the momentous nature of the story. One of the most glaring violations in credibility was in the movie's climax. After suffering for forty days, the will of the defenders had been tested. Their struggle to survive was rewarded with the arrival of the French (Allied) naval fleet. On film, the warships were represented by the sound of a distant explosion and the swoosh of a screaming shell marking the appearance of a miniature "warship" bobbing on what was supposed to be a shimmering sea. It was evidence of the film's inadequate production budget.

Many names from the novel were changed: Iskuhi, whose love for Gabriel makes her a pivotal female role in the book, became Karoon; apparently pronouncing "Iss-koo-he" was too challenging. The Greek American Gonzague Maris became Maris Durand, a Frenchman. New roles were created and expanded, as in the case of the sympathetic Turk Jamal and the civil governor who becomes the single composite of collective Turkish villainy.

There were no subtleties, no nuances, no deft directorial touches, and no creativity in the 140-minute film. On Kurkjian's insistence, adjustments had been made to heighten the ethnic aspects of the film. It seemed that the film was shot from its inception for Armenian audiences. Kurkjian's rationale was to liven up a "heavy story." No matter, the significance and symbolism and the high drama of *The Forty Days of Musa Dagh* were not there

When "The End" came, there was no sustained applause, no cheering, no standing ovations, no encores for Kurkjian, Mouradian, cast or crew. There was only a crashing silence. People left the theatre numbed, as if departing from a funeral. In the vernacular of the movie business, it was a "bomb."

As he was held partially responsible for the film's failure, Sarky Mouradian's reputation as a film director suffered. Nevertheless, he does not regret the experience:

> *It's history and I'm in it. It's in the book and I was the director. I'm happy I was involved in it no matter what people say. As a matter of fact I would like to do it again with the proper budget, cast, and crew. In respect for Werfel and the novel, a six-hour mini-series similar to Roots would be preferable. It would reach a wider audience on a major television network and it's free.* [160]

The participation of all those involved in the star-crossed *Musa Dagh* went unnoticed by the studios and the television networks.

The film was another setback for Armenians in the long, arduous struggle to keep alive the memory of the twentieth-century's first genocide. Furthermore, the film did nothing to remind the world of the cruelty of the Turkish Ottoman government and the injustice of their successors who remain in a state of denial.

The only saving grace, now that the film had been screened, was that the permanent rights to Franz Werfel's *The Forty Days of Musa Dagh*, under copyright laws, belonged to an Armenian. Never again would there be hassles with Turkey, the State Department, MGM, or the Werfel estate; no more dealings with Hollywood nabobs and their satraps; no more promises made and broken; no more obstructions by unions and their rank and file. The main thing that mattered now was that an Armenian was the sole possessor of the Armenian treasure. Someday the movie could be made again. Hopefully next time it will be produced on the grand scale envisioned by Irving Thalberg and Pandro Berman.

The buffet and champagne reception that followed the world premiere was polite and subdued. The private comment by the editor of one of the local Armenian newspapers was terse and embellished with an unequivocal expletive. The fifty years of Werfel's *Musa Dagh*'s trials and tribulations had come to this—an Armenian treasure had been violated.

POSTSCRIPT

Kurkjian was deeply disappointed. His efforts for the Armenian cause had become a shattered dream. He should not have been surprised by the unenthusiastic audience reaction and the damaging word-of-mouth gossip that followed in the Armenian community and press. George Maksian, a syndicated television and radio columnist in New York, commented: "We waited forty years for *The Forty Days of Musa Dagh*. It should have been done right. Kurkjian has a wonderful heart, but he should have gone to an experienced director."[161] Kurkjian knew it would be very difficult to sell the movie to an American distributor. The immediate mission was to salvage as much of his expenditures as possible.

In the thirty months that followed the Beverly Hills premiere, Kurkjian made the necessary arrangements and personally introduced the movie in the prominent Armenian communities in the United States and Canada. There were five screenings in the Los Angeles area (the Armenian American heartland of Montebello, Glendale, Van Nuys, Pasadena, and Hollywood), two each in Fresno, San Francisco,[162] Detroit, Chicago, Philadelphia, New York City, and Montreal. There was one screening each in Boston, Jersey City, Washington, D.C., Miami, Houston, and Toronto. Those "premiere" screenings grossed about $225,000.[163] For the Kurkjians, there was little comfort in the fact that some Armenians gave him credit for trying. The general reaction was a sad depression throughout the American and Canadian Armenian communities.

Racing against time and the grapevine, his only recourse now was to tap the overseas market before the adverse publicity killed off his chances. An American distributor considered showing *Musa Dagh* in Europe, but because of the ethnic nature of the film and its anti-Turkish theme, he backed off. Kurkjian believed that the Turkish government applied pressure throughout the world to prevent its screening. He thought that *Musa Dagh* had been screened in Greece, India, the Middle East, and Soviet Armenia. He was never informed as to where exactly the movie was shown or how often or how much was collected at the box office. The expected foreign market gross just did not materialize.[164] Distributing American movies overseas requires additional expenses. For non-English-speaking audiences, the movie must either be dubbed or carry subtitles. Foreign taxes are much higher than in the United States. At least 50 percent of the net has to remain in the host country, and then it will take anywhere from six to twelve months for the producer to realize the remaining 50 percent. An American filmmaker must count on at least 60 percent of his gross income from American audiences. Turning a deaf ear to Mouradian's protests, Kurkjian cut the original movie version from two hours and twenty minutes to an hour and a half to make it profitable as a videocassette. [165]

In early 1987, Kurkjian received a phone call from an interested party expressing willingness to show the movie on television. The date was set for Armenian Martyrs Day, April 24. Kurkjian was elated to be offered $200,000 to show it on nationwide television for one night. He was cognizant of the fact, that once you televise a film, viewers will tape it on their VCRs and the market value will depreciate considerably, if not evaporate completely. But he needed the money. His answer was an immediate affirmative.

About a week later, he received a telegram informing him that the deal had fallen through. He was thoroughly upset and his reaction was swift. Pursuing the matter, Kurkjian discovered that an unidentified person in the State Department had requested the cancellation of the movie on network television. The reason offered was that *Musa Dagh* would be harmful to the national defense. Kurkjian took exception to the State Department's intervention. He cited the clout of the Jewish lobbies and the many Holocaust movies and television programs. He called the Armenian Assembly, a nonprofit American organization espousing Armenian concerns and interests, in Washington. The Assembly spokesman asked Kurkjian to find out the name of the State Department agent who had applied the pressure. Following through, Kurkjian was rebuffed. The party he was dealing with to televise *Musa Dagh* informed him that it was impossible to secure the name of the State Department spokesman who had intervened. [166] Kurkjian was out $200,000.

Eventually *The Forty Days of Musa Dagh* was made available on VHS cassettes. The edited ninety-minute version failed to elicit any genuine public response. In November 1987, *Variety* reviewed the *Musa Dagh* video cassette: "… a dreary little film that does no justice to its weighty subject … low grade pic … hokey dialogue … too simplistic and one-dimensional … it's simply cheesy."[167]

During an interview with the author in 1988, Kurkjian shrugged his shoulders in a gesture that seemed to indicate the unloading of a massive weight. He took comfort in the thought, "Thanks be to God. I don't owe anyone, anything, anymore."[168]

Kurkjian retained legal ownership of the original 35 mm. 140 minute film and the edited 35 mm. ninety-minute version, plus the trailers, posters, lobby cards, fliers, and numerous screenplays. At home were two copies of the original 35 mm. long version and one copy of the 35 mm. edited version and trailers. They were the souvenirs of John Kurkjian's dream movie.

In pursuit of a dream John Kurkjian was run through a gauntlet that began with illusions of movie grandeur, only to suffer a punishing baptism in the real world of Hollywood. His inexperience in dealing with the powerful studio bosses and the labor unions set him up as a novitiate ripe for the fleecing. He found himself and his *Musa Dagh* film production caught in a bind. If Kurkjian had not made the movie in the prescribed time, the rights to Werfel's *The Forty Days of Musa Dagh* would have reverted to Anna Mahler. But he was so determined in his intent to make Werfel's novel into a film that he lost sight of the fact that there were several accounts of the Musa Dagh incident. He could have relied on those primary sources, credited their authors, and saved himself a considerable sum of money along with the chronic haggling with the Werfel estate. But in fairness to Kurkjian, in doing so he would have sacrificed the unique nature of Werfel's characters and an incomparable story line. High Investments, Inc., a small family private enterprise, was just too poorly equipped financially to create a major motion picture. Nevertheless, where others feared to tread, it is to the credit of John and Mary Kurkjian that they made a valiant effort to bring *The Forty Days of Musa Dagh* to the silver screen. Once John Kurkjian had made up his mind to produce the film, he pursued his passionate obsession to the final cut.

NOTES – BOOK VI
THE SEDUCTION OF THE SILVER SCREEN

Chapter 21
THE FORTY "YEARS" OF *MUSA DAGH*

1. *MGM Archives, Musa Dagh File*, Exhibit "A," Chronology of *Musa Dagh* Copyright History, 9/3/70.

2. Ibid., Office Memo, 7/21/69.

3. The foreign copyright of *The Forty Days of Musa Dagh* in Austria and Germany was due to expire seventy years after the last day of the year in which Franz Werfel died, to wit, December 31, 2015. In all Berne (Switzerland) member countries, the international copyright lapsed December 31, 1995, fifty years from the year of Werfel's death. Currently S. Fischer Verlag, Frankfurt am Main, Germany, retains the rights to Werfel's *The Forty Days of Musa Dagh* and Alma Mahler Werfel's *And the Bridge is Love.*

4. *MGM Archives, Musa Dagh File*, Exhibit "A," Chronology of *Musa Dagh* Copyright History, Letter: Felix Guggenheim, Esq., to Edith Tolkin, MGM Legal Department, 2/10/70.

5. Ibid., Memo: Saul Rittenberg to Edith Tolkin, 2/13/70.

6. Correspondence: George Mason to the author, Tracy Investment Co., Las Vegas, Nev., 12/8/70.

7. Among Frankenheimer's credits were *The Manchurian Candidate* ('62), *Birdman of Alcatraz* ('62), *Seven Days in May* ('64).

8. *MGM Archives, Musa Dagh File*, Memo from Frank Davis, 8/29/70.

9. Interview of John Kurkjian by the author, Thousand Oaks, Calif., 1/12-13/81.

10. Brochure, *Folk Dance Ensemble of Soviet Armenia*, sponsored by John Kurkjian and Harry Diramarian, San Francisco performance, 7/5/74.

11. Kurkjian interview, Thousand Oaks, Calif., 1/12-13/81.

12. Ibid., Letter: Frank Davis to Frank Rosenfelt, 8/18/70.

13. *MGM Archives, Musa Dagh File*, Chronology of *Musa Dagh* Copyright, Legal Department, received by Karla Davidson, 5/6/75.

14. Ibid., Letter: Edith Tolkin, MGM Legal Department, to Gary Cooper, Esq., representing John Kurkjian, 9/9/70.

15. Interview of Samuel Marx, MGM story editor, by the author, MGM Studio, Culver City, Calif., 1/28/81.

16. *MGM Archives, Musa Dagh File*, Letter: Rudi Monta, to Robert Weitman, 8/13/62.

17. Kurkjian interview, 1/12-13/81.

18. Ibid.

19. During the Cold War, the United States wanted bases in Turkey due to its strategic geographic position bordering the Black, Aegean, and Mediterranean Seas and the Caucasus in the East. Its possession of the vital waterway, the Dardanelles, was always a concern for the Soviet Union, Bulgaria, and Romania.

20. Samuel White had thirty years of film experience as producer, director, and film editor in seventy-five films with major studios and 175 hours of television (NBC, ABC, and CBS). He was one of the producers of the *Perry Mason* series.

21. Kurkjian interview, 1/12/-13/81.

22. Among Dino De Laurentiis' productions are *Bitter Rice* ('48), *La Strada* ('54), *Barrabas* ('62), *The Bible* ('65), and *Barbarella* ('68).

23. Kurkjian interview, 1/12/-13/81.

24. Ibid.

25. High Investments, Inc., consisted of John Kurkjian as president and his wife Mary Sarness Kurkjian as secretary. Initially, most of the money invested was theirs. The rest came from banks, business firms, and friends who were to be reimbursed with interest from the profits of the completed film. In a play on words, the word for "Armenian" in the Armenian language is pronounced "high;" only an Armenian would know that the company's name had a double meaning.

26. *MGM Archives, Musa Dagh File*, Letter: Greg Bautzer, Esq. to Frank Rosenfelt, 1/22/74.

27. Ibid., Letter: John Kurkjian to Greg Bautzer, Esq., Chronology of MGM-Kurkjian co-venture, May 20, 1974 to October 6, 1976; 10/29/76.

28. Ibid., Conference: John Kurkjian, Sam White, Frank Rosenfelt, Frank Davis, and Dan Melnick. Topic: Kurkjian-White script, 11/25/74.

29. Kurkjian interview, 1/12-13/81

30. Ibid.

31. *MGM Archives, Musa Dagh File*, Memo: Frank Davis to Karla Davidson, 1/14/75.

32. Kurkjian interview, 1/12-13/81.

33. *MGM Archives, Musa Dagh File*, Security Agreement and Financing Statement, Wyman, Bautzer, Rothman & Kuchel, Esq., to MGM, Karla Davidson, Associate General Counsel & High Investments, Inc., John Kurkjian, 8/7/75.

34. Ibid., Meeting at MGM: John Kurkjian, Sam White, Frank Rosenfelt, and Dan Melnick, 7/17/75.

35. Leslie Halliwell, *The Filmgoers Companion*, 6th ed., New York: Hill and Wang, 1977, p. 21. Edward Anhalt wrote the screenplays for *Becket* ('64) and *The Boston Strangler* ('68) and with his wife Edna wrote the screenplays for *Panic in the Streets* ('50), *Not As a Stranger* ('54), *The Pride and the Passion* ('56), and *The Young Lions* ('58).

36. Ibid., p. 298. James Goldman's screenwriting credits included *The Lion in Winter* ('68) and *Nicholas and Alexandra* ('72).

37. Ibid., p. 544. John Osborne's screen writing credits include *Look Back in Anger* ('59), *The Entertainer* ('60), and *Tom Jones* ('63).

38. *MGM Archives, Musa Dagh File*, Chronology of MGM-Kurkjian Co-venture, May 20, 1974 to October 6, 1976; Letter: John Kurkjian to Greg Bautzer, Esq., 10/29/76.

39. Ibid.

40. Ibid.

41. Leslie Halliwell, *The Filmgoers Companion*, Ronald Harwood's screenplays include *High Wind in Jamaica* ('65) and *One Day in the Life of Ivan Denisovich* ('71). In 2003, he won an Academy Award for his screenplay of *The Pianist* ('02).

42. *MGM Archives, Musa Dagh File*, Chronology of MGM-Kurkjian Co-venture, 5/19/74-10/6/76, Letter: Kurkjian to Bautzer, 10/29/76.

43. John Douglas Eames, *The MGM Story, The Complete History of Fifty Roaring Years*, New York: Crown Publishers, 1975, p. 368. On the occasion of MGM's 50th anniversary in 1974, Rosenfelt informed the celebrants that "One of our principal objectives will be to provide a climate at MGM which will attract creative film makers … contrary to recent public speculation, the roar of Leo the Lion will not be reduced to a weak meow."

44. *High Investments, Inc., Musa Dagh File*, Promotional brochure, *The Forty Days of Musa Dagh*, 1975.

45. Ibid.

46. Ibid.

47. The author's conversations with Richard Demirjian, Moraga, Calif., 11/27/93 and Armen Aroyan, in Oakland, Calif., 1/30/94, recounting their visit to the Musa Dagh region in September 1993.

48. *Oakland Tribune*, "Armenian Ordeal to Be a Film," 12/21/75, Sec. E, p. 10.

49. Kurkjian interview, 1/12-13/81.

50. *MGM Archives, Musa Dagh File*, Letter of Agreement, 1/27/76, between MGM (Producer), and Ronald Harwood, Ltd., (Writer), Contract Office File

Copy, 2/9/76.

51. Ibid., Letter: Kurkjian/Bautzer, 10/29/76.

52. Ibid.

53. Kurkjian interview, 1/12-13/81.

54. *MGM Archives, Musa Dagh File,* Memo: Frank Davis to Frank Rosenfelt, 4/23/76.

55. Ibid., Letter: Kurkjian/Bautzer, 10/29/76.

56. Ibid., Cont. 9076, News Release: *Musa Dagh,* 8/23/76.

57. Ibid.

58. Ibid., Memo: Sherry Lansing to Karla Davidson, 10/21/76.

59. Ibid., Memo: Karla Davidson to Frank Davis, 11/9/76.

60. Ibid., Letter: Kurkjian/Bautzer, 10/29/76.

61. Ibid., Memo: Karla Davidson to Frank Davis, 11/9/76.

62. Ibid., Memo: Patricia Healy to Frank Davis, 10/26/76.

63. Kurkjian interview, 1/12-1/13/81.

64. *MGM Archives, Musa Dagh File,* Letter: Kurkjian to Bautzer, 10/29/76.

65. Ibid., Letter: Karla Davidson to Frank Davis, 11/9/76.

66. Ibid.

67. Ibid.

68. Kurkjian interview, 1/12-13/81.

Chapter 22

SEARCHING FOR ANGELS

69. John Kurkjian, president; Paul Schreibman, legal counsel; Sam White, producer; Ika Panajotovic, producer; and screenwriter Clarke Reynolds made up the High Investments, Inc., production team.

70. *High Investments, Inc., Musa Dagh File,* Musa Dagh, Ltd., Promotional brochure, 1977, 12 pages.

71. Ibid., Letter: John Kurkjian to MGM, 7/12/78.

72. *MGM Archives, Musa Dagh File*, Letter: Harcourt Management Corp. to Karla Davidson, MGM Legal Dept., 5/23/77.

73. Kurkjian interview, 1/12-13/81.

74. *Variety*, 2/8/79.

75. Kurkjian interview, 1/12-13/81.

76. Letter: Dr. Dennis Papazian, Southfield, Mich., to the author, 8/17/92.

77. Ibid.

78. Kurkjian interview, 1/12-13/81.

79. Ibid.

80. *MGM Archives, Musa Dagh File*, Exhibit A, 9/3/70, Chronology of *Musa Dagh* Copyright history, Anna Mahler appointed Werfel estate administrator, 11/9/60.

81. Ibid., Letter: Samuel W. Tannenbaum, Esq. (Johnson & Tannenbaum, Attorneys at Law), New York, to MGM, Culver City, Calif., Attn: Mrs. Mildred Basch, responding to MGM's inquiry re: the copyright history of *Musa Dagh*, 5/6/75.

82. *High Investments, Inc., Musa Dagh File*, Contract: Anna Mahler and John Kurkjian, Re: Rights to *Musa Dagh*, signed by Mahler in London, England, witnessed by John J. Degan, Jr., Consul of the USA at London, England, 11/29/74.

83. Kurkjian interview, 1/12-13/81.

84. *High Investments, Inc., Musa Dagh File*, Letter: A. Kim Guggenheim, Esq. to Paul Schreibman, Esq., 8/17/78.

85. Ibid., "Memos to remember for letter to New York," John Kurkjian's handwritten outline detailing his experience with MGM and Anna Mahler, 1978.

86. Kurkjian interview, 1/12-13/81.

87. *High Investments, Inc.*, Musa Dagh, Ltd., Promotional Brochure, *Musa Dagh*, 1977, 12 pages.

88. Kurkjian interview, 1/28/81.

89. *High Investments, Inc.*, Musa Dagh, Ltd., Promotional Brochure, *Musa Dagh*, 1977, 12 pages.

90. Kurkjian interview, 1/28/81.

91. Since 1950, there had been a small but steady exodus of Armenians from Romania, some of whom found their way to North and South America via Beirut, Lebanon.

92. Kurkjian interview, 1/28/81.

93. Ibid.

94. Ibid.

95. Ibid.

96. Ibid.

97. Kurkjian interview, 1/12-13/81.

Chapter 23

THE FINAL CUT

98. Kurkjian interview, 1/28-30/81.

99. Kurkjian interview, 8/29/88.

100. Interview of Sarky Mouradian by the author, Van Nuys, Calif., 6/15/92.

101. In 1981, Los Angeles was home to more than 300,000 Armenians. It had the largest metropolitan Armenian population outside the Soviet Union. It ranked as the third largest Armenian center after Yerevan and Leninakan, Soviet Armenia.

102. Kurkjian interview, 1/28-30/81.

103. Ibid; Promotional brochure, *The Forty Days of Musa Dagh.*

104. *High Investments, Inc., Musa Dagh File,* Contract: High Investments, Inc. and Thomas Selden, 3/9/81.

105. Over the years David Lean had carved his niche in the pantheon of film geniuses with *Great Expectations* ('46), *The Bridge on the River Kwai* ('57), *Lawrence of Arabia* ('62), and *Doctor Zhivago* ('65).

106. Kurkjian interview, 8/30/88.

107. Leslie Halliwell, *The Filmgoer's Companion,* p. 635. Sarafian's credits: In England: *Run Wild, Run Free* ('69), John Mills, Bernard Miles, Gordon Jackson, p.748; *Fragment of Fear* ('70), Flora Robson, Wilfred Hyde-White, Roland Culver, p. 308. In the United States: *Vanishing Point* ('71), Dean Jagger, p. 929; *Man in the*

Wilderness ('71), Richard Harris, John Huston, p. 554; *The Man Who Loved Cat Dancing* ('73) Lee J. Cobb, Jack Warden, p. 558; *Lolly Madonna XXX* ('73), Rod Steiger, Robert Ryan, Jeff Bridges, p. 521.

108. Kurkjian Interview, 1/12-13/81.

109. *Hoosharar* (Armenian General Benevolent Union monthly magazine), "Talk Show Focuses on Armenian Image in the American Performing Arts," Vol. 69, No. 10, Dec. 1982, p. 6.

110. Mouradian interview, Van Nuys, Calif., 6/15/92.

111. Ibid.

112. *The Armenian Observer*, 12/16/87, p. 3.

113. Mouradian interview, 6/15/92.

114. *High Investments, Inc., Musa Dagh File*, Kurkjian/Mouradian Contract, 10/15/80.

115. Mouradian interview, 6/15/92.

116. Ibid.

117. *High Investments, Inc., Musa Dagh File*, Kurkjian/White Productions, July 1978.

118. In the archives of the American Film Institute, Louis B. Mayer Library, Los Angeles, are seventeen boxes containing more than 105 outlines, treatments, adaptations, various drafts of scripts, and complete screenplays of *The Forty Days of Musa Dagh*, covering the period from 1935 to 1981.

119. Mouradian interview , 6/15/92.

120. Ibid.

121. Kurkjian interview, 1/28-30/81.

122. *Variety*, Videocassette Film Review, *Forty Days of Musa Dagh*, 11/28/87, p.22.

123. James Monaco, *Who's Who in American Film Now*, New York, Baseline Book, 1987, p. 340. Mendoza-Nava scored the music for *The Boys in Company C* ('77), and *The Norsemen* ('78).

124. Mouradian interview, 6/15/92.

125. Ibid.

126. *High Investments, Inc. Musa Dagh File*, Agreement: High Investments, Inc., and Kenney/Travis & Associates, 3/81.

127. Mouradian interview, 6/15/92..

128. *Variety*, "Film and TV Casting News," 4/13/81, p. 9.

129. Mouradian interview, 6/15/92.

130. Interview of Hank Moonjean by the author, Los Angeles, Calif., 6/17/92.

131. Kurkjian interview, 8/29-30/88.

132. Mouradian interview, 6/15/92.

133. Kurkjian interview, 8/29-30/88.

134. Interview of Edward Vasgersian by the author, Moraga, Calif., 8/8/89.

135. *The 40 Days of Musa Dagh*, World Premiere Program, 4/82.

136. Mouradian interview, 6/15/92.

137. A veteran character actor who carried many a Western for John Wayne, Roy Rogers, et al.

138. Mouradian interview, 6/15/92.

139. *The 40 Days of Musa Dagh*, World Premiere program, 4/82: Karen Kondazian, Manuel Kichian, Sid Haig, Joseph Gostanian, Mark Tombazian, and Michael Tootikian.

140. Kurkjian interview, 8/28-29/88.

141. Mouradian interview, 6/15/92.

142. Vasgersian interview, 8/8/89.

143. Ibid.

144. Kurkjian interview, 8/28-29/88.

145. In most movies, scenes are not shot in sequence with the script. Most often to cut expenses, priority in shooting revolves around the principal actors because of their salaries.

146. Kurkjian interview, 8/29-30/88, confirmed by Mouradian, 6/15/92.

147. Kurkjian interview, 8/29-30/88.

148. Ibid.

149. Mouradian interview, 6/15/92.

150. Vasgersian interview, 8/8/89.

151. Kurkjian interview, 8/29-30/88.

152. Ibid.

153. Ibid.

154. Mouradian interview, 6/15/92. Ryder Sound Services was owned by Levon Chaloukian, former president of the Academy of Television Arts and Sciences

155. Kurkjian interview, 8/29-30/88.

156. Ibid.

157. *Armenian Mirror-Spectator,* "*40 Days of Musa Dagh* Movie May Premier in LA This Spring," 3/6/82, p. 1.

158. The author attended the world premiere at the Kurkjians' invitation.

159. The Los Angeles premiere grossed $31,115; expenses were $14,860.

160. Mouradian interview, 6/15/92.

161. *Hoosharar* (AGBU monthly magazine), "Talk Show Focuses on Armenian Image in the American Performing Arts," Vol. 69, No. 10, December 1982, p. 6.

162. In San Francisco the author made the arrangements at the Palace of Fine Arts Theater, 8/20/82 and 8/22/82.

163. *High Investments, Inc., Musa Dagh File*, List of Theater Presentations, October 1984.

164. Kurkjian interview, 8/29-30/88.

165. Mouradian interview, 6/15/92.

166. Kurkjian interview, 8/29-30/88.

167. *Variety,* Videocassette Film Review, *Forty Days of Musa Dagh*, 11/28/87, p. 22.

168. Ibid.

46 Dino De Laurentiis, proposed a joint *Musa Dagh* production with John Kurkjian, but MGM did not want him as a competitor.

47 Sarky Mouradian, directing *Musa Dagh* was the opportunity of a lifetime.

48 John Kurkjian, President of High Investments, Inc. and Frank Rosenfelt, Chairman of MGM, at the signing of the $8,000,000 contract to film *The Forty Days of Musa Dagh*, July 1975.

EPILOGUE

Epilogue

It's a political hot potato

Six years had passed since the world premiere of *The Forty Days of Musa Dagh*. On the author's initiative John and Mary Kurkjian were gracious to consent to a follow-up interview in August 1988. The intention was to trace the period after the MGM debacle that preceded the movie's premiere and the events that followed that unique occasion.

As we were wrapping up the last session the author was startled to hear Kurkjian say, "I no longer own the rights to Werfel's *Musa Dagh*. I sold them to a German outfit in Frankfurt (presently S. Fischer Verlag owns the rights to Werfel's novel.) I believe they want to make the movie again, this time as a television mini-series." Considering the hassles and the expenditures to secure the rights from MGM and the Werfel estate and the ordeal he suffered in making the movie, it was hard to believe that Kurkjian had surrendered his ownership to *Musa Dagh* for $25,000.[1] John Kurkjian's movie-making experience had embittered him so severely to do the unthinkable.

Upon further investigation in 1989, the author learned that Ottokar Runze, a German filmmaker in Berlin and Hamburg (Gmbh & Co., Film herstebing KG) was involved in a project to fund the filming of *The Forty Days of Musa Dagh*. Three years later, Runze informed Professor

Emeritus Avedis K. Sanjian, University of California, Los Angeles, that he was trying to raise $40 million to make the movie. Runze did not want any publicity because he was concerned about Turkey's attempts to undermine his project. It was his intent to keep his *Musa Dagh* project a secret.[2] With over two million Turks residing in Germany, how Runze expected to run a covert *Musa Dagh* production there or anywhere else is debatable.

Seeking financial support in the Armenian American community, in 2003 composer Michelle Ekizian and Runze met with Archbishop Khajag Barsamian, Primate of the Eastern Diocese of the Armenian Church of North America, in New York City. Unfortunately, Runze's pre-production plans were vague, subsequently nothing came of the meeting. The same was true with Runze's meeting with Howard Kazanjian, producer of *Raiders of the Lost Ark*. Later on, Runze employed Thom Mount, an executive at RKO International, to assemble a pre-production package with a $2 million budget. A husband and wife team, screenwriters Julian and Judith Plowman, had already submitted a first draft screenplay. Tentatively, Ekizian was the designated composer to score a $60 million film. To firm up the project, producer Arthur Sarkissian joined the production team. Alas, by summer 2004, this particular team disbanded.[3]

In July 2005 Arthur Chorbanian, who had served on Sylvester Stallone's *Rocky II* production, informed the author that Runze had contacted him.[4] After eighteen years on the project, the German producer was still short of his $60 million goal for the project. In 2006 he was seeking financial support in economically prostrated Armenia. His intention at the time was to film the production in Germany and Armenia.

If John Kurkjian's co-venture with Kirk Kerkorian's MGM studio failed to raise the necessary funds in the Armenian American community and abroad, it is questionable that the German producer will be successful. *Musa Dagh* is a motion picture production that demands much more than a $60 million budget.

* * *

That the *Musa Dagh* issue was still on the Turkish "watch" was evident as recently as November 2002. *The Turkish Forum*'s Mahmut Esat Ozam, castigating anyone contemplating a new *Musa Dagh* film, launched a campaign on the basis of a rumor. In his diatribe, Ozam condemned Werfel's novel as "a pitiful work of science fiction."[5] This is the same *Turkish Forum* in conjunction with the Turkish government that demanded Atom Egoyan's genocide film, *Ararat,* be banned from movie theaters in the United States and Canada that same year. As a result, *Ararat* was denied a national distribution by the Weinstein Brothers' Miramax Company. In all of northern California, it was restricted to a San Francisco art house for a limited engagement. In 2006, the Taviani Brothers refused to give into similar pressures applied on the Italian government by Turkish Premier Erdogan. Turkey demanded the elimination of any mention of the Armenian Genocide from their film, *Lark Farm*, in order to maintain cordial relations between Turkey and Italy.[6]

In the past, there was always the Turkish threat to boycott all American movies because of *Musa Dagh*. What is more topical is the possibility to cancel U.S.-Turkish agreements regarding the U.S. military presence in Asia Minor. In Washington, the Turkish menace to remove the American air base at Incirlik and other installations in Turkey carries more weight compared to the recognition of the Armenian Genocide or a *Musa Dagh* movie and Turkey knows it. Since the end of World War II, regardless of the political party in the White House, the situation in the Middle East has given Turkey immense leverage over the United States and more so now with our presence in Iraq and Afghanistan.

The billions of U.S. dollars showered upon Turkey since the passage of the Truman Doctrine have influenced U.S. and foreign corporations and governments to recognize that "they gain most from Turkey when they do the least for Armenia and Armenians."[7] The current stalemate caused by the Turkish-Azerbaijan blockade of Armenia due to the Nagorno-Karabagh issue is one case in point. Another factor is the oil pipeline from Baku through Georgia to Ceyhan, Turkey, circumventing landlocked Armenia.

Ironically, the monetary aid granted to Turkey since 1947 made it possible for Ankara to set aside funds to employ American public relations firms to lobby the Congress and the White House.[8] Would Turkey be willing to forfeit the American cornucopia if the Congress and the administration recognized the Armenian Genocide and ceased its opposition to a *Musa Dagh* movie? When the European Union, the Vatican, and France recognized the Armenian Genocide, Turkish Prime Minister Bulent Ecevit blustered,[9] but the Turkish government went on to conduct business as usual. Is there a diplomatic dichotomy here, or is it a game of Turkish bluff? Considering Ankara's refusal to support the U.S. and British coalition efforts in Iraq in March 2003, Congress and the White House must realize that they cannot buy cooperation from Turkey even when it comes to protecting American troops. The time is long overdue for the Congress and the White House to honor the pledges made so often during presidential election campaigns to pass and sign the Armenian Genocide resolution. In effect it would eliminate opposition to the future film production of Franz Werfel's *The Forty Days of Musa Dagh*.

In the past decade, the pro-Turkish-Azerbaijan lobby in Washington has been successful in retaining the services of former Secretaries of State Lawrence Eagleburger, Alexander Haig, and James Baker, former Senate

Majority Leader Howard Baker, former Congressmen Stephen Solarz and Greg Laughlin, former Senator Don Riegle, and other retired members of previous administrations and the U.S. Congress.[10] Recently the Livingston Group (a firm founded by former Louisiana Republican congressman, Robert Livingston) had a two-year $600,000 contract with Azerbaijan to promote U.S. political and economic ties. As Turkey's top Washington lobbyist, Robert Livingston, in September 2005, accused Armenian Americans of seeking to impose a "tyranny of the minority" for urging the Congress to pass the Armenian Genocide resolution. For its services in the past, the Livingston Group received over $10 million from Turkey[11] and was instrumental in securing $1 billion in federal loans for Turkey.[12]

As a result of the November 2006 election giving the Democrats control of the Congress, Turkey, to protect its interests, signed a new contract with the Glover Park Group. It is composed of former Clinton administration members among whom is Clinton's former press secretary, Joe Lockhart.[13] Previous to this, former National Security Advisor Brent Scowcroft, chairman of the American Turkish Council (ATC) denounced the debate about the Armenian Genocide in the United States Congress. In a September 17, 2005 press release, the Armenian National Committee of America reported that both the ATC and the Assembly of Turkish American Associations (ATAA) officials were engaged in illegal efforts to defeat the Armenian Genocide legislation. Based on whistle-blower Sibel Edmond's reports, contributing editor David Rose of *Vanity Fair* revealed that the Turkish government and its allies boasted of bribing members of Congress to stop the Armenian Genocide resolution.[14] The Turkish-Azerbaijan lobby has been the leading opponent of Armenian American efforts to secure recognition of the Armenian Genocide and Armenian Martyrs Day (April 24), to lift the Turkish-Azerbaijan blockades of Armenia, to defend Nagorno-Karabagh's (Artszak) right to self-determination, to retain Section 907 of the Freedom Support Act restricting United States assistance of Azerbaijan, and the continuation of U.S. foreign aid and military assistance to Armenia.[15]

Despite Amnesty International charges that Turkey is the only member of the North Atlantic Treaty Organization still using torture, employing censorship, prohibiting the creation of authentic political parties, harassing and persecuting Kurds, and hiring assassins, official American support of Turkey continues.[16]

The political reality not only lies in the deficiency of Armenian political influence in the United States but abroad as well. It was evident when Swedish Prime Minister Goran Persson's invitation to forty-eight nations to participate in the Stockholm International Forum on the Holocaust in January 2000 excluded Armenia due to direct pressures from the Turkish government.[17] Similarly, a conference in Vienna, Austria, titled "A Century of Genocide" scheduled for April 2000 excluded the Armenian Genocide.

There can be no doubt that the Turkish lobby in Washington would be in the vanguard to derail any new attempt to pass the Genocide resolution and to produce a movie of *The Forty Days of Musa Dagh* since that has been Turkey's policy for over seventy years. Turkey and its people need to understand that the Armenian struggle for justice is a fight for their rights as Turkish citizens. They must demand that they have the right to be fully informed of the unvarnished truth of their history, particularly the period from 1890 to 1923 vis-à-vis the Armenian inhabitants of Turkey. The fact is that Armenians have been striving for more than ninety years for the liberties of those who are against them.

* * *

Although more than seventy years have passed since the publication of Werfel's epic novel, it is still in print and continues to have a life of its own in the movie industry. How many novels or potential movies have had that kind of staying power? In 1997, movie critic Michael Wilmington of *The Chicago Tribune* reported in an interview with Sylvester Stallone that the action star was interested in the Armenian holocaust of World War I as described in Franz Werfel's novel.[18] In December 2006, Stallone restated his desire to create as both screenwriter and director an epic motion picture of *The Forty Days of Musa Dagh*. In an interview with Michael Booth of *The Denver Post* Stallone emphasized "the Turkish genocide of its Armenian community 1915" and described it as "the complete destruction of a civilization." He admitted that it is a "political hot potato" and that "the Turks have been killing the subject for eighty-five years."[19]

There was an immediate response to Stallone's statement. Sava Egilmez implored Turkish organizations of "The Association of the Struggle Against Acknowledgement of the Armenian Genocide" to send protest letters to Stallone.[20]

On the eve of the publication of *MUSA DAGH* the author learned of Hrant Dink's assassination in Istanbul, January 19, 2007. Dink, 53, was the prominent newspaper editor of his bilingual weekly *AGOS*. A Turk of Armenian descent, he was the voice for Turkey's ethnic Armenians. He had become a marked man for challenging the official Turkish position of the 1915 Armenian Genocide. A seventeen-years-old Turk admitted the crime and was arrested.

Will this tragic event adversely affect future Turkish-Armenian relations? It also begs another question: If this young man had been educated as to the true history of the Armenians in Turkey, particularly the period from 1890 to 1923, would he have committed the crime? It is certain to be another setback to Turkeys' desire for membership in the European Union.[21] Until Turkey officially recognizes the Armenian Genocide it will remain an outsider.

Considering the pap coming out of the movie industry for the last thirty years, *The Forty Days of Musa Dagh* deserves reconsideration. If Shakespeare, Austen, Tolstoy, Hugo, Ibsen, the *Titanic* and *The Lord of the Rings* trilogy can still generate movie productions and blockbuster profits, so can Werfel's masterpiece in the hands of a courageous and respected production team. It has the same powerful box-office and Academy Award potentials as demonstrated by David Lean's *Lawrence of Arabia* and Steven Spielberg's *Schindler's List*. One has only to acquaint oneself with the history of the *Musa Dagh* film project to appreciate the caliber and credits of those producers, directors, screenwriters, and actors who were genuinely interested in bringing *The Forty Days of Musa Dagh* to the big silver screen to know that it merits reconsideration.

Another indication of the novel's drawing power was evident in November 2005. Five thousand patrons of the arts chose to attend the world premiere performance of Michelle Ekizian's symphonic suite, *The Place of Beginnings*, in New York City's Cathedral of St. John the Divine. The event was sold out. Ekizian was inspired by Franz Werfel's *The Forty Days of Musa Dagh*. Her composition included a narration by Eric Bogosian based on Werfel's section of the novel describing the enduring beauty and spirituality of the lands around Musa Dagh. The audience was so moved by the performance that it gave Ekizian a five-minute standing ovation.[22] The attendees that evening demonstrated that there will always be an audience supporting Franz Werfel's *The Forty Days of Musa Dagh*. No matter the form – lecture or concert or play – they and others will be there too, for the motion picture of Werfel's novel.

The time is opportune for Franz Werfel's *The Forty Days of Musa Dagh* film project to be assumed by a new American production team composed of an esteemed producer, director, and screenwriter (Steven Zaillian, Academy Award winner for *Schindler's List* screenplay).

It should be someone with the fortitude and daring of Ridley Scott (*Gladiator*, 2000) or Mel Gibson (*Braveheart*, 1995) or Alejandro Gonzalez Inarritu (*Babel*, 2006) who can raise the necessary finances to carry out the production. It should not be the fate of *The Forty Days of Musa Dagh* to be the greatest motion picture never made.

The history of Werfel's *Musa Dagh* in Hollywood serves as an object lesson in avoiding the pitfalls of the past by anyone contemplating a new *Musa Dagh* motion picture. One must be prepared to deal with immense pressures exerted by Turkey, the Turks and their lobbyists on the White House, Congress, the State Department, the Motion Picture Association of America (MPAA), Hollywood studios and their employees, foreign governments, American and foreign corporations, and the American media. It is an absolute necessity to provide for a budget worthy of an epic novel/film. *Musa Dagh* merits at least $150 million in today's film industry to stay true to Werfel's novel.

The bi-partisan Armenian Caucus in the House of Representatives co-chaired by Frank Pallone (D, N.J.) and Joseph Knollenberg (R, Mich.), pro Armenian senators led by Richard Durbin (D, Ill.) and John Ensign (R, Nev.), the Armenian National Committee, the Armenian Assembly and the Armenian American Political Action Committee (ARMENPAC) must stay on alert to counter Turkish protests. Once a *Musa Dagh* motion picture production is underway, it is imperative that there be a worldwide publicity campaign through all aspects of the media similar to Russell Birdwell's approach with *Gone With The Wind*.[23] It will diminish the opposition and simultaneously create an eager potential audience. The controversial nature and history of the film must be emphasized similarly to Mel Gibson's *The Passion of the Christ* and Michael Moore's *Fahrenheit 9/11*. Civil libertarians, film historians, and advocates of *The Forty Days of Musa Dagh* should see that Franz Werfel's masterpiece finally makes it to the screen as a quality motion picture worthy of a Best Picture Academy Award.

Taking into account the number of times *Musa Dagh* was terminated, its proponents should be aware that many of the pressures, numerous delays, and terminations suffered by *The Forty Days of Musa Dagh* project were initiated by the Turkish government and its allies. If Turks were so successful in bribing members of Congress on the Armenian Genocide issue as reported by Sibel Edmond and revealed in *Vanity Fair*, we can expect them to do the same to stop *Musa Dagh* from ever reaching the screen?[24] *Musa Dagh* advocates must see that they do not prevail.

The record is clear. The seventy-four-year controversy surrounding the novel/film *The Forty Days of Musa Dagh* generated unprecedented internal political intervention and strident foreign opposition to the production of the motion picture. Historians, lawyers and politicians preoccupied with semantics may argue that the *Musa Dagh* case smacks of a conspiracy or complicity or collusion or blatant censorship or is much to do about an insignificant minority. The author contends that it is not a matter of either or, but that all four factors – conspiracy, complicity, collusion, and censorship run rampant throughout the *Musa Dagh* case and that minority of Armenians has served as the bulwark of Christianity and the west for 2000 years. A foreign government must never be permitted to stop production of an American motion picture. And the United States government should never be party to catering to the prejudice of a foreign government.

Presently there is a ray of hope. To honor the martyred Hrant Dink, more than 50,000 Turkish citizens attended his funeral (January 23, 2007), including many high government officials.[25] Perhaps in this gesture there is an opportunity to advance Turkish-Armenian relations to a higher plane. Europe and North America look to Turkey to seize the initiative.

NOTES – EPILOGUE

1. Interview of John Kurkjian by the author, Thousand Oaks, Calif., 8/29-30/88. (John Kurkjian died in Los Angeles in 1996, at the age of ninety. Mary Sarness Kurkjian died at the Ararat Armenian Home in Woodland Hills in 1999.)

2. Interview of Avedis K. Sanjian, Prof. Emeritus, University of California, Los Angeles, by the author, 6/18/92.

3. Telephone conversation with Michelle Ekizian by the author, 1/11/05.

4. Telephone conversation with Arthur Chorbanian by the author, 7/18/05.

5. *The Turkish Forum*, 11/30/02.

6. *The Armenian Observer*, "Taviani Brothers, Turkish Pressures on Their Genocide Film, " 3/22/06, p.1.

7. Ara Kalaydjian, "April 24, Armenians Worldwide Remember Genocide Victims of 1915," *AIM, American International Magazine*, Vol. I, No. l, July 1990, pp. 6-10.

8. Kevork Imirzian, "Turkish Lobby in America," *AIM, American International Magazine*, Vol. I, No. 1, July 1990, pp. 30-32. Organizations that have represented Turkey in the United States: Hill & Knowlton, Inc., International Advisors, Inc., Thompson & Co. jointly with McCauliffee, Kelly, Rafaelli, & Siemens, Doremus, Inc.

9. *The Armenian Observer*, "Turkish PM Warns France Against Endorsing Armenian Genocide Bill," 2/23/2000, p. 3.

10. Ibid., Moorad Mooradian, Ph.D., "Our Ally Turkey," 4/9/03, p. 3.

11. Ibid., "Bob Livingston's Group Received $10 Million from Turkey to Lobby Against Armenian Issues," 3/29/06, p.1.

12. *The California Courier*, "Ankara Hires New Agent in Washington," 12/14/06, p. 3.

13. Ibid.

14. Armenian National Committee of America, press release, "House International Relations Committee Overwhelmingly Adopts Armenian Genocide Legislation," Washington, D.C., 9/15/05.

15. *The Armenian Observer*, "House of Representatives Asks Key Committee to Maintain Aid," 4/23/03, p.12.

16. Susan Fraser, "Turkey Says its Government Spent $50 Million on Assassins," *Contra Costa Times*, 1/24/98, p. A22.

17. *The Armenian Observer*, "Abp. Vatche Hovespian Expresses Anger to the Swedish Government for Armenia's Exclusion from the Conference," 1/2/00, p.1.

18. Michael Wilmington, "Sly vs. Sly, His Apocalyptic Battles Have Fueled 20 Years of Over-the-Top Movie Action," *The Chicago Tribune*, 8/10/97.

19. Michael Booth, "Stallone's Deft as Rocky in the Q&A Ring," *The Denver Post*, 12/16/06.

20. *Pan Armenian.Net*, 12/21/06.

21. Elif Shafak, "The Murder of Hrant Dink," *The Wall Street Journal*, 1/22/07.

22. Pellegrino D'Acierno, "Concert of Remembrance," *Armenian Mirror-Spectator*, 2/11/06, p. 11.

23. Russell Birdwell, a former police reporter for Hearst's *Los Angeles Examiner* was David Selznick's public relations chief for *Gone With The Wind*. He advertised the world over in search of an actress to play Scarlett O'Hara. His endeavors won immense newspaper and magazine space. It was a victory for maximum press at minimum cost.

24. Armenian National Committee of America, press release, "House International Relations Committee Overwhelmingly Adopts Armenian Genocide Legislation," 9/15/05.

25. Sebnem Arsu and Suzanne Fowler, "Armenian-Turkish Unity at Slain Editor's Funeral," *New York Times*, 1/24/07.

APPENDIX

APPENDIX

I. Declaration issued on July 13, 1915 by Antioch District Lieutenant Governor Zeki Maaruf

1. Let it be noted that, seven days from the date of this announcement, all Armenians living in the Kaza (district) of Antioch must leave Antioch and its surrounding villages. Everyone must, during this period, arrange his or her personal affairs and means of transportation.

2. During the relocation of the Armenians to areas determined by the government and during the course of the journey, their comfort, peace, and protection against all kinds of extortion will be insured by the gendarmes.

3. Transportation and food for families whose poverty has been established will be provided by the government.

4. Possessions and items remaining behind will be registered, one by one, in a ledger and stored in secure places and protected by the government. Later, the monies acquired from the sale of these items will be deposited in government safes and then sent to the owners.

5. The personal rights of the refugees will be protected after they comfortably inhabit their assigned locations.

6. Under my chairmanship, I have formed a committee to make certain that the relocation does take place, that it will be conducted

properly, that personal rights will be protected, and that possessions and movable items are registered in ledgers.

7. Individuals subject to the relocation must support the government's operation with complete trust. Other Ottoman subjects must respect and observe this right, which is protected in every way, since the pending relocation is going to be an ordinary migration.

8. Warning! Be it the people or the officials, both must behave in an orderly fashion. Whoever is found negligent in these matters will immediately be arrested and court-martialed.[1]

II. Declaration issued on July 17, 1915 by the Sub-district Suedia Mudir (minor civil official)

To the village mukhtar (mayor) and his members, according to the kaimakam's (district governor) proclamation, I proclaim that in the next seven days you must have your personal affairs arranged and be ready for deportation.[2]

III. The Reverend Dikran Andreasian's plea for Allied intervention, September 2, 1915

To any English, American, French, Italian, or Russian admiral, captain, or authority whom this petition may find, we appeal in the name of God and human brotherhood.

We, the people of six Armenian villages, about 5000 souls in all, have withdrawn to that part of Musa Dagh called Damlajik, which is three hours' journey northwest from Suedije along the seacoast.

We have taken refuge here from Turkish barbarism and torture, and most of all from the outraging of the honor of our women.

Sir, you must have heard about the policy of annihilation which the Turks are applying to our nation. Under cover of dispersing the Armenians, as if to avoid rebellion, our people are expelled from their houses, deprived of their gardens, their vineyards, and all their possessions.

This brutal programme has already been applied to the city of Zeitoun and its thirty-two villages, to Albustan, Geoksun, Yarpouz, Gurin, Diarbekir, Adana, Tarsus, Mersin, Deort Yol, Hadjin, etc. And the same policy is being extended to all the two and a half million Armenians in different parts of Turkey.

The present writer was the Protestant pastor in Zeitoun a few months ago and was an eyewitness of many unspeakable cruelties. I saw families of eight or ten members driven along the highway, barefooted children six or seven years old by the side of aged grandparents, hungry and thirsty, their feet swollen from the toilsome journey. Along the road one heard sobs and curses and prayers. Under the pressure of great fear, some mothers gave birth to children in the bushes by the side of the road. Immediately afterward they were compelled by the Turkish guards to continue their journey till kind death arrived to give an end to their torture.

The remainder of the people who were strong enough to bear the hardships of the march were driven on under the whips of the gendarmes to the plains of the south. Some died of hunger. Others were robbed along the way. Others were stricken with malaria and had to be left by the roadside; and, as a last act of this dark and foul tragedy, the Arabs and Kurds massacred all the males and distributed the widows and girls among their tribes!

The Government some forty days ago informed us that our six villages must go into exile. Rather than submit to this we withdrew to this mountain. We now have little food left, and the troops are besieging us. We have had five fierce battles. God has given us the victory; but the next time we will have to withstand a much larger force.

Sir, we appeal to you in the name of Christ!

Transport us, we pray you, to Cyprus or any other free land. Our people are not indolent. We will earn our own bread if we are employed.

If this is too much to grant, transport at least our women, old people, and children, equip us with sufficient arms, ammunition, and food, and we will work with you with all our might against the Turkish forces. Please, sir, do not wait until it is too late!

Respectfully your servant, for all the Christians here.

Dikran Andreasian, September 2.[3]

IV. Chronology: Siege and deliverance at Musa Dagh, July 13 to September 14, 1915 Prepared by the author based on "A Red Cross Flag That Saved Four Thousand," *The Outlook*, 12/1/15, Vol. CXI, pp. 790, 799-803.

Tuesday, July 13	Official order to evacuate the six villages of Musa Dagh (population about 6000) within eight days (by July 21, 1915) delivered in YoghunOluk.
Wednesday, July 14	Meetings are held and decision is made to establish a defense on Musa Dagh.
Thursday, July 15	Ascent of Musa Dagh begins. More than 4000 Armenians atop Musa Dagh by Sunday, July 18, 1915. The Rev. Dikran Andreasian considers July 15, 1915 as the first day of Musa Dagh's defense.
Sunday, July 18	Defenses prepared; Central Administrative Council elected by secret ballot and a Committee of Defense appointed.

Wednesday, July 21	The first Turkish attack is launched (This is the same day the deportations were to begin).
Sunday, August 15	The Rev. Harutiun Nokhudian and sixty families from Bitias joined by 30 families from Haji Habibli begin "relocation" march to Der-el Zor.
Thursday, September 2	The Rev. Andreasian sends swimmers with messages to Allied ships in the Mediterranean, efforts are futile. A runner is sent to Aleppo to alert U. S. Consul Jesse Jackson. Two banners displayed: (1) Red Cross on white field (2) "Christians in Distress—Rescue" on cliff overlooking Mediterranean Sea.
Sunday, September 5	French armored cruiser *Guichen* sighted on fifty-third day of defense, joined by the flagship *Jeanne d'Arc* and three French armored cruisers and a British warship.
Monday, September 6– Sunday, September 12	French naval personnel evacuate 4049 Musa Dagh survivors who are put aboard French warships.
Sunday, September 12	Embarkation from Musa Dagh.
Tuesday, September 14	Arrival at Port Said, Egypt.[4]

V. The Musa Dagh Martyrs

Hagop Karageozian 1880-1915	Krikor Nekroorian 1875-1915
Hovannes Kojian 1874 -1915	Jabra Kheyoyan 1887-1915
Hovhannes Loorchian 1891-1915	Samuel Markarian 1891-1915

Sarkis Shannakian 1880-1915	Missak Bayramian 1897-1915
Samuel Boyajian 1874-1915	Baghdassar Mardikian 1886-1915
Hapet Vanayan 1889-1915	Barsoom Khoshian 1874-1915
Bedros Havatian 1882-1915	Boghos Andekian 1894-1915
Abraham Seklemian 1898-1915	Hagop Havatian 1885-1915
Krikor Kebourian 1854-1915	Bedros Penenian 1855-1915[5]

VI. Some of the events during the siege and deliverance at Musa Dagh incorporated by Werfel in *The Forty Days of Musa Dagh* from Andreasian's account; Prepared by the author

- The tragedy at Zeitun. The Reverend Dikran Andreasian ("Aram Tomasian" in the novel) was the pastor of the Armenian Protestant church in Zeitun and was in charge of the mission orphanage there.
- Andreasian (Tomasian) was allowed to go home to YoghunOluk with his pregnant wife.
- Description of Musa Dagh's economy: agriculture, industry, and trades.
- The Turkish government's directive ordering the evacuation of the Armenian villages within eight days.
- Village leaders meeting in YoghunOluk to discuss the options and consequences of the Turkish directive.
- The decision to withdraw to Musa Dagh, taking food, livestock, arms.
- Reverend Harutiun Nokhudian's decision to obey the Turkish summons, leading some 90 families from Bitias and Haji-Habibli into exile.
- Reliance on the success of the Allied Dardanelles campaign.
- Violent cloudburst, first night on the mountain.

- Defense preparations: scouts, messengers, reserve group of sharpshooters, et al, appointed.
- Mass meeting on Musa Dagh: Governing Council and Committee of Defense are elected by secret ballot.
- Turks attack using a field gun; Armenian sharpshooter kills Turkish gunners.
- Muslim villagers supplied arms by the Antioch arsenal.
- Turks threaten the Armenian encampment on Musa Dagh at Damlayik; Armenians counterattack at night while enemy is resting; familiarity with terrain is an Armenian advantage. Turks routed.
- Andreasian's son ("Tomasian's son" in the novel) born on Musa Dagh.
- Supplies running out. Plans made to escape by sea; swimmers and runners appointed to contact Allied ships and American Consul Jesse B. Jackson in Aleppo. Andreasian's message mentions Armenian villagers on Damlayik atop Musa Dagh for forty days, having fought fierce battles.
- Two large banners are made, one with a red cross the other with a message in English, "Christians in Distress—Rescue".
- Armenians let loose an avalanche of boulders and logs on encroaching Turks.
- French cruiser *Guichen* sighted. Musa Dagh delegation welcomed aboard.
- French (Allied) naval task force arrives, led by flagship *Jeanne d'Arc*.
- Musa Dagh survivors embark for Port Said.[6]

VII. Literary critics' reviews (excerpts) of *The Forty Days of Musa Dagh*, 1934-1935

John Chamberlain, *New York Times*:
Will invade your senses and keep the blood pounding. Once read it will never be forgotten.

Hendrik Willem Van Loon:
To me it is worth everything that has appeared in the last two years.

R. M. Gay, *The Atlantic Monthly*:
So full of suspense and excitement, so majestic in its presentation of the tragedy of a whole people ... one cannot fail to find it remarkable.

Harry Hansen, *Harper's*:
The story grows on one, the whole dark, useless tragedy born of racial and religious differences, is indelibly impressed upon the memory.

Horace Gregory, *New York Herald Tribune*:
Unequaled in modern history ... I know of no contemporary novel where historical incident is given such complete reality.

William Soskin, *New York American*:
This is undoubtedly Franz Werfel's masterpiece and as such the masterpiece of one of the greatest living novelists.

Clarence Dane:
Written with such power, with such restraint, that though you cannot bear to read you cannot put it down.[7]

New Statesman & Nation:

Overtones of Old Testament characters and story of human heroism ... gives life to the long Armenian struggle.[8]

New York Herald Tribune:

In no other modern novel may we find a better interpretation of the motives behind mass movement nor shall we find a better portrayal of mass in action. The Armenian nation has survived by that power which is obtained by minority and disenfranchised races throughout the world.[9]

Newsday:

Werfel has done something for the Armenians that no one has managed for Europe's Jews: he has romanticized, in the best sense of the word, their destruction.[10]

Time:

Werfel gave the word "Armenian" a new and heroic significance ... takes its place with *All Quiet on the Western Front* ... that makes it unwelcome in Germany.[11]

American Heritage:

In a 1992 survey requesting noted writers to discuss their favorite historical novel, Mark Helprin, author of *A Soldier of the Great War* and *A Winter's Tale* had this to say: A great difference exists between a work of fiction that is a vehicle for the teaching or exploration of history—what I would call a historical novel—and one that is set, vividly or otherwise, in the past ... By this standard, then, my favorite historical novel is not a historical novel. Nonetheless, it is

Franz Werfel's *The Forty Days of Musa Dagh*. Though neither author nor subject matter is American, the underlying theme certainly is: a fortress manned by the weak, who triumph over the strong solely by virtue and ingenuity.[12]

VIII. MGM Survey regarding *Musa Dagh*'s appeal to a movie audience at the Screen Directors Guild Theater, February 19, 1963[13]

	Females	Males
I would be eager to see it right away	11.7%	9.3%
I want to see it soon as possible	5.0%	7.4%
I probably will see it soon as possible	13.3%	18.5%
I probably will see it sometime	28.3%	18.5%
I am not sure I would see it	20.3%	31.5%
I probably will not see it	8.3%	11.1%
There's no doubt that I'm not interested in seeing it	5.0%	3.7%
No opinion	8.1%	0.0%

The title, *The Forty Days of Musa Dagh*, gave the following impressions as a film:

	Females	Males
Adventure	31.7%	38.9%
Biblical	30.0%	24.0%
Historical	26.0%	18.0%
Action	23.0%	18.0%
Drama	18.0%	18.0%
Spectacular	15.0%	
Adult Film	13.0%	

Religious	13.0%	
Re-make of Old Movie	10.0%	
Romance	8.0%	
Science Fiction	8.0%	
Animal	5.0%	
Mystery	5.0%	
Comedy	3.0%	1.9%
Musical	3.0%	
Children	0.7%	
Western	1.7%	1.9%

IX. Press and prejudice, *The Forty Days of Musa Dagh*

La Republique, September 4, 1935

Mr. Numan Rifat, the Secretary General of Foreign Affairs, told us," ... the film shall not be exhibited in friendly countries." On June 9, 1935, a communication was received ... signed by Mr. Hull, the Minister for Foreign Affairs, saying that the Government had forbidden the production of the film without the consent of the Turkish Ambassador at Washington

La Republique, September 6, 1935

Statements made by an American in our city: MGM is an essentially Jewish concern with Jewish managers endowed with a different commercial mentality ...

Son Posta (Turkish language), Istanbul, September 6, 1935

The Forty Days of Musa Dagh ... containing nothing but hostile propaganda and inaccuracies ... This film, taken from the work of a Jew ... simply renews the vile accusations concocted by the Jew

Morgenthau, former American Ambassador to Turkey, with the help of Master Schmavonian, former dragoman of the Embassy ...

La Republique, September 7, 1935

The New York press is carrying on an intense propaganda for the distribution of Franz Werfel's book ... which portrays us in a false and disadvantageous light ... This state of affairs is of such a nature as to blacken our reputation before world public opinion ... Up to now 170,000 copies of this book have been sold.

La Republique, September 8, 1935

In the new world ... we are looked upon as barbarians ... We allow a Jew, driven from Germany, to publish a book full of carefully planned insults against us ... [14]

X. A partial list of personnel costs for Pandro S. Berman's projected *Musa Dagh* production, "Operation Roxbury" in Greece, June 1964. An example of a very small "tip of the iceberg" (Hank Moonjean's comment) for the edification of movie buffs

Extras: Weekly salary for a six-day week $120   each.
(Even though this was very low by Hollywood standards, it was ten times the pay of the Greek soldiers).

Production Unit Manager:	$6000
Assistant Director:	4000
Assistant Accountant:	3000
Cashier:	3000
Security Watchman:	2000
Assistant Film Editor:	2000
Assistant Sound Director:	3000

Sound Mix Recorder:	3000
Camera Operator - Sound:	3000
Boom Operator:	1500
Master Carpenter:	1500
Master Painter:	1500
Chaperon/School Teacher:	1200
Interpreter:	1500
English-speaking Secretary:	1500
Draftsman:	1500
Scenic Artist:	2000
Set Dresser:	2000
Carpenters, painters, plasterers, riggers, engineers and upholsterers:	$1500 each.[15]

XI. Screenwriter Ronald Harwood's expense account, May 10 to September 6, 1976 (An expenditure of the Kurkjians' High Investments, Inc.)

Apartment rental:	$4024.13
Staples, food:	595.00
Auto rental:	1375.00
Auto (gas, oil, wash, parking):	128.00
Restaurants/meals:	3486.57
Restaurant tips (20% of the bill):	693.70
Clothing purchases:	82.15
Laundry, dry cleaning:	180.00
Telephone, telegraph:	152.14
Periodicals, barber, shoeshine, cigarettes, and tobacco:	140.00

Recreation: 198.00
Misc.:   322.85
$11,377.54 [16] + $50,000 for screenplay

XII. Kurkjian/White Musa Dagh "Game Plan" co-venture with MGM

Phase I Development Period

September 18 - October 7, 1975: In this two-week period a new writer was to be selected whose initial assignment was just to read the book.

October 8 - October 22, 1975: After the writer had read the book, he had another two weeks to make up his mind to accept or reject the assignment to write the screenplay. If his answer was in the affirmative, then meetings would be held to discuss his feelings and possible approach to scripting *Musa Dagh*.

October 23, - November 13, 1975: Within three weeks the appointed scriptwriter had to come up with a detailed description of how he planned to treat and adapt the book to the screen, especially the interrelationships of the principal characters as well as the elimination of characters he considered expendable.

November 14 - November 21, 1975: In the next seven days the writer's presentation was to be read, digested, and discussed. If there was a consensus, then he would proceed to write a full and complete treatment before going into the script.

November 22 - December 13, 1975: In this period the writer would deliver the treatment.

December 13 - December 20, 1975: Another week in which to read, digest and discuss the treatment. If a consensus was reached, the writer proceeds with the script.

December 20 - January 31, 1976: This six-week period was the longest interval in Phase I, which would give the writer time to deliver the script's first draft.

February 2 - February 9, 1976: A week would follow to allow for reading, digesting, and discussing the first draft.

February 10, 1976: One day only to meet with the writer to discuss changes, etc.

February 11 - March 10, 1976: Within the next month, the writer was expected to complete all revisions and polish and deliver the final script. The total elapsed time for the writer had come to twenty-three weeks.

March 11 - March 18, 1976: Although the contract to read the final shooting script had called for a four-week period, one week was all that was needed. If approved and accepted by MGM and High Investments (Kurkjian and White) as per agreement, Phase I, Development Period, was to be concluded, setting the stage for Phase II.

Simultaneously, during the Phase I, Development Period, a detailed survey and analysis would take place in the search for a foreign country that would best qualify for the picture's production. Qualifications would include all exterior locations, studios for interior sets (if needed), governmental cooperation, production personnel, extras, equipment, animals, and other requirements. Once the decision about the country was made, crucial locations were to be pinned down and incorporated into the shooting script to save time and money. Once the director was assigned, then they would proceed with Phase II.

Phase II Further Development Period

March 19 - June 5, 1976: In this eleven-week period, preparation for principal photography would take place. The director would be assigned to read and digest the script and make agreed-to changes; a line producer would be assigned; the budget breakdown and schedule would be prepared; key roles would be cast; an art director would be appointed, and key production personnel and all other customary production planning would be in place.

June 7 - September 30, 1976: Principal photography was to begin and be completed in this period of sixteen weeks and four days. The schedule called for one hundred shooting days based on a six-day week.

October 1 - December 30, 1976: In this three-month period post-production was to be completed and the final print made ready.[17]

NOTES

APPENDIX

1. The Rev. Dikran Antreassian (Andreasian), *Escape to Musa Dagh or The Banishment of Zeitoun and Suedia's Revolt,* translated by Knarik O. Meneshian,

Paramus, N.J.: Armenian Missionary Association of America, 1993, p. 31.

2. Ibid., p. 32.

3. Dikran Andreasian, "A Red Cross Flag That Saved Four Thousand," *The Outlook*, 12/1/15, Vol. CXI, p. 802.

4. Ibid.

5. *75th Anniversary of the Heroes of Mousa Ler, 1915-1990, Directory*, translated from the Armenian, Mousa Lertzis Bay Area and Fresno, CA., 1990.

6. Knarik O. Meneshian, *Escape to Musa Dagh or the Banishment of Zeitoun and Suedia's Revolt*. Translated from Dikran Andreasian's *Zeituni Antsnadviutuin yev Suedia Inknabashbanatuin (The Surrender of Zeitun and the Self-Defense of Suedia)*, Cairo, Egypt, 1915, 68 pages. Paramus, N.J.: Armenian Missionary Association of America, 1993, p. 37.

7. *New York Times, Book Review*, "Book-of-the-Month Club, Advertisement," Comments of Chamberlain, Van Loon, Gay, Hansen, Gregory, Soskin, and Dane, 8/18/35, p. 20.

8. *New Statesman & Nation*, 12/29/34, Vol. 8, p. 972.

9. *New York Herald Tribune*, "Books," 12/2/34, p. 3.

10. National Association for Armenian Studies and Research (NAASR), Armenian Book Clearing House, Advertisement on the occasion of the republication in paperback of *The Forty Days of Musa Dagh*, New York: Carrol & Graf, 1985.

11. University of California, Los Angeles, Special Collections Library, *Franz Werfel Papers*, Box 21; *Time*, 12/3/34.

12. Mark Helprin, "Truth and Fiction, The Power of the Historical Novel," "My Favorite Historical Novel," *American Heritage*, Special Issue, Vol. 43, No. 6, October 1992, pp. 84-107.

13. *MGM Archives, Musa Dagh* File, Research Department, *Musa Dagh* Test Survey, Screen Actors Guild Theater, Hollywood, Calif., 2/19/63.

14. *U.S. Department of State, Division of Near Eastern Affairs*, Document 811.4061, Embassy of U.S.A., Istanbul, Turkey, Musa Dagh/35: Dispatch No. 768, "Press

Campaign Against MUSA DAGH Film," 9/10/35, Attached: Clippings from Turkish newspapers with translations.

15. *MGM Archives, Musa Dagh* File, Berman Production, Outside Production No. 16, "Operation Roxbury," Memo: Hank Moonjean to Pandro S. Berman, 6/22/64.

16. *MGM Archives, Musa Dagh* File, Inter-office Communication: *The Forty Days of Musa Dagh*, Ronald Harwood's Expense Account, 5/10/76 - 9/6/76.

17. *MGM Archives, Musa Dagh* File, Inter-office Communication: *The Forty Days of Musa Dagh*, Samuel White to Raymond Wagner, 9/18/75.

BIBLIOGRAPHY

PRIMARY SOURCES

GOVERNMENT DOCUMENTS

Great Britain

Bryce, Viscount James, *The Treatment of Armenians in the Ottoman Empire, 1915-1916,* Documents presented to Viscount Grey of Fallodon; also known as *The Blue Book,* Arnold Toynbee, ed., London: H.M.S.O., 1916.

_____, "Report of Musa Dagh Rescue by Bishop Torkom of the Gregorian Community of Egypt," *The Blue Book,* Document 131.

United States

National Archives and Records, Department of State, File 811.4061-Motion Pictures, Musa Dagh File, Nos. 1-64, Washington, D.C.

_____, Communique: *J. B. Jackson to Secretary of State, May 27, 1918*; RG 59, File 867.4016/386 in Vahram Shemmassian's "The Armenian Villagers of Musa Dagh, A Historical-Ethnographic Study, 1840-1915," Ph.D. diss., University of California, Los Angeles, 1996.

_____, U. S. Congress, Senate, *Report of the American Military Mission to Armenia.* Maj. Gen. James G. Harbord; 66th Cong., 2d sess., Rept. 266, Washington, D.C., 1920.

Los Angeles, Calif., County Recorder, Death Certificate: Franz Werfel, September 25, 1945. Copy provided by Dr. William Mandel, September 3, 1985.

ARCHIVAL SOURCES

American Film Institute, Louis B. Mayer Library, *The Forty Days of Musa Dagh* File,   Special Collection No. 37, Los Angeles, Calif.

_____, Interview of Pandro S. Berman, tape recording, prepared and conducted by Mike Steen, August 4, 1972, Los Angeles, Calif.

High Investments, Inc., Musa Dagh File, Thousand Oaks, Calif.

Metro-Goldwyn-Mayer, Archives, *The Forty Days of Musa Dagh* File, Culver City, Calif.

Story No. 5807, Irving Thalberg production, 1934-1935.

Julian Blaustein *Musa Dagh* production, 1958-1961.

Pandro S. Berman *Musa Dagh*, Outside Production No. 16, "Operation Roxbury," 1962-1966.

Jerry Gershwin/Elliott Kastner *Musa Dagh*,Gina Productions, 1968-1970.

Metro-Goldwyn-Mayer/Kurkjian High Investments, Inc., *Musa Dagh* Joint Venture Production No. 9076, 1974-1976.

University of California, Los Angeles, Special Collections Library, Collection 512,

Franz Werfel Papers (Boxes 1-38).

MEMOIRS

Andreasian, Reverend Dikran. *Zeituni Antsnadviutuin yev Suedia Inknabashbanatuin (The Surrender of Zeitun and the Self-Defense of Suedia)*, Cairo, 1915.

Antreassian, Reverend Dikran, *Escape to Musa Dagh* or *The Banishment of*

Zeitoun and Suedia's Revolt, translated by Knarik O. Meneshian, Armenian Missionary Association of America, 1993.

Baronian, John (Medford, Mass.) and Richard Demirjian (Moraga, Calif.). *A Traveler's Account of a Sentimental Ethnic Journey* (an unpublished memoir), September 1993.

Boyadjian, Haroutune P. *Musa Dagh and My Personal Memoirs*, Fairlawn, N. J.: Rosekeer Press. 1981.

Morgenthau, Henry. *Ambassador Morgenthau's Story*, Memorial Edition honoring Henry Morgenthau and to commemorate the 60th Anniversary of the Armenian Genocide, Plandome, N.Y., New Age Publishers, Originally published in 1919, Garden City, N.Y.: Doubleday, Page & Co.

INTERVIEWS by the author

Armen Aroyan, January 30, 1994, Oakland, Calif.

John Baronian, August 8, 1996, Moraga, Calif.

Richard Demirjian, January 30, 1994, Oakland, Calif. and August 8, 1996, Moraga, Calif.

John Kurkjian, January 12-13, 28, 1981 and August 29-30, 1988, Thousand Oaks, Calif.

Samuel Marx, Metro-Goldwyn-Mayer, January 28, 1981, Culver City, Calif.

Joseph Matossian, October 6, 1989, Berkeley, Calif.

Hank Moonjean, June 16, 1992, Los Angeles, Calif.

Sarky Mouradian, June 15, 1992, Van Nuys, Calif.

Avedis Sanjian, Prof. Emeritus, University of California, Los Angeles, June 18, 1992.

Edward Vasgersian, August 8, 1989, Moraga, Calif.

CORRESPONDENCE

George Mason, Tracy Investment Co., Las Vegas, Nev., to the author, December 8, 1970.

Dr. William Mandel, San Pablo, Calif., to the author, September 3,1985. Re: Hitler's statement in 1939 about the Armenian massacres of World War I.

To Ottokar Runze, Hamburg, Germany, by the author, March 17, 1992.

Dr. Dennis Papazian, Southfield, Mich., to the author, August 17, 1992.

UNPUBLISHED MANUSCRIPTS (Theses)

Minasian, Edward, "They Came From Ararat, The Exodus of the Armenian People to the United States," master's thesis, Berkeley, University of California, 1961.

Sanjian, Avedis K., "Sanjak of Alexandretta (Hatay), A Study of Franco-Turco Relations," Ph.D. diss., Ann Arbor, University of Michigan, 1956.

Shemmassian, Vahram L., "The Armenian Villagers of Musa Dagh, A Historical-Ethnographic Study, 1840-1915," Ph.D. diss., Los Angeles, University of California, 1996.

BOOKS

Auron, Yair. *The Banality of Indifference, Zionism and the Armenian Genocide*, New Brunswick, N.J. and London, U.K.: Transaction Publishers, 2000.

Beauchamp, Cari. *Without Lying Down, Frances Marion and the Powerful Women of Early Hollywood*, New York: A Lisa Drew Book, Scribner, 1997.

Brown, Gene. *Movie Time, A Chronology of Hollywood and the Movie Industry from Its Beginnings to the Present*, New York: Macmillan, 1995.

Dadrian, Vahakn N., *German Responsibility in the Armenian Genocide, A Review of the Historical Evidence of German Complicity*, Watertown, Mass.: Blue Crane Books, 1996.

_____, *The History of the Armenian Genocide: Ethnic Conflict from the Balkans to Anatolia to the Caucasus*, Providence, R.I.: Berghahn Books, 1995.

Dickens, Homer. *The Films of Marlene Dietrich*, Secaucus, N.J.: Citadel Press, 1968.

Dooley, Roger. *From Scarface to Scarlett, American Films in the 1930s*, New York: Harcourt Brace Jovanovich, 1979.

Eames, John Douglas. *The MGM Story--The Complete History of Fifty Roaring Years*, New York: Crown Publishers, 1975.

Emin, Ahmed. *Turkey in the World War*, New Haven: Yale University Press, 1930.

Gabler, Neal. *An Empire of Their Own--How the Jews Invented Hollywood*, New York: Anchor Books, Doubleday, 1988.

Gardner, Gerald. *The Censorship Papers, Movie Censorship, Letters from the Hays Office, 1934 to 1968*, New York: Dodd, Mead & Co., 1987.

Garth, Jowett. *Film, The Democratic Art*, American Film Institute, Boston: Little, Brown and Co., 1976.

Gibbons, Herbert Adams. *The Blackest Page of Modern History: Events in Armenia in 1915, The Facts and Responsibilities*, New York: G. P. Putnam's Sons, 1916.

Gold, Mary Jayne. *Crossroads Marseille, A Memoir 1940*, Garden City, N.J.: Doubleday, 1980.

Halliwell, Leslie. *The Filmgoer's Companion*, 6th ed., New York: Hill & Wang, Division of Farrar, Straus and Giroux, 1977.

Hovannisian, Richard G., ed., *The Armenian Genocide, History, Politics, Ethics*, New York: St. Martin's Press, 1992.

Hovannisian, Richard G., ed., *Remembrance and Denial, The Case of the Armenian Genocide*, Detroit: Wayne State University Press, 1998.

Katz, Ephraim. *The Film Encyclopedia*, New York: Perigee Book, Putnam Publishing Group, 1979.

Korda, Michael. *Charmed Lives, A Family Romance*, New York: Random House, 1979.

Leylani, A., *Movses Der Kaloustian*, Boghos Snabian, ed., Anjar, Lebanon: A.R.F. Red Mountain Committee, 2004.

Lloyd, Ann and Graham Fuller, eds., Arnold Desser, cons. ed., *Illustrated Who's Who of the Cinema*, New York: Portland House, 1987.

Lochner, Louis P., *What About Germany*, New York: Dodd, Mead & Co., 1942. cited by Kevork Bardakjian in *Hitler and the Armenian Genocide*, Special Report No. 3, Cambridge, Mass.: Zoryan Institute, 1985.

Marx, Samuel. *Mayer and Thalberg, The Make-Believe Saints*, New York: Random House, 1975.

McBride, Joseph. *Frank Capra, The Catastrophe of Success*, New York: Simon & Schuster, 1992.

McClelland, Doug. *Hollywood on Hollywood, Tinsel Town Talks*, Winchester, Mass.: Faber and Faber, 1985.

Monaco, James. *Who's Who in American Film Now*, New York: A Baseline Book, 1987.

Monson, Karen. *Alma Mahler: Muse to Genius, From Fin-de-Siecle Vienna to Hollywood's Heyday*, Boston: Houghton-Mifflin Co., 1983.

Morris, L. Robert and Lawrence Raskin, *Lawrence of Arabia, The 30th Anniversary Pictorial History*, New York: Anchor Books, Doubleday, 1992.

Reinhardt, Gottfried. *The Genius*, New York: Alfred Knopf, 1979.

Taylor, John Russell. *Strangers in Paradise, The Hollywood Émigrés, 1933-1950*, New York: Holt, Rinehart & Winston, 1983.

Thomas, Bob. *Thalberg, Life and Legend*, Garden City, N.Y.: Doubleday, 1969.

Thomas, Tony. *The Films of Henry Fonda*, Secaucus, N.J.: Citadel Press, 1983.

Toynbee, Arnold J., *Armenian Atrocities--The Murder of a Nation*, London: Hodder & Stoughton, 1915.

Trumpener, Ulrich. *Germany and the Ottoman Empire, 1914-1918*, Princeton, N.J.: Princeton University Press, 1968. Cited by Kevork Bardakjian in *Hitler and the Armenian Genocide*, Special Report No. 3, Cambridge, Mass.: Zoryan Institute, 1985.

Vertanes, Charles A., *Armenia Reborn*, Armenian National Council of America, New York: Delphic Press, 1947.

Wade, Dorothy and Justine Picardie. *Music Man, Ahmet Ertegun, Atlantic Records, and the Triumph of Rock 'n' Roll*, New York: W. W. Norton & Co., 1990.

Walker, Alexander. *Garbo, A Portrait*, authorized by Metro-Goldwyn-Mayer, New York: Macmillan, 1980.

Webster, Donald E., *The Turkey of Ataturk*, Philadelphia: American Academy of Political & Social Science, 1939.

Werfel, Alma Mahler. *And the Bridge Is Love, Memories of a Lifetime*, in collaboration with E. B. Ashton; New York: Harcourt, Brace and Co., 1958. © Frankfurt am Main: S. Fischer Verlag.

Werfel, Franz. *Die Vierzig Tage des Musa Dagh*, 2 Vols., Vienna: Zsolnay Verlag, 1933.© Frankfurt am Main: S. Fischer Verlag.

_____. *Die Vierzig Tage des Musa Dagh*, One Volume, German edition, Biography of Werfel by Dr. Helga Watzke, Frankfurt am Main: S. Fischer Verlag GmbH, G.B. Fischer, 1965.

_____. *The Forty Days of Musa Dagh*, Geoffrey Dunlop translation from the German, New York: Viking Press, 1934.

_____. *The Forty Days of Musa Dagh*, New York: Pocket Books, Giant Cardinal Edition, 1961, 1962.

_____. *The Forty Days of Musa Dagh*, New York: Carroll & Graf, 1983, 1985.

_____. *The Song of Bernadette*, New York: Viking Press, 1942.

_____. *A Star of the Unborn*, translated by Gustave O. Arlt, New York: Viking Press, 1946.

Wilder, Thornton, *The Bridge of San Luis Rey*, © 1928, by arrangement with the Wilder Family LLC and the Barbara Hogenson Agency, Inc., All rights reserved.

Zinnemann, Fred. *An Autobiography, A Life in the Movies*, A Robert Stewart book, New York: Charles Scribner's Sons, Maxwell Macmillan International, 1992.

ARTICLES (BOOK EXCERPTS)

Aron, Yair. "*The Forty Days of Musa Dagh*: Its impact on Jewish Youth in Palestine and Europe," *Remembrance and Denial, The Case of the Armenian Genocide*, Richard Hovannisian, ed., Detroit: Wayne State University Press, 1998.

Hoss, Annette. "The Trial of Perpetrators by the Turkish Military Tribunals: The Case of Yozgat," *The Armenian Genocide, History, Politics, Ethics*, Richard Hovannisian, ed., New York: St Martin's Press, 1992.

Moranian, Suzanne Elizabeth. "Bearing Witness: The Missionary Archives as Evidence of the Armenian Genocide," *The Armenian Genocide, History, Politics, Ethics*, Richard Hovannisian, ed., New York: St. Martin's Press, 1992.

Reid, James J., "Total War, the Annihilation Ethic and the Armenian Genocide, 1870-1918," *The Armenian Genocide, History, Politics, Ethics*, Richard Hovannisian, ed., New York: St. Martin's Press, 1982.

Smith, Roger W., "The Armenian Genocide: Memory, Politics and the Future,"

The Armenian Genocide, History, Politics, Ethics, Richard Hovannisian, ed., New York: St. Martin's Press, 1982.

PERIODICALS, PAMPHLETS, BROCHURES, PRESS RELEASES

Andreasian, Dikran. "A Red Cross Flag That Saved Four Thousand," translated by Stephen Trowbridge, *The Outlook, An Illustrative Weekly Journal of Current Events*, Vol. CXI, December 1, 1915.

Armenian National Committee of America, press release, "House International Relations Committee Overwhelmingly Adopts Armenian Genocide Legislation," Washington D.C., 9/15/05.

The Armenian Review, "Remnants of the Turkish Genocide," December 1949. Item in the Armenian newspaper, *Azdak*, Beirut, Lebanon.

Baljian, Levon-Garabed (the future Vasken I, Catholicos of All Armenians) Essay: "The Living Power of Art, Musa Dagh Armenians in Franz Werfel's Novel," translated from the Armenian by Joseph Matossian.

Bardakjian, Kevork B., *Hitler and the Armenian Genocide*, Special Report No. 3, Cambridge, Mass.: Zoryan Institute, 1985.

Bennetts, Leslie. "Ahmet Ertegun," *Vanity Fair*, January 1998.

Blumenthal, Warner. "Father and Son in the East: A New Look at Werfel's *The Forty Days of Musa Dagh*," West Georgia College: *Mountain Interstate Foreign Language Conference*, Vol. 23, 1973.

Brochure, *Folk Dance Ensemble of Soviet Armenia*, Sponsored by John Kurkjian and Harry Diramarian, San Francisco performance, July 7, 1974.

Brochure, *The 40 Days of Musa Dagh*, World Premiere Program, Academy of Motion Pitcures, Arts & Sciences Theater, Beverly Hills, Calif., April 30, 1982.

Dadrian, Vahakn N., "The Armenian Genocide in Official Turkish Records," (Collected Essays), *Journal of Political and Military Sociology*, Vol. 22, No. 1, Summer, 1994.

_____, "A Review of the Main Features of the Genocide," *Journal of Political and Military Sociology*, Vol. 22, No. 1, Summer, 1994. Taken from a monograph in *The Yale Journal of International Law*, Vol. 14, No. 2, Summer, 1989.

Directory, *75th Anniversary of the Heroes of Mousa Ler, 1915-1990*. Translated from the Armenian, *Mousa Lertzis Bay Area and Fresno, Calif.*, Musa Dagh Commemorative Album, The Musaler Martyrs, 1990

Guttman, Joseph. " Brief Account of the Armenian Massacres in World War I," *The Beginnings of Genocide*, N.Y.: Armenian National Council, 1948. (Taken from *Yivo Bleter*, Journal of the Yiddish Scientific Institute).

Helprin, Mark. "My Favorite Historical Novel: Truth and Fiction, The Power of the Historical Novel," *American Heritage*, Special Issue, October 1992.

Hoosharar, "Talk Show Focuses on Armenian Image in American Performing Arts," Armenian General Benevolent Union (AGBU) monthly magazine, December 1982.

Housepian, Marjorie. "The Unremembered Genocide," *Commentary*, New York: American Jewish Committee, Vol. 42, No. 3, September 1966.

Imirzian, Kevork. "Turkish Lobby in America," *AIM (Armenian International Magazine)*. Los Angeles, Calif., July 1990.

Kalaydjian, Ara. "April 24, Armenians Worldwide Remember Genocide Victims of 1915," *AIM (Armenian International Magazine)*, Los Angeles, Calif., July 1990.

Kazarian, Haigaz. "*The Forty Days of Musa Dagh* and Its English Translation," *The Armenian Review*, Vol. XVI, September 1963. Originally published in *Hairenik Monthly*, Boston, June 1951.

Minasian, Edward. "The Forty Years of Musa Dagh: The Film That Was Denied," *Journal of Armenian Studies, National Association for Armenian Studies and Research* (NAASR) Vol. II, No. 2, Fall/Winter, 1985-1986; Vol. III, Nos. 1 and 2, 1986-1987; Cambridge, Mass.: Armenian Heritage Press.

Motion Picture Herald, "The Case of Musa Dagh," December 7, 1935.

New Stateman & Nation, Book Review: *The Forty Days of Musa Dagh*, December 29, 1934.

Publishers Weekly, February 13, 1961.

Saroyan, William. "Forty Days of Good and Evil," *Saturday Review*, December 8, 1934.

Saryan, Levon A., "The Arrest and Incarceration of the Armenian Intellectuals at Ayash: April 24, 1915-July 25, 1915," *The Armenian Review*, Summer, 1975.

Schulz-Behrend, George. "Sources and Background of Werfel's Novel, *Die Vierzig Tage des Musa Dagh*," *The Germanic Review*, April 1951.

Time, Book Review: *The Forty Days of Musa Dagh*, December 3, 1934, *Franz Werfel Papers*, Box 21, Special Collections Library, University of California, Los Angeles.

Walker, Christopher J., "Anatomy of a Genocide," *AIM (Armenian International Magazine)*, Los Angeles, Calif., Vol. I, No. 1, July 1990.

The Week in Germany. A Weekly Publication, German Information Center, New York:

"Kohl Sends Message to Holocaust Survivors," July 22, 1988.

"Moravian, Bohemian Writers Featured in New German-Language Textbook," October 18, 1991.

"Numerous Events Mark the 60th Anniversary of Nazi BookBurning," May 14, 1993.

"Commissioner: Over Seven Million Foreigners Now Living in Germany," January 16, 1998.

NEWSPAPERS

Armenian Mirror-Spectator. An English language Armenian weekly, Watertown, Mass.

"'*40 Days of Musa Dagh*' Movie May Premier in LA This Spring," March 6, 1982.

"The Forty 'Years' of Musa Dagh, January 24, 1987.

"News From Armenia," July 28, 1990.

Pellegrino D'Acierno, "Concert of Remembrance," January 11, 2006, p. 11.

Armenian Observer. An English language Armenian weekly, Los Angeles, Calif.

"Fresno and San Francisco Musa Dagh Union," August 20, 1986.

"Historic Pilgrimage to Moussa Dagh," September 3, 1997.

"Ceremony in Honor of Three Great Friends of Armenia: Dr. Johannes Lepsius, Viscount James Bryce, and Franz Werfel," April 15, 1998.

"Abp. Vatche Hovsepian Expresses Anger to the Swedish Government for Armenia's Exclusion from the Conference," January 2, 2000.

"Genocide Conference in Vienna May Be Postponed," February 16, 2000.

"Turkish PM Warns France Against Endorsing Armenian Genocide Bill," February 23, 2000.

Moorad Mooradian, "Our Ally Turkey, April 9, 2003.

"House of Representatives Asks Key Committee to Maintain Aid," April 23, 2003.

"Taviani Brothers, Turkish Pressures on Their Genocide Film," March 22, 2006.

"Bob Livingston's Group Received $10 Million from Turkey to Lobby Against Armenian Issues," March 29, 2006.

Boston Evening American

"Louella Parsons," November 22, 1938.

California Courier. An English language Armenian weekly, Los Angeles, Calif.

"Elie Wiesel's Introduction to the New French Edition of Werfel's *The Forty Days of Musa Dagh*." May 21, 1987.

"Ottoman Empire Hero Taken Home, Re-buried," August 8, 1996.

"Ankara Hires New Agent in Washington," December 14, 2006, p. 3.

Chicago Tribune

Michael Wilmington, "Sly vs. Sly, His Apocalyptic Battles Have Fueled 20 Years of Over-The-Top Movie Action," August 10, 1997.

Christian Science Monitor

Kenneth Waring, "Armenians on the March Again," September 16, 1939.

Contra Costa Times. Walnut Creek, Calif.

"Remains of Enver Pasha Given Military Honors in Istanbul," August 5, 1996.

Susan Fraser, "Turkey Says It's Government Spent $50 Million On Assassins," January 24 1988, p. A22

Denver Post

Michael Booth, "Stallone's Deft as Rocky in the Q&A Ring," December 16, 2006.

Daily Telegraph, London

May 29, 1922.

Hairenik Weekly. An English language Armenian weekly, Boston, Mass.

Vartkes Aharonian, *The Forty Days of Musa Dagh*, January 18, 1935.

A. Antrasian, "Memories of a Survivor of Musa Dagh," (13 years old at the time of the siege), September 27, 1935.

_____, "Armenians Repulse Two Turkish Attacks," September 27, 1935.

"Mamoulian Grants Interview to the 'Weekly' Reporter," October 4, 1935.

"Turkey Alarmed Over Filming of Musa Dagh," October 4, 1935.

"Franz Werfel's Speech at Mekhitarist Celebration of Bible in Vienna," October 20, 1935.

"Rumor Says 40 Days Will Be Filmed," November 1, 1935 (Information based on news report in *New York Evening Journal*, October 25, 1935).

"Current Events by Politics, His Master's Voice," November 1, 1935.

"Minister of Musa Dagh Fame to Bring Suit Against Werfel," Based on the November 13, 1935 interview of the Rev. H. Nokhudian by Zoe B. Fales, *Albany Times Union*, November 22, 1935.

"Memories of a Survivor of Musa Dagh, The Rescue, The Sojourn, and the Return," November 22, 1935.

"Werfel Grants Interview to Armenian Press Bureau Representatives, Famous Author to Stay Three Months in U. S.," November 22, 1935.

Vartkes Aharonian, "An Hour with Franz Werfel," November 29, 1935.

"MGM Decides To Film *Musa Dagh*," December 6, 1935.

"Franz Werfel Is Feted by Armenians in New York," December 13, 1935.

"Herr Werfel's Speech, Delivered at Recent New York Banquet," December 13, 1935.

"A. R. F. Representative Extols Author of Musa Dagh," December 13, 1935.

"Werfel Meets Survivor of Musa Dagh," December 13, 1935.

"The Turkish Press Roused Against Franz Werfel," January 3, 1936.

"Franz Werfel Leaves U.S.," February 28, 1936.

"Werfel Arrives in Paris," March 13, 1936.

"Armenians Abroad-France," March 13, 1936.

"Apropos Musa Dagh," April 3,1936 (Excerpted from *Variety*, March 1936).

"Pathetic," April 3,1936 (Excerpted from *Variety*, March 1936).

"*Musa Dagh* Thrills Overflow House in New York," April 24, 1936.

Vartouhie Calantar Naldbandian, "A Historic Crime and Its Motive," April 24, 1936.

"Franz Werfel," September 6, 1945.

"On the Occasion of the 80th Anniversary of the Heroic Epic: Musa Lehr—*The Forty Days of Musa Dagh* (*Herosmardin Ootsoon Amiyagin Areetov Musa Lehren Karasnarya Herossamardeh*)," September 21, 1995.

Hollywood Reporter, re: ***The Forty Days of Musa Dagh***

"Musa Dagh to be Filmed," April 20, 1935.

July 11, 1940.

November 29, 1951.

January 23, 1961.

June 29, 1961.

November 4, 1966.

September 1, 1967.

April 10, 1969.

Los Angeles Examiner

July 3, 1961.

Los Angeles Times

"*The Forty Days of Musa Dagh*," December 11, 1950.

"*The Forty Days of Musa Dagh*," October 23, 1962.

Aram Arax, "Jews: Pressured on Issue of Armenian Genocide," April 22, 1985.

New York Herald Tribune

    Books, "Werfel and *The Forty Days of Musa Dagh*, Comment by Survivors of the Tragedy on the Novel's Authenticity in Spirit and Fact," Interview of the Reverend Harutiun Nokhudian by Avedis Derounian, Reporter: *The Armenian Spectator*, March 24, 1935, *Franz Werfel Papers*, Collection 512, Box 9; Special Collections Library, Los Angeles, University of California.

    Books, Review, *The Forty Days of Musa Dagh*, December 2, 1934.

New York Times

    "Armenians Slain in Great Numbers," April 26, 1915.

    "Kurds Massacre More Armenians," April 26, 1915.

    "Great Exodus of Christians," April 26, 1915.

    "Appeal to Turkey to Stop Massacres," April 28, 1915.

    "Allies to Punish Turks Who Murder," May 24, 1915.

    "Defense Committee (Turkish) Corners Supplies," September 14, 1915.

    "An Autocratic Triumvirate," September 14, 1915.

    "Would Send Here 550,000 Armenians," September 14, 1915.

    "Plans Armenian Corps To Fight For The Allies," September 19, 1915.

    "German Missionary Aids," September 25, 1915.

    "Missions Board to Appeal," September 25, 1915.

    "Says Extinction Menaces Armenia," September 25, 1915.

    "Government Sends Plea For Armenia," October 5, 1915.

    "800,000 Armenians Counted Destroyed," October 7, 1915.

    "Already Has $75,000 To Help Armenians," October 7, 1915.

    "Thousands Protest Armenian Murders," October 18, 1915.

    "Turkey Bars Red Cross," October 19, 1915.

    "Only 200,000 Armenians Left in Turkey," October 22, 1915.

    "Beat Off 4,000 Turks," March 12, 1916.

    "Franz Werfel's Heroic Novel," Louis Kronenberger, December 2, 1934.

Advertisement, *The Forty Days of Musa Dagh*, December 2, 1934.

"Reich Bans Film Writer," August 13, 1935.

Book Review, Advertisement, *The Forty Days of Musa Dagh*, Book-of-the-Month Club, August 18,1935.

"Armenians Fete Werfel," January 6, 1936.

"Hollywood's Censor Is All the World, Should Turkey Ban American Films Because It Disliked *The Forty Days of Musa Dagh*?" March 29, 1936.

June 16, 1938.

June 26, 1938.

"Franz Werfel, Noted Author Dies," August 27, 1945.

Sebnem Arsu and Suzanne Fowler, "Armenian Turkish Unity At Slain Editors Funeral," January 24, 2007.

Oakland Tribune, Calif.

"Armenian Ordeal To Be a Film," December 21, 1975.

March 26, 1981.

PanArmenian.net (electronic media)

December 21, 2006

San Francisco Chronicle

"Kurt Waldheim Opens Festival at Salzburg," July 29, 1988

John Stanley, "Hollywood's Daring Defiance of '30's 'Code'," *Datebook*, July 31, 1988.

Gerald Nachman, "Roars, Rants, and a Rave or Two," *Datebook, Show Business*, April 19, 1992.

Datebook, "Black Stars Help Spike Lee," May 20, 1992.

Datebook, "BBC's Mao Film Fuels Battle with China," December 18, 1993.

***Turkish Forum*,**

November 30, 2002.

Variety, re: ***The Forty Days of Musa Dagh.***

November 17, 1935.

February 3, 1961.

June 29, 1961.

June 12, 1968.

April 4, 1969.

April 10,1969, p. 187.

April 16, 1969.

February 8, 1979.

"Film and TV Casting News," April 13, 1981.

Forty Days of Musa Dagh, Videocassette Film Review, November 28, 1987.

Wall Street Journal

Elif Shafak, "The Murder of Hrant Dink," January 22, 2007.

Washington Herald

"Musa Dagh To Be Filmed," April 17, 1935.

REFERENCE WORKS

Encyclopaedia Britannica, Vol. 16, 1961. Chicago: Encyclopaedia Britannica, Inc., 1961.

The Holy Bible, The Revelation of St. John the Divine, Oxford Self-Pronouncing Bible, Containing the Old and New Testaments, Authorized King James Version, New York: Oxford University Press, Date omitted.

MISCELLANEOUS

Advertisement: On the occasion of the re-publication in paperback of *The Forty Days of Musa Dagh*, New York: Carroll & Graf, 1985. Belmont, Mass.: Armenian Book Clearing House, National Association for Armenian Studies and Research (NAASR).

ILLUSTRATIONS:
SOURCES/CREDITS

1. Frontispiece: Project SAVE, Armenian Photograph Archives. Watertown, Mass.; Cartographer: Mardy Minasian.

2. *New Armenia*, Vol. XXI.

3. *New Armenia*, Vol. X.

4, 18, 21. Courtesy of Mousa Ler Association of California, Calendar 1999.

5, 11, 13, 14, 15. Courtesy of Dr. Vahram L. Shemmassian, Musa Dagh Photograph Archives.

6. Courtesy of Armine Antreassian and Dr. Vahram L. Shemmassian

7, 8, 12, 16. Courtesy of Dr. Vazken K. Der Kaloustian and Red Mountain Committee (ARF), *Movses Der Kaloustian* (A. Leylani), Bedros Snabian, ed., Ainjar, Lebanon, 2004.

9, 10, 17, 19, 20. Courtesy of Rev. Gregory Haroutunian and Varack Haroutunian.

22, 23, 25, 26. University of California, Los Angeles (UCLA) Special Collections Library, Franz Werfel Papers.

24. *New Armenia*, Vol. XIX.

27–32, 39–46. Courtesy of Marc Wanamaker, Bison Productions.

33–37. National Archives and Records Administration.

38. United States State Department, Musa Dagh File.

47. Courtesy of Sarky Mouradian.

48. Courtesy of John Kurkjian, High Investments, Inc.

Sturges, John, 226–27
Suedia district, 27n3
Surmelian, Leon, 210–11
Syria, resettlement in, 50

T
Tabakyan, Haiganoush Naldjian, xx
Talaat, Mehmet, xxviii, xxx, 58, 200
Tan (Turkish newspaper), 117, 118
Tarasseff-Torossian, Levon (Henri
    Troyat), 226
Taviani Brothers, 321
Tears of Happiness (film), 282
Tekeyan, Charles Diran, 20, *37*
"telephone boys," 10
television movies, proposed, 266, 319–21
television screening of 1981 film, 304
Thalberg, Irving G., *169*
    background, 92
    and censorship, 132, 133, 137, 142
    filmmaking credo, 100–101,
        130–31
    and Mamoulian, 123
    pressures on, 107–8, 110
    and Wilson, 98
Thompson & Co., 329n8
Tito, Josip Broz, 270
Tolan, John H., 141
Tombazian, Mark, 286, 314n139
Tootikian, Michael, 314n139
Tor, Vedat Nedim, 122–24
Tovmassian, Krikor, 29n28
Treaty of Lausanne, 164n167
Treaty of Sevres, 140, 164n167
Troyat, Henri (Levon
    Tarasseff-Torossian), 226
Truman Doctrine, 193, 195, 321
Trumbo, Dalton, 256
Turkish Armenians, 113–15,
    159n92, 325

Turkish Embassy. *See also* Ertegun,
    Mehmet Munir; Turkish
    Government
    concerns about film, 97, 100, 101,
        103, 110
    and Kurkjian, 279–80
    and "Operation Roxbury," 194,
        200, 218, 226
    and press, 117, 118, 120, 135–36,
        138, 146
The Turkish Forum, 321
Turkish Government. *See also*
    Ottoman Turkey; Turkish
    Embassy; Young Turks movement
    ban of MGM films, 104, 106–7,
        112, 115, 123, 127, 128,
        131–32, 140, 148, 192, 321
    and Cold War politics, 250, 307n19
    concerns about film, 75–76, 105–6
    and distribution of 1981 film,
        302, 304
    lobbying efforts, 322–24
    military bases in, 200, 228, 250,
        307n19, 321
    and "Operation Roxbury," 193,
        195, 197–98, 223, 225, 227–28
    relations with U.S., 95
    threats to Romania, 270–71
    in WWII, 229n2
Turkish Jews, 129–30
Turkish press
    campaign against film, 106, 117–25,
        343–44
    pressure on MGM, 110, 139
    and Turkish Armenian responses,
        113–14
Turkish "watch list" as of 2002, 321
Tyrell, Lord, 127, 147–48

U
Ullman, Liv, 255

Printed in the United States
75663LV00006BA/73-219